PARTNERING

The New Face of Leadership

EDITED BY

Larraine Segil
Marshall Goldsmith
James Belasco

AMACOM

AMERICAN MANAGEMENT ASSOCIATION

New York | Atlanta | Brussels | Buenos Aires | Chicago | London | Mexico City
San Francisco | Shanghai | Tokyo | Toronto | Washington, D.C.

Special discounts on bulk quantities of AMACOM books are available to corporations, professional associations, and other organizations. For details, contact Special Sales Department, AMACOM, a division of American Management Association, 1601 Broadway, New York, NY 10019.
Tel.: 212-903-8316. Fax: 212-903-8083.
Web site: www.amacombooks.org

This publication is designed to provide accurate and authoritative information in regard to the subject matter covered. It is sold with the understanding that the publisher is not engaged in rendering legal, accounting, or other professional service. If legal advice or other expert assistance is required, the services of a competent professional person should be sought.

Library of Congress Cataoging-in-Publication Data
Partnering : the new face of leadership / edited by Larraine Segil, Marshall Goldsmith, James Belasco.
    p. cm.
    Includes bibliographical references and index.
  ISBN 0-8144-0757-9
    1. Strategic alliances (Business) 2. Leadership. I. Segil, Larraine.
II. Goldsmith, Marshall. III. Belasco, James A.
HD69.S8 P37 2002
658—dc21   2002011116

Printing number

10 9 8 7 6 5 4 3 2 1

DEDICATION

This book is dedicated to the true heroes of September 11, 2001—those people who spent what they knew were the last moments of their lives in dedicated and urgent work focused on helping others. The long list of "lifesaving partners" includes firefighters, police, Port Authority workers, passengers on United flight 93, workers who stayed with disabled fellow employees, and the countless, nameless people who put others first in the race down the stairs to possible safety. These people, with their actions, redefined the concept of "partnership" we write about in this book. They sacrificed their lives so that others may live. We honor their sacrifice by donating our profits from this book to charities supporting the families of September 11 victims.

CONTENTS

PART TWO *Partnerships and Teambuilding: Emerging Dimensions for the Leader as Partner*

PART THREE *Becoming a Global Leader Through Partnerships*

PART FOUR *The Leader as Partner:
Succeeding in a Complex World*

PREFACE

Why did some of the most important visionaries in management science join forces to produce this book? Because this is a very special moment in time, the cause the book supports is worthy and valid, and the idea of partnering as a leadership and management mandate is appropriate and important.

THE MOMENT IN TIME

The early years of the decade 2000–2010 have already brought major shifts in global and domestic awareness. Not since World War II has there been such an urgent need to link people, thoughts, knowledge, and information. During the Great War, world populations came together to overcome the threat to the very principles on which many religions, societies, and communities were based, including the freedom to live life without destroying the rights of others; the defense of beliefs and a way of life that protected those who were different; and the opportunities for self-actualization that Abraham Maslow wrote and taught. Out of that war came economic opportunities, as well as moments of great courage as individuals and countries fought against evil. The world of business rose to the occasion, and then the postwar, baby boomer population exploded the macro- and microeconomic scene as corporations grew and fed the huge consumer demand that still drives growth worldwide.

[ix]

September 11, 2001, epitomized the change in global dynamics. Worlds of difference imploded as conflicting beliefs, suicidal bombers, corporations, communities, individuals, and government converged into one horrific event that has changed the world forever. No longer will business consider its employees "people for hire." Now they see them as their community. No longer will employees consider their place of work as just the place they earn a living. Now they see it as possibly the last place they may go that day. Everyone says goodbye to their loved ones as they leave home in the morning with a different sense of what the day might bring. Most of all, we realize that we live in a community—a world community, in which the actions of those far away from us can quickly become our loss, our tragedy.

THE CAUSE THIS BOOK SUPPORTS

The moment in time described in the preceding paragraphs impacted the three of us as we sat together one day in the middle of September 2001, talking about how we could do something to make a difference for those affected by the tragedy of September 11. We talked about how we could use our skills, our contacts, and our positions in the world business community. We realized that the best thing we could do would be to call upon our colleagues in the Financial Times Knowledge Dialogue group, in which we participate as Thought Leaders,* as well as others with whom we have worked, including calling in some favors from friends. We started to do exactly that. We contacted each one of the authors who have contributed to this amazing collection of writings. Every one of them unreservedly said "yes." Regardless of their own new and existing book schedules, teaching and student responsibilities, onerous keynote and speaking schedules, conference commitments, even family weddings and sadly, family

---

*Two hundred individuals have been selected to be part of this group, FTKD, organized by The Financial Times, UK (part of Pearson Publishing); each person is considered by FTKD to be the leading luminary in their particular field, and has been asked to be available as a resource to CEOs and managing directors of global organizations through this group. For more information, see www.Financialtimesknowledgedialogue.com

funerals, not one of our author-friends declined. They lent their personal brands to this book, in the hope that you, our readers, would gain from our insights, and in buying the book, would contribute your money to the thousands of people who were touched, damaged, destroyed, and forever changed by the events of September 11, 2001. People from around the world are affected by this tragedy, thus we have included in this book our friends and colleagues from many countries; we are one people and our contribution is neither nationalistic nor patriotic—it is our human obligation.

PARTNERING AS A LEADERSHIP
AND MANAGEMENT MANDATE

Partnering is an overused term. So is leadership. When connected together, the meanings of these two terms change, and it becomes clear that there are many interpretations and applications of partnering and leadership. The various contributors to this book have each looked at the subject from their own perspectives. The diversity of angles and richness of interpretation is the competitive edge that this book brings to you. Partnering is a corporate term, but it is also a personal term. Leadership is a challenge whether in the entry level, middle or top of an organization, or, indeed, as part of a family or community.

The first part of our book, *Building Successful Organizations Through Partnerships,* looks at the organizational application of these two concepts. Marshall Goldsmith begins the section with a discussion of the changing role of leadership; in particular he focuses on the increasing importance of developing partnerships both inside and outside the organization. Robert Kaplan and David Norton offer a strategy-focused portrayal of how the Balanced Scorecard measurement and management system can be used to facilitate partnerships inside and outside organizations. In her chapter, Sally Helgesen describes how the celebrity-style leadership of the past will give way to a new era of leaders as partners. Through an account of military actions on September 11, Major General (USAF, Ret.) Donald W. Shepperd illustrates how an instilled management philosophy will be tested during crises. Elizabeth and Gifford Pinchot complete this section with a comparison of the various ways of creating order within organizations and a discussion of how leaders can implement productive partnerships within and across the boundaries of formal organizations.

Part Two delves into the subject of *Partnerships and Teambuilding: Emerging Dimensions for the Leader as Partner* with contributions from visionaries in the field. Ken Blanchard begins this section with a description of how leaders can use Situational Leadership II® to lead their people to magnificence. John Alexander and Russ Moxley continue with a new definition of leadership: *personal power*. The purpose of Jon Katzenbach's chapter is to describe where and how team performance fits into an overall leadership approach. Jim Kouzes and Barry Posner explain the mutual dependence and need for partnering between the leader and the led. In their chapter, Judy Rosenblum and Cheryl Oates explain their framework of successful partnerships for learning leaders and they also put forth some common obstacles to successful partnerships. Debra Noumair and Warner Burke clarify four theories of how leaders can handle partnerships and relationships with those in positions both above and below them in the organizational hierarchy. In his fresh account of the importance of partnering, Harvey Robbins depicts four leadership styles with which the "accidental leader" can approach partnerships. Bob Nelson gives a step-by-step guide to partnering with employees to promote commitment and excitement within organizations. The last chapter in this section is by R. Roosevelt Thomas, Jr. Roosevelt uses his "The Giraffe and Elephant Fable" to illustrate obstacles to partnerships and the characteristics of a partner–leader.

Part Three addresses the critical issues of *Becoming a Global Leader Through Partnerships*. Larraine Segil begins this section with an examination of leadership and alliances and describes Dynamic Leadership and the Ten Essential Traits of Dynamic Managers and Leaders. Robert Rosen continues the section with intriguing insights into the issue of cultural literacy and its importance to leaders who partner globally. The next chapter, a collaborative effort by Stephan A. Friedrich, Hans H. Hinterhuber, D. Quinn Mills, and Dirk Seifert, discusses global leadership and the many different styles of leadership around the world; it also compares Europe's standard of partnering leadership with America's "celebrity" leadership style. Maya Hu-Chan and Brian Underhill continue the section with an exploration of cross-cultural partnering and give some specific actions leaders should take on the path to global success. In his chapter, Fariborz Ghadar parallels a leader's role as partner in the global environment to that of the leader of a NASCAR pit crew. Fons Trompenaars and Peter Wooliams discuss seven dilemmas of leadership for global leaders and give examples of leaders and companies that have been successful at working through each dilemma. The Rt. Hon. Kim Campbell provides us with a political bent on the subject of the leader as partner by giving personal examples of how partnering enabled her to succeed in passing legislation. Concluding this section is Nancy Adler, who illustrates the importance of working together for global success with an account of the leaders at Norske Skog's successful attempt to try something totally different in their efforts to enhance leadership and promote peace.

Part Four moves into the very personal issues and the role of the leader as partner as we look at *Succeeding in a Complex World.* Jim Belasco opens this section with a description of the leader's responsibility to focus on coaching and partnerships and examples to that effect. In his chapter, Brian Tracy explains five key areas of focus important to leading and partnering effectively. Kevin Cashman depicts five touchstones of partnering and gives five specific skills the leader will need to partner successfully. Phil Harkins offers us the "dos" and "don'ts" of leadership; he explains how to use communication to build partnerships and thus be a better leader. Elliott Masie continues this section by illustrating how we can use technology to communicate and build partnerships throughout our organizations. Beverly Kaye and Betsy Jacobson explore the crucial component of legacy (leaving something of enduring quality to the organization and its people) to leadership and to partnering with others now and into the future. In his chapter, Richard Leider encourages us to hear our inner calling and follow it, thus partnering who we are with what we do. Nathaniel Branden concludes this section, and our book, with a look at two essential qualities of successful leaders, self-esteem and integrity.

We thank you for buying this book. We thank you on behalf of the many families who cannot thank you personally themselves, but who will benefit from the proceeds of your generosity. And it is our fervent hope that there is great and lasting value for you in our thoughts and teachings.

Our E-mail and website addresses are listed within our bios at the end of the book. We hope you will contact us with your comments and thoughts.

Larraine Segil
Marshall Goldsmith
James Belasco

ACKNOWLEDGMENTS

Many people help convert the sketchy dreams of a book into the hard reality of the pages you hold in your hand. The single most important "dream converter" was Sarah McArthur. She took the ill-formed idea and midwifed, nursed, mothered, raised, dressed, and clothed it, and created what you see here today. In all the myriad of "things to do done" to make a book a book, Sarah exceeded every expectation. Whether it was dealing with publishers or authors, editing the authors' sometimes turgid words or gently reminding us that we had a deadline to meet, she always delivered more than we even knew to ask.

Moreover, Sarah is a joy to work with. She possesses an unerring sense of what it takes to make words and ideas into a successful book. Her pleasantness and positive attitude shone like a lighthouse on a dark night and helped us through the often difficult and trying times inevitable in any book preparation. She magically converted the most difficult problems into solvable, rewarding activities. This book now sees the light of day thanks to Sarah McArthur's magic. We, and all the readers of this text, are forever indebted to her for her efforts.

We are also deeply indebted to our contributing authors. All of these individuals are busy professionals, with more on their plates than they can swallow. Client calls, presentations, and personal research and writing commitments fill their calendars. Yet, in the midst of all that busyness, these 41 individuals, giants in their fields, took the time to support our cause and share their gems of wisdom with us all. The chapters that follow are gems of wisdom produced by wise and caring people, giants in their profession and giants in life. As editors, we are humbled by the privilege of working with these giants in our cause to commemorate the heroes and support the victims of September 11, 2001.

In the end, we owe the most acknowledgment to our families, those most important people in our lives that the events of September 11 reminded us so forcibly about. We thank Clive, Lyda, and Candy for their support. You are the wind beneath our wings.

PART ONE

Building Successful Organizations Through Partnerships

◀◉▶

CHAPTER 1

THE CHANGING ROLE OF LEADERSHIP

Building Partnerships Inside and Outside the Organization

MARSHALL GOLDSMITH

In a recent study (sponsored by Accenture), we completed in-depth interviews with more than 200 specially chosen, high-potential leaders from around the world. When compared to colleagues at their level in their organizations, all of these participants were seen as being at the very top. They were asked to describe how the ideal leader of the future would differ from the leader of the past. The results clearly portrayed this individual as someone skilled at building partnerships inside and outside the organization. Although these skills were seen as having been somewhat important in the past, they were viewed as critically important for the future.[1]

Much has been written on *how* leaders can build partnerships (including several chapters in this book). This section builds on our research and focuses on *why* the leader of the future will need to be a builder of partnerships. Six different types of partnerships are explored: three inside the organization (direct reports, co-workers, and managers) and three outside the organization (customers, suppliers, and competitors).

BUILDING PARTNERSHIPS INSIDE THE ORGANIZATION
Partnering with Direct Reports

The traditional assumptions that have "bonded" employees with organizations are changing rapidly. Employees no longer expect that

[3]

their organizations will provide them with job security. As the expectation of security has diminished, so has the blind loyalty that was implicit in this security. Almost all of the high-potential leaders whom we interviewed saw themselves as "free agents," not "employees" in the traditional sense.[2] They saw the leader of the future as a person who could build "win–win" relationships and who could be sensitive to their needs for professional growth and development. They then felt not only a desire but also a responsibility to deliver value in return, to the leader and to the organization. In simple terms, they saw the leader of the future as their *partner,* not their *boss!*

As Peter Drucker has noted on many occasions, one of the great challenges for leadership in the future will be the management of knowledge workers. Knowledge workers are people who know more about what they are doing than their manager does.[3] The high-potential people we interviewed painted a very clear picture. The managers of the best knowledge workers of the future will have to be good partners. *They won't have a choice!* If they are not great partners, they won't have great people.

Partnering with Co-Workers

Another great challenge for the leader of the future is breaking down boundaries. The successful leader of the future will be able to share people, capital, and ideas across the organization. As the world becomes more complex, this type of integration becomes more important, a concept that is easy for the CEO to understand.[4] The CEO is rewarded by the success of the entire organization, not just that of any one unit. The CEO can understand that people need to be shared so that they can develop the expertise and breadth needed to manage the entire organization. Capital needs to be shared so that mature businesses can transfer funds to high-growth businesses. Ideas need to be shared so that everyone in the organization can learn from both successes and mistakes in the most efficient way possible. The high-potential leaders we interviewed saw themselves as potential CEOs and recognized the value of this perspective.

Although these advantages are easy to see from the vantage point of the CEO, they can be more difficult to execute from the position of the lower level manager. Leaders at all levels will need to develop the skills to negotiate and build "win–win" relationships with colleagues. In some cases they must choose to experience a short-term loss so that the organization can achieve a long-term gain. In the past, many leaders were taught to compete with colleagues for people, resources, and ideas. They had been rewarded for "winning" this competition. In the future, leaders will need to learn to collaborate and share with colleagues across the organization. The success of the larger organization will depend on the leaders' abilities to become great partners with their co-workers. In many cases, the participants in our research believed that developing partnerships with co-workers was an even greater challenge for leaders than developing partnerships with direct reports.

Partnering with Managers

Other than the CEO, every leader in the organization has a manager.

The changing role of leadership will mean that the relationship between managers and direct reports will have to change in *both* directions. Not only managers, but also direct reports (who also may be leaders), will need to change. Many leaders of the future will be operating more like the managing director of an office in a consulting firm than the operator of an independent small business. This is true not only in business, but also in the human services sector. The new leader of the United Way, Brian Gallagher, recently described the ideal future leaders of this organization as partners leading in a network, not managers leading in a hierarchy.[5]

A consulting firm that could be a benchmark in partnering between junior and senior people is McKinsey and Company. At McKinsey, a director may often have less detailed knowledge about a client than a more junior principal. Leaders at all levels are trained in the following philosophy: "When you believe that the direction you are being given is not in the best interest of our client, you do not have the *opportunity* to challenge, you do not have the *right* to challenge, you have the *obligation* to challenge." This philosophy teaches leaders at all levels to have very adult and responsible relationships with their managers.

Our high-potential participants saw the leaders of the future as working with their managers in a team approach that combined the leader's knowledge of the unit operation with their managers' understanding of the larger needs of the organization. Such a relationship requires taking responsibility, sharing information, and striving to see both the micro- and macro-perspective. While partnering with management can be much more complex than "taking orders," it is becoming a requirement, not an option. When direct reports know more than their managers, they have to learn how to influence "up" as well as "down" and "across."

BUILDING PARTNERSHIPS OUTSIDE THE ORGANIZATION
Partnering with Customers

As companies have become larger and more global, there has been a shift from buying stand-alone products to buying integrated solutions.[6] One reason for this shift is economy of scale. Huge retail corporations, such as Home Depot or Wal-Mart, do not want to deal with thousands of vendors. They would prefer to work with fewer vendors who can deliver not only products but also systems for delivery that are customized to meet their needs. A second reason is the convergence of technology. Many customers now want "network solutions," not just hardware and software.

As the suppliers' relationships with their customers continue to change, leaders from supply organizations will need to become more like partners and act less like salespeople. Our participants noticed a shift toward building long-term customer relationships, not just achieving short-term sales. This change means that suppliers need to develop a much deeper understanding of the customer's total business. They will need to be willing to look at the "big picture" in terms of delivery and reliability and to make many small sacrifices to achieve a large gain.

Partnering with Suppliers

As the shift toward integrated solutions advances, leaders will have to change their relationships with suppliers. A great example is IBM. "A growing percentage of IBM's business now involves customized solutions incorporating non-IBM products and services. While the idea of IBM selling non-IBM products was almost unheard of in the past, it is now becoming commonplace—to the benefit of customers and, in the long run, IBM itself."[7] The same trend is occurring in the pharmaceutical and telecommunications industries.

In a world in which a company sold stand-alone products, partnering with suppliers was viewed not only as unnecessary, but also perhaps as unethical! The company's job was to "get the supplier down" to the lowest possible price to increase margins and profitability. Leaders who partnered with suppliers may well have been seen as "helping the enemy" or having a "conflict of interest." Today, many leaders realize that their success is directly related to that of their suppliers. Northrop Grumman, one of America's leading defense contractors, actually includes commitment to suppliers as one of their core values.

The leaders in our study saw suppliers as key partners. They realized that the leaders of the future would be able to transcend differences and focus on a common good—serving the ultimate end user of the product or service.

Partnering with Competitors

The most radical change in the role of leader as partner has come in the area of partnering with competitors. This previously unthinkable concept has now become commonplace. Most of the high-potential leaders who we interviewed saw competitors as potential customers, suppliers, and partners with few clear lines of demarcation. While there are still some noted exceptions to this trend (e.g., Coca-Cola and Pepsi), the direction of the curve is very clear. Most organizations that rely on knowledge workers have varied and complex relationships with competitors.

When today's competitors may become tomorrow's customers, the definition of "winning" changes. As people have memories, unfairly "bashing" competitors or striving to ruin their business could have harmful long-term consequences. While competitors should not expect collusion or unfair practices, they should expect integrity, respectful treatment, and fair dealing.

CONCLUSION

It becomes obvious in reading this chapter that the six trends toward more partnering reinforces each other. For example, as employees sense less job security, they begin to see suppliers, customers, and competitors as potential employers. The fact that leaders need to learn more about these other organizations, build long-term relationships, and develop "win–win" partnerships means that the other organizations are even more likely to hire the leaders. In many cases, this is seen as a positive, not a negative by both organizations. As the trend toward outsourcing increases, it becomes increasingly difficult to determine who is a customer, supplier, direct report, manager, or partner.

Almost every high-potential leader we interviewed believed that the leader of the future would need to be far more skilled than the leader of the past. In many ways the "old world" was simpler. Telling direct reports (who know less than we do) what to do is much simpler than developing relationships with partners (who know more than we do). Being able to work in a "silo" is much simpler than having to build partnerships with peers across the organization. "Taking orders" from managers is much simpler than having to challenge ideas that are not going to meet customer needs. Selling a product to customers is much simpler than providing an integrated solution. Getting the lowest price from suppliers is a lot simpler than understanding their complex business needs. Vying with competitors is a lot simpler than having to develop complex customer–supplier–competitor relationships.

The challenge of leadership is growing. The high-potential leaders of the future who we studied believe that many of the qualities considered important in the past, such as integrity, vision, and self-confidence, will be required in the future as well. They believe that in addition, building partnerships inside and outside the organization will become a *requirement*, not an *option*, for future leaders.

CHAPTER 2

USE THE BALANCED SCORECARD TO PARTNER WITH STRATEGIC CONSTITUENTS

Employees, Customers, Suppliers, and Communities

ROBERT S. KAPLAN AND DAVID P. NORTON

Often overlooked in essays on leadership is the role of the organization's measurement and management system. Effective leaders, however, know that measurement and management systems play a critical role in communication; in establishing the culture and values of the organization; and in aligning diverse units, employees, and constituencies. In this chapter, we describe how effective leaders customize their organization's measurement and management system to partner with their employees for strategy implementation. We also discuss how the new measurement and management system goes beyond intraorganizational partnerships, facilitating alignment and partnership with external constituents: customers, suppliers, and communities.

THE BALANCED SCORECARD: FROM MEASUREMENT TO MANAGEMENT

We introduced the Balanced Scorecard (BSC) in 1992.[1] The BSC measures organizational performance using financial and nonfinancial measurements in four perspectives: financial, customer, internal process, and learning and growth. The approach quickly evolved into a new system for describing and managing strategy.[2] Many of the organizations that adopted this new approach soon enjoyed breakthrough improvements in performance.[3]

[9]

We created the Balanced Scorecard because financial measurements had become insufficient for contemporary organizations. Strategies for creating value had shifted from managing tangible assets to knowledge-based strategies that created and deployed an organization's intangible assets, including customer relationships; innovative products and services; high-quality and responsive operating processes; skills and knowledge of the workforce; the information technology that supports the workforce and links the firm to its customers and suppliers; and the organizational climate that encourages innovation, problem-solving, and improvement. Yet, words were insufficient for describing and communicating such strategies. Statements such as "Delight the customer," "Offer superior service," or "Invest in our people" had very different meanings to different people. The power of measurement was to take the ambiguity out of words so that everyone had a clear, coherent picture of exactly what the strategy is.

PARTNERING WITH EMPLOYEES

Several forces highlight the importance of partnering with employees. Employees want to know that they are working for an organization that is contributing value to the world, that society benefits from the mission and strategy of their organization and its products and services. They need to understand how the success of the organization benefits not only its shareholders, but also its customers, suppliers, and the communities in which it operates. Employees also want to know where they fit within the organization and how they can contribute to helping it achieve its mission and objectives. Furthermore, leaders now recognize that their strategies, however brilliantly they may be formulated, will be successful only if everyone in the organization understands the strategy and helps to implement it.

The Balanced Scorecard provides a simple, clear message about organizational strategy that all employees can understand and internalize in their everyday operations. With such understanding, employees can link improvements in their daily processes to achievement of high-level strategic objectives.

The Balanced Scorecard framework describes strategy with strategic objectives, measures, targets, and initiatives. (See Figure 2-1.) Strategic objectives and measures can be imbedded in a general framework or template, which we call a "strategy map," that complements the Balanced Scorecard with a simple, succinct visualization of the hypotheses and interrelationships that are at the heart of strategy.[4] (See Figure 2-2.)

The strategy map enables leaders to communicate clearly to employees the nature of the organization's business and how the organization intends to succeed and outperform competitors. It articulates the critical elements for a company's growth strategy:[5]

➤Objectives for growth in shareholder value

➤Targeted customers through whom profitable growth would occur

➤Value propositions that lead customers to do more business and at higher margins with the company

➤Innovation and excellence in products, services, and processes

➤The capabilities and alignment of employees and systems that enhance important internal processes and customer relationships to generate and sustain growth

The strategy map and accompanying scorecard provide a powerful communication vehicle about the organization's vision and strategy. Rather than use measurement to *control* employees, leaders use strategy maps and Balanced Scorecards to *communicate* a vision for the future, often embodying new ideas and approaches that promote growth. Employees can become inspired with their understanding of how their organization creates value and intends to be a healthy, growing entity.

For example, at Duke Children's Hospital,[6] Dr. Jon Meliones had to cope with the open warfare between administrators on the one hand and caregivers—physicians and nurses—on the other. Administrators kept emphasizing, "Cut costs, save money." Caregivers replied, "We're not good at cutting costs; we cure children and save lives. That

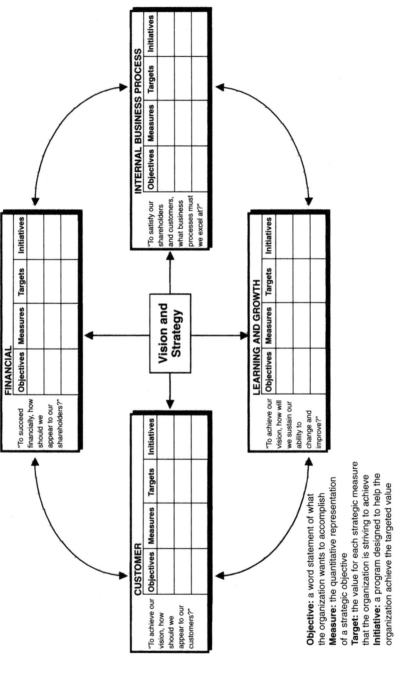

FINANCIAL

"To succeed financially, how should we appear to our shareholders?"

Objectives	Measures	Targets	Initiatives

CUSTOMER

"To achieve our vision, how should we appear to our customers?"

Objectives	Measures	Targets	Initiatives

INTERNAL BUSINESS PROCESS

"To satisfy our shareholders and customers, what business processes must we excel at?"

Objectives	Measures	Targets	Initiatives

LEARNING AND GROWTH

"To achieve our vision, how will we sustain our ability to change and improve?"

Objectives	Measures	Targets	Initiatives

Vision and Strategy

Objective: a word statement of what the organization wants to accomplish
Measure: the quantitative representation of a strategic objective
Target: the value for each strategic measure that the organization is striving to achieve
Initiative: a program designed to help the organization achieve the targeted value

FIGURE 2-1. THE BALANCED SCORECARD: TRANSLATING VISION AND STRATEGY INTO FOUR PERSPECTIVES

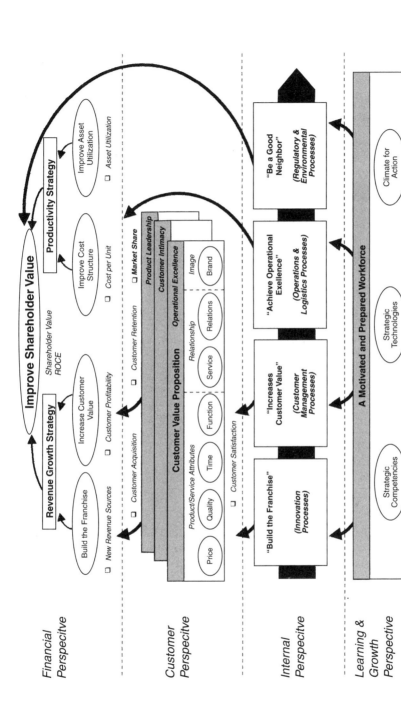

FIGURE 2-2. THE BALANCED SCORECARD STRATEGY MAP

is our mission." Staff members were demoralized, financial performance was terrible, and improvement programs kept failing. Meliones created a leadership team with representatives from each of the three employee groups to redefine the mission and to develop a Balanced Scorecard that incorporated two apparently conflicting objectives—lower costs, improve patient care. Meliones, the leader, continued to encounter conflict and resistance, but he kept repeating the balanced mantra, "No money, no mission," emphasizing the need to achieve harmony among these seemingly incompatible objectives. During the next three years, employees worked constructively together; they transformed large operating losses into positive operating margins, while achieving levels of patient care and satisfaction that were ranked best in their category.

Having constructed the high-level strategy map and scorecard, leaders cascade the strategy down to decentralized divisions, business units, and support functions. Rather than dictating the company-level measures down to the operating units, leaders encourage the operating units to define their own strategy—based on local market conditions, competition, operating technologies, and resources—to deliver on the high-level strategic themes. The business-unit managers choose local measures that *influence,* but are not necessarily identical to the corporate scorecard measures.

The most remarkable transformations and partnerships occur in support functions and shared services, such as human resources, information technology, finance, and purchasing departments. The process transforms these from functionally oriented cost centers into *strategic partners* with the line-operating units and the company. This alignment is often accomplished with a service agreement that defines the menu of services to be provided—including functionality, quality level, and cost—between each support department and the business units.

When this process is complete, the employees in all organizational units, whether a line-business unit or a staff function, understand how their unit contributes to overall organizational success. This process aligns the decentralized units to a strategic partnership with each other and the corporate parent to deliver an integrated strategy. Corporate-level synergies emerge in which the whole exceeds the sum of the individual parts.

For these scorecards to be effective, however, everyone in the organization must understand the strategies for their unit, division, and the overall corporation. CEOs understand that they cannot implement strategies by themselves. They need contributions—actions and ideas—from everyone. Individuals far from corporate and regional headquarters create considerable value by finding new and improved ways of doing business. This is not top-down direction. This is top-down communication, helping employees to learn how they can contribute to successful strategy implementation.

Leaders use many different channels to communicate the strategic message. The strategy map and Balanced Scorecard are communicated in newsletters, brochures, bulletin boards, speeches, videos, training, education programs, and the company intranet. The personal behavior of executives reinforces the message.

Employees become truly empowered by understanding *what* the organization wishes to accomplish, and *how* they can contribute to these accomplishments. This understanding generates intrinsic motivation. People now know that their work can make a difference to the organization. Employees come to work with energy, creativity, and initiative, searching to find new and better ways by which they can help the organization succeed. New information, ideas, and actions, aligned with organizational objectives, emanate from the organization's frontlines and back offices.

This new partnership with employees is reinforced with personal and team objectives linked to unit and corporate achievement, and, typically, with a new incentive plan that enables all employees to benefit financially as targets for strategic measures are achieved and economic value is created.

A final component occurs when the company implements the learning and growth objectives to upgrade the skills and capabilities of its employees. Employee skills and capabilities enhance internal processes and customer value propositions that are at the heart of the strategy. The strategy map reveals the strategic chain of cause-and-effect relationships that eventually links investment in employee skills to improved financial performance. As the senior executive of a major bank declared[7]:

> In the past, we found it hard to get and maintain focus on our employee training and skills. We talked about their importance but when financial pressure was applied, these were among the first spending programs to go. Now with the Balanced Scorecard, people can see the linkages between improving these capabilities and achieving our long-term financial goals. A focus on these infrastructure investments could be sustained even in a highly constrained environment for corporate spending.

PARTNERING WITH CUSTOMERS

The customer perspective is at the heart of the organization's strategy. Almost all companies want to grow revenues and reduce costs, so the objectives in the Balanced Scorecard's financial perspective are fairly generic across organizations. What differentiates the companies is how they define their customers and the value proposition for targeted customers. Often, this process leads to new strategic partnerships with targeted customers.

For example, Rockwater, an undersea construction company in the Halliburton organization, competed mainly on price, a typical practice in the construction industry. As it began to build its initial Balanced Scorecard, Rockwater managers took the somewhat unusual step of actually going out to talk to its existing and potential customers, the large integrated oil and gas companies. Rockwater learned that most of its customers did choose the lowest price bidder from among their qualified suppliers. Rockwater identified several important customers, however, who actually preferred suppliers capable of establishing a long-term relationship based on value added, rather than offering the lowest price on individual projects. Rockwater decided to implement a new strategy—to become the number one supplier to customers wanting a value-adding relationship. For Rockwater to become a strategic partner with its targeted customers required the development of several entirely new processes. The nature of the partnership was captured and communicated with measures in its Balanced Scorecard customer perspective (see Figure 2-3) and several new internal business objectives.

Mobil U.S. Marketing and Refining, like Rockwater, moved to a new "customer intimacy" strategy that would offer a superior buying experience for consumers. Mobil's market research had revealed that only 20 percent of consumers purchased gasoline on the basis of price alone. About 60 percent of consumers would be willing to pay a premium price if offered a superior buying experience, including immediate access to a gasoline pump, a convenient and rapid payment mechanism, a superior onsite convenience store, clean restrooms, and friendly employees. Mobil decided to focus its marketing efforts on building long-term relationships with such consumers. It developed loyalty programs, based on a new Speedpass™ payment mechanism (an employee innovation stimulated by communicating the customer value proposition to all employees through the Balanced Scorecard). Customer measures for the strategy included share of market among consumers in the targeted segments and a mystery shopper score to capture whether the desired value proposition was being consistently delivered in Mobil's 6,500 retail outlets.

Yet, Mobil had to forge a partnership with another set of customers. Like companies in many industries, Mobil's immediate customers were independent wholesalers and retailers. Franchised retailers purchased gasoline and lubricant products from Mobil and sold these products to consumers in Mobil-branded stations. If end-use consumers were to receive a great buying experience, then the independent dealers had to deliver that experience. Dealers were clearly a critical part of Mobil's new strategy.

In the past, Mobil did not consider their retailers or distributors as components of its strategy. Relationships could even be adversarial because for every cent that Mobil reduced the price of gasoline to the dealer, to reduce the dealer's cost of goods sold, one cent would be subtracted from Mobil's top line (revenues). This old strategic view put Mobil and its dealers in a zero-sum game situation. Mobil realized that its new customer-intimacy strategy could not possibly succeed

Strategic Objective	Measurement
Tier I: For Tier I customers, build longer-term relationships that are based on satisfying the following customer objectives • High perceived value for money • Hassle-free relationships • High-performance professionals • Innovative work approaches	**Market /Account Share:** Market share for Tier I clients and accounts **Customer Ranking Survey:** Tier I customers' perception and rating of our services, relative to our competition **Customer Satisfaction Index:** A measure specific to a Tier I customer's specific aims, on an individual project basis

Customer

FIGURE 2-3. STRATEGIC OBJECTIVES AND MEASUREMENTS FOR TARGETED, TIER I, CUSTOMERS

unless it stopped treating dealers as rivals. Dealers had to become partners in the strategy to deliver on the superior buying experience to millions of consumers each day.

In a sharp departure from the past, Mobil adopted an objective and measure to increase dealers' profitability. Mobil set a stretch target to have its dealers become the most profitable franchise operators in the country, so that it could attract and retain the best talent. The new strategy created a positive-sum game, increasing the size of the reward that could be shared between Mobil and its dealers; thus, the relationship would be win–win.

The higher reward came from several sources. First, the premium prices that Mobil hoped to sustain at its stations would generate higher revenues. Second, by increasing the market share in the targeted segments, a higher quantity of gasoline would be sold and a higher percentage of the purchases would be for premium grades. Third, the dealer would have an enhanced revenue stream from the sale of nongasoline products and services, convenience store, and auxiliary car services, a portion of which would also flow back to Mobil. In summary, the Balanced Scorecard provided the language, and subsequently the measurement and management system, to communicate the value from forging strategic partnerships with targeted customers: dealers and end-use consumers.

PARTNERING WITH SUPPLIERS

The success of many companies—retailers such as Sears, The Limited, and Wal-Mart; electronic companies such as Hewlett-Packard, Cisco, and Sun Microsystems; and automotive companies—depends on having outstanding suppliers and great relationships with their suppliers.[8] When strong supplier relationships are part of the strategy leading to breakthrough customer and/or financial performance, then outcome and performance driver measures for supplier relationships become incorporated on the Balanced Scorecard. Supplier objectives and measures are typically incorporated within the "Achieve Operational Excellence" theme in the Internal Process perspective. (See Figure 2-2.)

For example, a major fashion retailer, which we will call Kenyon Stores, knew that the excellence of its own performance was critically dependent on the ability of its key suppliers to manufacture goods quickly, responsively, and at low cost. Kenyon developed a sourcing leadership theme on its strategy map that stressed development and management of the supplier base, so that desired volumes and mix of merchandise could be rapidly produced and delivered at high standards of quality. Kenyon's in-store personnel examined merchandise from all incoming shipments. One measure recorded the percentage of items that could not be offered to customers because of quality-related defects. The scorecard measured the overall percentage of quality-related returns, and also the specific percentages for individual vendors. A second sourcing leadership measure came from a newly created vendor scorecard that evaluated suppliers along dimensions of quality, price, lead-time, and input into fashion decisions.

Strategic partnerships with suppliers arise when companies wish to select suppliers that offer not low prices, but low costs. Low-price suppliers may turn out to be extremely high-cost if they deliver in large quantities that require extensive storage space, receiving and handling resources, as well as tying up capital from buying and paying for materials and merchandise well in advance of when they are used. The quality of incoming items supplied by low-price suppliers may not be guaranteed to conform to buyer specifications, so the company must inspect incoming items, return those found to be defective, and arrange for replacement parts to arrive (which themselves have to inspected). The low-price supplier may also not have a stellar on-time delivery capability. Its failure to deliver reliably at scheduled times causes the buying company to order well in advance of need and hold protective stock in case delivery is not when expected. Late deliveries cause higher costs for expediting orders and rescheduling the plant around the missing items. Also, low-price suppliers may not be electronically connected to their customers, thereby imposing higher costs on customers when they order and pay for the purchased parts.

In contrast, a low-cost supplier may have slightly higher purchase prices, but it delivers defect-free products, directly to the end-use location, just in time, as they are needed, and uses electronic channels for ordering and payment. The buying company incurs virtually no costs for ordering, receiving, inspecting, storing, handling, expediting, rescheduling, rework, and paying for parts purchased from this low-cost supplier. A strategic partnership, therefore, can be defined by a cost measure (activity based) that motivates total cost reductions across the supply chain. It would also use measures related to the quality, lead-time, and on-time delivery performance for suppliers.

By elevating strategic objectives and measures for superior supplier relationships to the company's Balanced Scorecard, employees come to understand the value of forging strategic relationships with their key suppliers. This recognition and understanding provides the context for initiatives, resources, and performance feedback on the most critical elements of the supplier relationship.

PARTNERING WITH THE COMMUNITY

Companies, such as telecommunications and utilities, whose prices and operations are regulated to some extent by governmental authorities, must have excellent relationships with these authorities and legislatures. Companies whose operations entail environmental, health, and safety (EHS) risks need to comply with regulations in the nations and communities in which they operate. Beyond compliance, they may seek to achieve a reputation as a leader in EHS performance to enhance their ability to recruit and retain valuable employees and to maintain and expand their physical presence in communities. When such regulatory and EHS considerations are vital for a successful strategy, companies include several objectives in a "good corporate citizen" strategic theme in the internal perspective. (See Figure 2-2.) For example, Mobil, in its Balanced Scorecard, included measures on environmental and safety performance, stressing the importance of being a good employer and a good citizen in every community in which it conducted business.[9]

One chemicals company created a fifth perspective solely to reflect environmental considerations. They argued[10]:

> Our franchise is under severe pressure in many of the communities where we operate. Our strategy is to go well beyond what

current laws and regulations require so that we can be seen in every community as not only a law-abiding corporate citizen but as the outstanding corporate citizen, measured both environmentally and by creating well-paying, safe, and productive jobs. If regulations get tightened, some of our competitors may lose their franchise, but we expect to have earned the right to continue operations.

For them, the environmental perspective highlighted how outstanding environmental and community performance was a central part of its strategy and had to be an integral part of their scorecard. It communicated the priority to be the outstanding employer in every community in which it operated.

Thus, even though suppliers and the community are not explicitly one of the four perspectives of the Balanced Scorecard, their interests, when they are vital for the success of the business unit's strategy, are incorporated on strategy maps and Balanced Scorecards. These stakeholder objectives, however, should not be appended to the Scorecard via an isolated set of measures that managers must keep "in control." Their measures appear only when partnerships with suppliers and the community are critical to the success of the strategy and fully integrated into the chain of causal event linkages on a strategy map that define and tell the story of the business unit's strategy.

SUMMARY

Traditionally, competitive advantage came from access to low-cost raw materials, energy sources, or financial capital and an ability to invest in physical capital to achieve economies of scale and scope.[11] Today, value creation comes from mobilizing and managing the organization's intangible resources, especially loyal and profitable customer relationships; high-quality and responsive operating and supply-chain processes; information systems and knowledge; and motivated, skilled, and empowered employees. Leaders need new measurement and management systems to align their tangible and intangible assets to deliver a coherent and integrated strategy.

Strategy maps and Balanced Scorecards help leaders communicate the strategy to critical constituents—employees, suppliers, customers, and the community—and focus their entire organization on enhancing the strategic partnering relationships with these constituents that drive and sustain long-term value creation.

CHAPTER 3

THE DEMISE OF THE CELEBRITY-LEADER AND THE RISE OF PARTNERSHIP NODES

SALLY HELGESEN

How we think about leadership will undergo a subtle but significant evolution over the next few years. This change has already begun to manifest itself, though by means of confusing and even contradictory signals. It is being shaped primarily by a confluence of economic, technological, social, and demographic transformations that are altering the nature of every organization—business, governmental, educational, social sector, military, legal, medical, and religious. The changes these transformations effect will also be intensified by the events of September 11.

DEFLATING THE CELEBRITY-LEADER

To understand what is happening, let's first look briefly at the impact of September 11 on how we think about leadership, for a significant implication of the events has gone largely unmentioned. Our culture, which has in recent years increasingly identified celebrities as its heroes, suddenly found itself riveted by stories of everyday, and for the most part anonymous, heroes—the firemen, policemen, emergency service workers, and rescuers who put their lives on the line in the course of doing their duty; the people who died just because they went to the office on a sunny Tuesday morning; and the stalwarts who took early flights to a business conference.

[24]

The clarity with which we now discern heroism in lives we had been taught to view as ordinary has the potential to reverse the trend toward conflating heroism with celebrity. This trend has been widely noted in popular culture in recent years, and is easy to discern in the fields of media and entertainment, as well as in the marketing of products ranging from sportswear to magazines, retirement communities to cooking equipment. Yet, business and organizations have also become enmeshed in celebrity worship. In the same way that the popular media write about trends by tying them to movie stars, so too does the business media write about organizations and business trends by tying them to, and identifying them with, celebrity-leaders. In the process, these leaders assume the mantle of hero, which imbues them with a superhuman aura.

We see much evidence of this. During most of the 1990s, *Fortune* and *Business Week* seemed determined to press upon their readership the notion that Intel simply was Andy Grove (or later, Craig Barrett), while GE was in turn Jack Welch. At popular conferences and colloquies on leadership, these men's names were endlessly invoked, whereas the means by which their organizations operated and how the companies did (or did not) spur innovation rarely made it into the conversation.

It takes nothing away from these men in terms of the leadership they provided or the legacies they left to observe that equating a huge, complex, and decentralized organization with a single leader (especially a leader who did not found the enterprise) distorts the reality of how organizational life is lived and how extraordinary accomplishments are made. Focusing on the leader as hero, the leader as the story, may make life easier for business journalists and provide corporate publicists with a ready-made hook, but it also twists how we think about leadership, according it too much credit while paradoxically demeaning its true achievements.

In a similar vein, a good proportion of the overly optimistic market investment that occurred during the previous decade was fueled by the growing tendency to create celebrities out of stock analysts and portfolio managers with a successful record, making them into virtual cult figures at whose word and into whose portfolios individuals heedlessly flung enormous sums of money. The celebrity of the leaders whose companies these analysts touted, of course, only added to investors' willful confidence; the very names of such leaders seemed to harbor a kind of magic, and investing "in" them was assumed to confer both prestige and safety (as in, "I've got my money in Jack").

As a result, some of the major financial disasters that heralded the present downturn were the result of celebrity analysts setting up shop with virtually no oversight, with Long Term Capital Management being the most notorious example. Because the investment professionals (and the analysts who covered them) had become heroes, and because they were viewed as having a nearly infallible touch, people felt safe entrusting billions to their care with little knowledge of how the investments were being handled.

It is ironic that this trend toward the exaltation of the leader as celebrity-hero was reaching its zenith even as organizational reality was moving in the opposite direction. For the imperative of an economy built on networks—of producers, suppliers, customers, and technology providers—by its very nature undermines the concept of the lone hero-leader. Networks, on the contrary, flourish in an environment characterized by distributed talent, the open flow of information, and the creation and management of what might be called *partnership nodes* at all levels of the organization.

PARTNERSHIP NODES

I saw the power of this partnership model firsthand while doing a case study of the roots of the "Intel Inside" campaign. It may seem surprising that this model emerged at the very time that Andrew Grove was popularly viewed as synonymous with Intel, and so an apt representative of the celebrity syndrome in the world of business. Although this was true in the broader culture (and certainly played a role in how the market valued Intel), it was remarkably untrue within the company itself.

Ted Jenkins, the company's senior engineer, the sixth employee to be hired, and the informal steward of Intel's culture, explained the reason to me.[1] Jenkins's words have since come to seem a useful benchmark for determining how skilled and receptive an organization is when it comes to fostering partnerships.

"Intel's great strength," said Jenkins, "lies in the way the company allows resources to flow to wherever there's a problem. In many companies, this doesn't happen. I think that's because, in most organizations, resources tend to get stuck wherever someone is in a position of power. Power in such organizations is usually based almost solely upon position, on where someone stands on the org chart. The people at the top hold on tight, so no one else can establish any kind of alternate power base. And it's the *absence* of other power bases that causes resources to get stuck."

By contrast, at Intel, according to Jenkins, "There is no single way of being powerful. Position is just one aspect of power, and not necessarily the most important. Here we recognize—we even honor—nonpositional power." Jenkins enumerated the various kinds of nonpositional power. "The power of expertise, basically how much you know. The power of personal authority, how charismatic or believable you are. And the power of personal connections, the breadth and the depth of your relationships, both within and outside of the organization."

Thinking about Jenkins's remarks, I began to realize that in most organizations I had worked with or studied, the kind of non-positional power he described was viewed as subversive, a threat to the prerogatives of senior leadership. Those individuals who established alternate power bases in such companies, who wielded more authority than their job title necessarily reflected, or had a broad network of relationships that were not strictly bound by the chain of command, were viewed with suspicion, sometimes even hounded out of the organization.

It also became apparent that the "Intel Inside" campaign, which entirely repositioned the company in the marketplace, changing it from a manufacturer of a component for computers (albeit the component was the microprocessor) to a brand name that drove the sales of computers themselves, and thus lessened the company's dependence on computer manufacturers, resulted primarily from Intel's ability to let nonpositional power flourish.

This particular transformative innovation had not been borne of a decision by the executive committee, nor did it occur in response to a strategic planning initiative. Rather, it grew out of a series of improvisations that evolved at the grassroots of the company, as employees with diverse concerns attempted to meet a series of challenges. Those who devised the strategy that would become "Intel Inside" included a marketing team in Santa Clara, a couple of trademark lawyers in an office nearby, and a cadre trying to create visibility for Intel's product in Japan's crowded market.

These teams, individuals, and cadres—people at very different levels in the organization, who often shared little beyond the propensity to exercise nonpositional power, and whose network of relationships throughout the company was particularly broad—reflected an organizational structure based on partnership nodes, shifting relationships, and alliances that came together to reshape who the company was in the world.

The reshaping effected strategic-level change in the organization by migrating its customer base from computer-makers to consumers. This in turn created new partnership nodes and alternate power bases within Intel, as well as between Intel and its suppliers, producers, customers, and technology providers. These new nodes transformed both the structure and the operations of the company, enabling what had begun as a seat-of-the-pants experimental effort to become embedded in the company's purpose, mission, self-conception, and way of doing business.

The role of Intel's leadership in this reshaping was to give the individuals and teams who came up with the idea of marketing directly to the customer a license to experiment, a measure of financial support, and a framework within which to test their results. The leadership was able to do this because it had established a culture in which people in the ranks felt comfortable building relationships across lines and levels, units and divisions, and exploiting the power that resulted from these new alliances to partner on seemingly off-the-wall experimental projects. In many organizations, such informal partnerships based on converging ideas would have been considered disruptive of the basic power structure, illegitimate given the chain of command.

In such circumstances, the innovations that were the fruit of such partnerships at Intel would never have been able to take root.

CONCLUSION

The confluence occurring today between economic, technological, social, and demographic change is creating an organizational environment in which change is a constant, nimbleness an imperative, a broad base of talent an essential, and maintaining a balance between innovation and brand identity the key to survival. In such an environment, an organization's ability to nurture partnerships at various levels becomes a requirement. For innovation to flourish in the ranks, there must be "tolerance at the margins," as Arie de Geus has observed.[2]

The measure of leaders in such a world will increasingly lie in their ability to nurture organizational cultures that permit and encourage a rich variety of partnerships, alliances, and relationships to form—a situation that has the inevitable consequence of encouraging the development of alternate bases of power within the organization. Getting comfortable with this will be difficult for leaders, but the ability to do so will be the balancing act, the art, and the hallmark of appropriate leadership in the years ahead. The recent trend toward a celebrity culture of leadership, in which the leader embodies the organization, is clearly utterly responsible for its success. To assume that a leader has a magic touch that validates his or her decisions is not only inadequate to, but the antithesis of, what such an environment demands.

As Peter Drucker has noted, a knowledge organization is one in which knowledge (and thus power) is distributed throughout the organization.[3] But a culture that worships positional leaders makes it difficult for organizations to leverage this internal knowledge. As we have seen in the case of Intel, however, if the organization has a tradition of valuing nonpositional power, and the leader does not circumvent it, the consequences of the popular culture viewing the leader as celebrity will be blunted. At bottom, Andrew Grove never bought into his own publicity, but this takes unusual personal strength and is hard to come by.

Organizational failures, painful market reevaluations, and political flameouts are part of the 1990s legacy of the celebrity-leader. The price paid was unusually high this time around, because the model had become especially inappropriate to the circumstances. As the evolving economy and networked technologies that support it continue to foment radical change, partnership nodes will become the story in the years ahead.

Indeed, partnership nodes—informal, ad hoc, leaders acting as partners, individuals at the grassroots assuming responsibility and cooperating to lead in utterly unforeseen circumstances—is what we saw happening before our eyes on September 11. It is part of that experience's blessing and an as-yet rarely acknowledged aspect of its legacy. Thus, the events of that and subsequent days provide a model that will give energy, possibility, and value to networked organizations in years ahead.

◄○►

CHAPTER 4

LEADERSHIP PARTNERS: SEPTEMBER 11, 2001

MAJOR GENERAL (USAF, RET.) DONALD W. SHEPPERD

The most important book I have ever read concerning management philosophy was *Flight of the Buffalo* by Jim Belasco, which changed the way I led and managed organizations.

DEVELOPING A MANAGEMENT PHILOSOPHY

At the time, I was an Air Force Major General and had just taken over as head of the Air National Guard. I was stationed in the Pentagon and in charge of 110,000 people spread throughout the 54 states and territories. My organization was composed of 89 flying units, all the way from F-16 fighters to giant C-5 transports, and 250 nonflying units, mainly combat communications, tactical air control radar, weather, air traffic control, and intelligence personnel.

As I read Jim Belasco's book, I reflected on my problems: how to effectively control a large, widely dispersed organization spread all over the world; how to embed a management and leadership philosophy; how to set an agenda; how to communicate; and how to measure success. These are the same problems faced by CEOs in all large organizations.

Dialogue in this chapter is reconstructed based upon conversations with the participants and to protect security.

I also recalled my first day of class in 1985 at Air War College, the senior service school for Air Force officers at Maxwell AFB, AL. The school commandant marched on stage, issued a welcome, and then proceeded with his speech: "Ladies and gentlemen, you have been chosen to attend this school because you are one of the top 1 percent of Air Force leadership. What got you here was your ability to lead people, make things happen, and produce results. Many of you will go on to attain high rank. I want to assure you of one important thing: If you simply continue to do what has made you successful to this point in your career, you will now become a total and absolute failure!"

The commandant's message was simple, yet deep. As you move to positions of increasing responsibility, you must change the ways in which you lead, manage, and communicate. In my case, I had to learn to communicate and lead people whom I would never see, some halfway around the world. They had to know what I wanted, why I wanted it, how I wanted it done, and most importantly, they had to believe in me and I in them. Also, I was held responsible for their performance and success.

Before I read *Flight of the Buffalo,* I had always assumed that the most important responsibility of a leader was to get the "right tools" for people to do their work and accomplish their organizational goals. But Jim Belasco's book turns the organizational responsibilities upside down. Jim said the most important responsibility of a leader is to create an organization that makes it possible for the people to get the tools for themselves. In other words, leaders are responsible to create a vision and a culture that enables workers to be successful through their own efforts, not just through those of the boss.

It was obvious that if I allowed myself to be responsible to find the tools for all the workers in a large organization, my desk would pile high with one request after another and one excuse after another for why someone could not perform, because "I" could not get them the resources they needed to succeed. I had observed over the years that people are world-class problem finders, and if my job as CEO were to solve the workers' problems, the system would simply bog down.

Armed with my newfound philosophy, I set out to create a shared vision and culture for pride and success in a large and very complex organization. Who better to help me than Jim Belasco? I called Jim and sought his assistance. At the time the quality movement was in vogue throughout industry and government. I had been through many of the previous cycles, Zero-Defects, Management by Objectives, Quality Circles, Six Sigma, and so on. Although all of the philosophies were of some utility, few stood the test of time. I had always been suspicious of "management waves" and gurus, and was seeking a simple overarching philosophy to guide me. Jim provided a common-sense approach void of New Age management babble. He and we went to work trying to embed new thoughts and methods in our leadership team. I decided to focus on the elements of the quality movement that made the most sense to me:

➤Customer orientation

➤Continuous improvement

➤Empowerment of people

➤Measurement

Jim helped me arrange staff "off-sites," reading material, and other management tools that, when combined with a strategic plan, allowed me to measure and track the performance of our organization. It became clear that what gets measured gets better! But before you make the decision to measure something, take great care. Jim taught me there are many indicators of performance, but few indicators of success. He made me concentrate on an important question: What is it you as a CEO "really" want to watch? He helped me to create an electronic corporate dashboard that clearly laid out what was to be measured, what performance goals were expected, and most importantly, how people's performance compared to produce organizational goals. The dashboard was intended to be available at all levels of the organization, and I quickly saw the power of information widely distributed that "visually" compared the performance of units and people.

Jim also preached three things that I was determined to embed in our organization:

1. Passionate devotion to customers at all levels, including co-workers.

2. Learn more about your customer's business than your customer knows and offer him or her solutions that solve his or her problems, not yours.

3. Create relationships based on trust that last over time.

STANDING THE TEST OF TIME: SEPTEMBER 11, 2001

When I retired from the Pentagon four years later, I questioned whether or not the things in which I believed, the things I tried to emphasize and embed, would stand the test of time or make a difference. I had been told that when people and organizations are stressed, they revert to what they truly believe, rather than what they have been taught and told. I got the answer to my questions on September 11, 2001, when the airplanes hit the World Trade Center and the Pentagon.

At 8:55, on the morning of September 11, I was working in my home office when the phone rang. My wife was calling from her workplace. "Are you watching the TV? An airplane just hit the World Trade Center!"

I turned on the TV to witness the spectacle that has since haunted all of America, the World Trade Center engulfed in fire and smoke. The thought of terrorism occurred to me, but like most I assumed it was likely a tragic accident until the second aircraft hit; then there was no doubt in my mind that this was an act of terrorism. My home is close to the Pentagon, and I actually "felt" the concussion when the third aircraft hit the Pentagon.

Earlier in the day, Lieutenant Colonel Marc "Sass" Sasseville and Major Dan "Razin" Caine reported for work to the operations building at the 113th Fighter Wing, District of Columbia Air National Guard, stationed at Andrews Air Force Base Maryland, 11 miles from the nation's Capitol and the White House. The unit is commanded by Brigadier General Dave Wherley, a superb officer, pilot, and commander, and is equipped with supersonic F-16 fighter aircraft. It was a beautiful day, not a cloud in the sky. Sass and Razin anticipated a normal day of flying, gunnery practice, and "pulling-Gs" in mock air-to-air combat. Like the rest of America, their day was to be anything but normal.

Sass was the operations supervisor for the day, the senior officer in charge of desk duties to supervise all operations activities. Razin performed duties as the supervisor of flying (SOF) in charge of desk duties, specifically involving flying activities. Three of the unit airplanes were airborne on a practice gunnery mission over a North Carolina gunnery range 100 miles to the south of Andrews. Sass was conducting a scheduling meeting, planning for future unit-deployment training. The meeting was attended by Captain Brandon "Igor" Rasmussen, First Lieutenant Heather "Lucky" Penny, and Technical Sergeant Dave "Chunks" Callaghan, all of whom would play roles in the evolving events of the day.

Razin was at the operations desk trying to avoid starting on some of the paperwork all fighter pilots detest. "Hey, Razin, switch on the TV to CNN. You won't believe it!" shouted a voice from the other end of the operations building. When Razin saw what all of America was watching, that an aircraft had impacted the World Trade Center in New York City, he shouted to Sass and the others attending the scheduling meeting.

Because they are stationed at Andrews Air Force Base, the 113th flying operations are regularly affected by the movements and flights of Air Force One, the President's airplane. When the President moves, all operations stop and air traffic into and out of Andrews comes to a halt, often when 113th F-16s are airborne, while the Secret Service scours the area on foot, in cars, and from helicopters. Thus, over time and out of necessity, the 113th had to develop close relationships with the Secret Service, which manages the President's moves. Razin had just returned from attending a course with a Secret Service agent, who on September 11 happened to be working in the joint operation center (JOC) in the White House.

When the second aircraft impacted the WTC, Razin and Sass swung into action. They called Brigadier General Dave Wherley to come immediately to operations (he was already on his way). Razin called his Secret Service friend in the JOC. Although Razin did not know about the third aircraft inbound to the Pentagon, the thrust of the conversation was, "This is obviously terrorism, are you guys thinking about the defense of DC and do you want us to do something about it? We have a flight of three F-16s airborne and we can generate the rest of our fighters."

"Jesus, hang on! BUT DON'T HANG UP, we're busy!" was the answer.

Razin held the phone line open while Sass and General Wherley gave orders to begin generating airplanes, to arm guns, and to move air-to-air missiles out of munitions storage areas. Maintenance troops raced on the flight line to pull covers off jet engine intakes and canopies to ready the fighters for takeoff. Razin contacted the three aircraft on the gunnery range and told them to turn for home immediately!

An alert female FAA Dulles Radar Approach Controller, who was aware of the New York situation and had been notified that it was likely a third airliner had been hijacked, noticed an unidentified high-speed target west of Dulles International Airport headed back east towards Washington on her radar screen. The order "ALL AIR TRAFFIC IN UNITED STATES AIRSPACE, PROCEED IMMEDIATELY TO THE NEAREST SUITABLE AIRFIELD AND LAND" had been issued by Norm Mineta, the Secretary of Transportation and broadcast on all FAA radio air traffic control and emergency frequencies. The FAA controller asked an Air Force C-130 that was proceeding to land if he saw the unidentified aircraft. The C-130 pilot replied he had an aircraft in sight that appeared to be "an airliner at high speed and descending." The FAA controller called the Secret Service, who reportedly immediately whisked the Vice President (the President was on a trip to Florida) into a secret secure location.

By this time, three 113th F-16s were returning from practice gunnery missions and landing back at Andrews AFB in response to the FAA and radio calls from Razin on their discreet operations radiofrequency.

Razin was feverishly working the phone. The gist of the call was historic, "THE NATIONAL COMMAND AUTHORITY URGENTLY REQUESTS THE ASSISTANCE OF ANY ARMED AIRCRAFT! IMMEDIATELY LAUNCH ANYTHING YOU HAVE AND DEFEND

THE CAPITOL! USE OF DEADLY FORCE IS AUTHORIZED! THIS IS ON THE AUTHORITY OF THE PRESIDENT!"

Razin asked General Wherley to listen and verify the request. Sass then assigned Lieutenant Colonel Phil "Dog" Thompson the duties of supervisor of flying and handed over the duties of operations supervisor to Festus Chase. Sass, Lucky, Razin, and Igor began to assemble briefing materials, including takeoff data and flight lineup cards, and donned their anti-G suits in anticipation of a rapid launch. These people were pros who regularly flew together. They were familiar with standard procedures, hand signals, radio call signs, and so on. Thus, a detailed briefing was unnecessary; however, none of them realized that a third hijacked airliner was, at that very instant, headed directly for the White House.

Dog and General Wherley quickly conferred. Dog grabbed the operations radio. Major Billy "Testy" Hutchison was the leader of the flight that was just landing after their gunnery range mission. "Billy, how much gas you got left?" queried Dog.

The flight members had been informed of the situation in New York during its return. The dribbles of information being passed on the operations radiofrequency, combined with the FAA order to clear America's airspace, made them aware that a serious situation had arisen across America. Testy Hutchison replied, "Not much. I got twenty-four hundred pounds."

The Arab terrorist Hani Hanjour was at the controls of American Airlines Flight 77 that the FAA controller saw streaking past Dulles toward Washington, D.C. His target was the White House. A retracing of the aircraft flight path shows Hanjour making a pass over the Washington Monument, then turning back west. The White House is very difficult to spot from the air, even for experienced pilots. Hanjour's limited training did not enable him to find it, so he went for his secondary target and crashed into the west side of the Pentagon. Billy Hutchison could see smoke rising from the area of the Pentagon, 11 miles northwest.

General Wherley issued the order: "Billy, launch! Go max endurance. Stay airborne as long as you can while we're getting other aircraft ready. Terrorists in hijacked airliners have hit the World Trade Center in New York and the Pentagon. Others may be headed here. Orbit the Capitol and defend it. Use of deadly force is authorized." Billy understood.

Meanwhile, Sass and Lucky raced for their airplanes. As there had not been time to load missiles, they taxied for takeoff with only non-explosive training ammunition in their guns rather than delay take-off to rearm.

The first flight airborne from Andrews to defend the Capitol was Testy Hutchison, alone in an F-16 and almost out of gas. He re-launched after landing from his gunnery mission with only ten to 15 minutes of fuel available. After takeoff, he headed straight for the burning Pentagon and made a low pass that was seen on TV across America, confirming the fire and flames coming from the west side over his operations radiofrequency. He circled over downtown Washington awaiting help from the next flight.

The second flight consisted of Sass Sasseville, an experienced F-16 Fighter Weapons School Graduate, and Lucky Penny, a 90-pound female F-16 fighter pilot. Sass and Lucky established radio contact with Approach Control at Reagan Airport and began to sort through targets on their radar, looking for any unidentified aircraft heading for the Capitol. Sass quickly assumed command of the developing situation. He established combat air patrols (CAPs) with spokes oriented northeast, southeast, southwest, and northwest of the Capitol, using Reagan Airport as "Bullseye," a ground reference control point.

The first airplane airborne fully armed with missiles was Razin. Also a graduate of the Air Force Fighter Weapons School, which offered the equivalent of a Ph.D. in fighter tactics, Razin turned FAA civilian radar approach controllers into combat weapons controllers in a five-minute briefing. He briefed them on terminology, "Friendly," for radar targets that were identified, "Bogey" for targets that could not be positively identified, and "Bandit" for known hijackers. The hastily assembled team scoured the skies, desperately looking for United Airlines Flight 93, which was surely headed for the Capitol.

As the world now knows, the fateful action to shoot down an airliner with Americans onboard did not have to be performed by the F-16 pilots from Andrews. Civilian passenger heroes onboard the flight took matters into their own hands. They recited the Lord's Prayer, said "Let's roll," and attacked the hijackers, causing the airplane to crash in Pennsylvania before it reached Washington, DC, and the orbiting F-16s.

General Wherley, Sass, Razin, Igor, Dog, Festus, Testy, Lucky, and Chunks were only the first of many military members and flights from my old organization who swung rapidly into action across America that day as we turned our air defenses to "look inward" for the first time in history, rather than outward for foes attacking our country.

CONCLUSION

I have thought about what Jim Belasco taught me, what I preached to my organization, and how it worked on September 11:

➤The job of the leader is not to get tools for the workers, but to create vision and a culture that allows them to get the tools for themselves.

➤Passionate devotion to "customers" at all levels, including co-workers.

➤Learn more about your customer's business than your customer knows and offer him or her solutions that solve his or her problems, not yours.

➤Create relationships based on trust that last over time.

On September 11, the fighter F-16 pilots of the DC Air National Guard did not ask their leaders for tools. They got their own.

They had a clear idea of who their customer was—the American public—and had a passionate devotion to that customer. They knew more about their customer's business than the customer knew. When the time came, they brought solutions to the customer's problems.

They created relationships based on trust that that lasted over time. Razin's and Dog's relationship with a Secret Service agent in the White

House, and the pilots' relationships with each other enabled them to spring rapidly into action, trusting each other in a complicated, intense, high-risk situation fraught with danger and the very high risk of error or failure.

What Jim Belasco advocated and I tried to embed in my organization stood the test of time. In a crisis, this group of people saw what was happening and leaped into action, without asking for permission. Rather they intended to ask for forgiveness if they were wrong. They reverted to what they truly believed, philosophies that were vindicated on September 11.

CHAPTER 5

LEADING ORGANIZATIONS INTO PARTNERSHIP

ELIZABETH PINCHOT AND GIFFORD PINCHOT

The era of the "divine right" of leaders is passing. The economic conditions in which autocratic leadership worked well are giving way to a more complex economy in which effective leaders share power with those they influence. Highly dominant leadership styles passed muster in the fear-based hierarchies that worked for controlling a hastily assembled army of peasants or an industrial enterprise in which unskilled workers performed simple, repetitive tasks. Today's complex, knowledge-based organizations require leaders who relate to their teams not as subjects to be assigned tasks, but rather as partners in a shared enterprise. The partnership challenge goes beyond the quality of relationships between leader and subordinate, critical as that is. We address how leaders at all levels of the organization can increase organizational performance by helping evolve a lateral network of partnerships across the boundaries of the formal organization.

Informal lateral networks are the emerging brains of highly intelligent twenty-first century organizations and will gradually take over some of the responsibility for coordinating work from the chain of command. These horizontal partnerships will include teams that buy and sell with each other in internal service networks, and individuals and groups that are given the freedom of choice to self-organize to accomplish tasks in innovative and efficient ways.

DISSOLVING BUREAUCRACY WITH PARTNERSHIP

The increasingly complex and interconnected challenges organizations face are driving the need for new organizational systems and leaders skilled in partnership. Large organizations act in and through many cultures, technologies, suppliers, customer segments, geographies, functional specialties, professional associations, and so forth. No one person can have more than a superficial understanding of all the interacting issues and challenges. Horizontal networks of teams and individuals integrated through partnership relationships create the necessary organizational integration and intelligence. Many companies have fostered long-term success by pioneering organizations integrated by horizontal partnerships.

Partnering with Freedom at Hewlett-Packard

Hewlett-Packard's printer business of the last two decades gives us a classic model of a distributed organization bound together by voluntary partnership relationships. In 1981, rather than using their printers to sell HP computers, they bucked the tide of centralization by stepping outside HP to partner with Canon to make a laser printer that worked with their competitors' computers as well as HP's. In the early 1990s, the printer business, which was then producing 40 percent of HP's income, employed 9000 people across six sites. Rick Belluzzo "ran" that business out of a small leased office with four people: himself, a research and development manager, and two secretaries. This arrangement worked because they had progressed far beyond bureaucracy. Most of the tasks and responsibilities, including coordination between teams running the five separate businesses within the inkjet group, were delegated to the teams themselves, who handled everything they could with partnership and collaboration.

How a group of 9000 employees and five separate businesses managed to integrate itself with almost no staff is a triumph of partnership skills. The research and development manager worked with the teams to share technology and to encourage collaboration in designing a part (such as a common inkjet print head) where economies of scale suggested the teams should work together. He did not tell them what to do, and, needless to say, top-down integration would be impossible with a staff of four. When a common problem arose, a team assembled itself from the different subgroups and handled it. Often the teams identified and solved problems themselves, although sometimes Rick Belluzzo and his three staff members were the impetus for the groups' tackling collaborative solutions. Given their extremely limited staff time, they chose well to focus on inspiring partnership solutions among the network of teams and helping strengthen their group's sense of community.

Because very few orders were issued from above, it might seem as though this HP business group was composed of independents who only occasionally partnered. In fact, the subgroups tended to be highly interdependent and worked as a team on a regular basis, even when this involved sacrifices. For example, as years went by, responsibility for generating profit shifted from one area to another within the business. Each area took its turn shouldering the burden of producing profit, so the whole inkjet business was a reliable profit generator, while certain parts at various times needed to spend more on research and development or shave their margins to be competitive. Sharing the load without worrying about who was ahead was a critical piece of the HP partnering system. It was based on knowing each other, trusting that everyone would be treated fairly, and strong personal friendships.

AN ORGANIZATION IS RELATIONSHIPS

An organization is largely made up of people and their relationships with each other. These relationships include both vertical and horizontal relationships within the organization as well as those with outsiders, such as customers and suppliers. The quality of relationships in this complex web of interconnections largely determines the quality and effectiveness of the organization. If they are uncooperative, untruthful, angry, uncaring, or unduly constrained, the organization will be out of touch with its customers, unable to coordinate internally, and unresponsive to both opportunities and threats. The highest quality relationships are those of partnership, mutual support, and mutual respect for autonomy, not those in which one party dominates another. For this reason, more effective knowledge-intensive organizations work to encourage partnerships rather than dominance and submission.

Many of today's leaders have earned their promotions through high-order individual contributions and ability to stand out from the crowd. They are better at authority than teamwork. They have little experience with the partnering skills, habits, and attitudes that will make them effective in their new roles, much less to teach partnership to their people.

The explosive growth of the executive coaching industry, which often helps individual contributors improve their relationship skills, illustrates the depth of the gap between the supply and the demand for leaders with partnering skills. Yet, every human is born with the capacity to build partnerships. The emerging partnering style of work hooks directly into humans' innate need for connection and collaboration, and the inherent pleasure we derive from working together. Those leaders who can create an environment of partnership for all their people will infuse energy and meaning into their workplaces.

In the conversion to post-bureaucratic organizations, teams with autonomy to manage their areas of work form the basic unit of partnership, small enough for efficient high involvement and large enough for the collective strength and synergy generated by diverse talents. Teams handle complexities collaboratively by the partnership quality of their internal and external relationships.

Endenburg Electrotechniek: A Classic Partnership Story

The collapse in the early 1970s of the Rotterdam shipbuilding industry threatened the existence of many departments in Endenburg Electrotechniek, especially the one that performed electrical work for local shipbuilders. Management came to the electrical department and told them what they had dreaded to hear: they would probably need to shut down the department and reduce staff.

Deliberations in the department focused on these painful changes, until one electrician suggested an alternative: The department members could dress up in shirts and ties and solicit business for the other departments of the company. Departmental staff developed a plan, submitted it to management, and got the go-ahead. It wasn't long before business they found for other departments compensated for lost business in their own department. In addition, the other departments soon referred business for related electrical work to them and they were back in business themselves. Without much help from management, the members of the department changed the function and form of their organization to generate value in a changing marketplace.

Why did this happen there and then? For decades, the leadership in Endenburg had been preparing their company members for partnership. Everyone in the company was in one or more self-managing workgroups. The leadership at the top of the organization didn't know what to do about the decline of the shipbuilding industry; however, they had created the embedded intelligence of a partnership organization so those closest to the problem could figure out how to deploy the underemployed resources. By moving beyond hierarchical systems of management, they had created an organization capable of responding constructively to sudden changes.

Grow Partnerships with Freedom, Not Hierarchy

Oddly, there is no command and control way to create a partnership culture in an organization. Command and control works against partnership in many ways, the most basic of which is a violation of human autonomy. Effective partnerships are always voluntary relationships. If one can leave if his or her interests are not served, the chances increase that one will be treated with equity and fairness. The bureaucratic form of organization, which is the predominant industrial flavor of command and control organization, works against partnership, because it prohibits freedom of choice in work relationships. The individual employee does not choose which projects to work on, who to team with, how to do the work, which vendors to use, which customers to serve, which mentors to recruit, and so on.

In a chain-of-command organization, the game is rigged to reward dominance (and submission), staying within one's box, and competing for upward mobility rather than helping one's co-workers. An organization that overemphasizes the role of a formal chain of command cannot embrace the multidimensional nature of the challenges organizations face today. Attempts to upgrade the bureaucratic system to a multidimensional matrix organization often fail because a matrix organization, when combined with a hierarchical mindset, produces gridlock. How then are all those big bureaucratic corporations staying alive? All large organizations with bureaucratic structures are dependent on the informal partnerships that integrate projects and functions across boundaries.

Organizations can be formally designed and informally led to increase the probability of partnership relationships within and between units significantly. Leaders can support teamwork, workplace community, and internal services provided by *intra*preneurial teams of volunteers. More generally, leaders can implement productive partnerships within and across the boundaries of the formal organization.

Over the past few decades, the empowerment and participation movements have spread through most organizations, influencing leaders to listen more and trust their people to make more decisions. Yet, evolution continues in the organizational world, and we are moving again, from a time when the most effective leaders handed down vision and direction to their followers, to a time when effective leaders evoke a collective vision, rather than create it alone. This move from individual brilliance toward a collective intelligence brings the leader, and everyone else, into partnerlike relationships with subordinates, peers, bosses, customers, and suppliers. Learning to support the emergence of collaborative visions that integrate the visions of others is at the core of twenty-first-century leadership skills.

THREE METHODS OF BRINGING ABOUT ORDER IN ORGANIZATIONS

One important role of leadership is to educate people about what it takes to create the detailed thinking capacity of an effective knowledge-based organization. If organizational intelligence is more a product of the informal network than the chain of command, reeducation is needed to replace certain common beliefs about what must be done to create order. Most people still believe that relying on the chain of command is the only possible way to coordinate individuals at work. Misplaced trust in the power of the chain of command can justify everything from laziness to cruelty. There is a new story for leaders to tell: the truth about the great human capacity for directing and co-ordinating their own work through effective partnerships, teams, networks, and markets.

Consider the greatly superior performance routinely achieved by self-organizing teams when compared with the system of "foreman and reluctant, but obedient, workers." Think of the extraordinary performance of groups of people facing a challenge such as Apollo 13, the effectiveness of guerillas against foreign aggression, or a community disaster needing thousands of volunteers. The strictures of bureaucracy are set aside and people work together as partners. Even in ordinary times, people in high-performance teams, egalitarian new ventures, and nonprofit organizations often accomplish extra-ordinary amounts of innovative work with few resources and little time, and have fun as well.

When it comes to large-scale systems, such as large nations, chain-of-command bureaucracy fails miserably. Despite vast natural resources and very bright, often well intentioned people striving to make it work, the centralized Soviet economy was unable to produce decent food, clean manufacturing, good cars, or personal computers. As knowledge-based work and innovation became the key to productivity and military effectiveness, the Soviets fell so far behind that they gave up on their unraveling empire. What had started as an experiment in people working together as equals ended in a failure, largely because the command-and-control nature of the centralized state economy destroyed the partnership relationships it was intended to create. The same fate awaits any large organization in a knowledge-intensive business that re-lies on the effectiveness of a system dominated by a chain-of-command method of bringing order, even with the most caring leadership.

In addition to command and control, we examine two more ways of bringing order that reduce the need for bureaucratic hierarchy and increase effective partnership relationships within organizations:

1. Organizational Community: The human propensity to form mutually supportive bonds and to contribute to the workgroups, teams, and organizations of which they are a part.

2. Internal Choices: The self-organizing power of freedom of choice in systems, such as the voluntary buying and selling by customers and entrepreneurial vendors in an internal market economy.

Both these forces, community and choice, contribute to partnership relationships that create a more productive and satisfying place to work. Increasing community and choice within organizations, and limiting the power of the chain of command, can greatly increase an organization's ability to arrange resources and people to respond to customers, to innovate, and to adapt to local conditions.

The first, organizational community, emerges from the generosity of people in a "gift economy," and from the effective partnership relationships in high-performance teams. We look at each in turn.

Building Community Via the Gift Economy

We humans are social beings with an innate capacity for cooperation and partnership. We take pleasure in working together and seek to make contributions to the group even if we will not always get a larger share by doing so. When unhindered by the fear that excess hierarchy imparts, we naturally discuss what the group is doing and seek better ways to do it.

The human instinct for cooperation and even altruism contains a surprising competitive aspect. In his breakthrough book, *The Gift,* Lewis Hyde contrasts what he calls "the gift economy" with what he calls "the exchange economy."[1] In the *exchange economy* with which we are all familiar, whoever *gets the most* has the highest status. In *a gift economy,* the rules are almost the opposite: *whoever gives or contributes the most* without expecting anything in return has the highest status.

For example, consider two professors at a conference. One gives an outstanding paper that others will be quoting for years; however, she has only a moderate knowledge of the field and spends the rest of the time in the hall. The other takes extensive notes of everything that happens in the conference and goes away with more knowledge that anyone else in his field but gives no papers. One professor *has the most knowledge;* the other *contributes the most* to the field. Which one has higher status? Obviously the one who makes the largest contribution to science, not the one who knows the most science. Science has traditionally operated according to the gift economy, not the exchange economy. (This fact helps to explain why scientists and business people typically have such difficulties in communicating with each other. They have fundamentally different ways of measuring success.)

The gift economy drives much of the partnership activities in an organization. People help each other across organizational boundaries. They often receive nothing in return for that help except the sense of having contributed and the regard of others for having made the contribution. Leaders can develop the gift economy by making voluntary contributions visible—by an attitude of gratitude, which notices and publicizes extraordinary efforts and contributions, and by adding to annual appraisals gifts of service outside one's job description or area.

High-Performance Teams

Partnership is learned and practiced in teams. A group of people with a common purpose and the prospect of sharing the rewards of success will naturally form a team. Team members earn the regard of other members by being productive and contributing to the progress of the group, and thus are naturally motivated to find the best way to contribute. Much of the time, they don't need the direction of a boss, because they can see for themselves what needs to be done. They take turns leading the discussion and respect each other's roles.

Although the team leader is not always apparent, leadership exists. Whether the roles are formal or situational, shared or rotated, leaders emerge. A leader may be the one they turn to in emergencies or for major decisions for which consensus is not possible. The leader's role may be to provide the broad view of what is going on or keeping the team humming by bringing his or her wisdom to process and relationships.

Leaders can bring out partnership in an organization at both micro- and macro-levels—by creating strong self-organizing teams, and inspiring everyone to work with commitment to the greater whole. Leaders can implement reward and selection systems that honor partnership and self-organization. They can take advantage of the emergence of large group planning techniques to build a culture of participative decision-making.

New techniques for large-scale, participative planning processes have revolutionized the size of systems in which integration can occur by participatory democracy. Many hundreds of people can now participate in finding a vision and designing their own work systems. We can see the superiority of democratic partnerships over hierarchy when people given responsibility for the new design and implementation of their work systems perform in ways that are creative, effective, efficient, and wise.

THE SELF-ORGANIZING PRINCIPLE OF CHOICE

It may seem bizarre that freedom of choice is a powerful principle for supporting and bringing coherent order to partnerships in large systems, but in fact it can be. For instance, marketplace choice has served to integrate the activities of thousands of companies around the globe to design and produce a jetliner. Neither Boeing nor Airbus has one tenth of the intellectual capital or coordination capacity to cost effectively mine metals, create alloys, make fasteners, cast and machine parts, design avionics, produce control systems, make engines, and so on. The complex systems we call airplanes come together through the voluntary agreements and collaborations of thousands of companies operating in the global marketplace.

The relationship between customer and vendor is formally one of equals. In some cases the buyer has all the power—consider General Motors and one of their smaller suppliers. In others, the seller has more power—consider your relationship with your local utility company. But, in a well functioning market, both have choice and something far closer to equality than found in a hierarchical relationship between boss and subordinate. For this reason, a free market with the power between participants in relative balance provides a better base for partnership than a chain-of-command structure.

We have been experimenting with suffusing large organizations with partnership networks by bringing the free market inside. We do this by helping clients to set up the institutions, rights, and responsibilities of a market for certain internal services. People in what used to be staff groups and support functions voluntarily form teams and look for internal customers for their services in other parts of their company.

One of our clients moved a number of its information technology (IT) activities from functional staff groups with budgets to internal businesses with internal customers. The businesses, which we called "intraprises," included functions such as web hosting, application development, human factors engineering, graphics design, mechanical engineering for electronic products, and writing and editing instruction manuals.

At the core of this transition was the Intracapital Bank. The bank made loans to the intraprises when they began or expanded, maintained internal "bank accounts" for each, processed the transfer of payments from the customers to the intraprises, and subtracted the intraprises' expenses and salaries from their accounts. In addition, the bank helped manage the corporate immune system for the ventures, provided training, helped solve teamwork and organizational growth issues, and generally made the whole system work.

All these tasks were clearly too much for the small bank staff. Instead of building an empire, the bank contracted out parts of many tasks to partners in this organizational transformation, often to the intraprises themselves. For example, rather than wrestling with teaching basic finance to the various teams, the bank turned to an intraprise that helped other ventures to set up their books and prepare financial statements. Whenever the bank had difficulty getting well organized financial reports from one of its customers, it recommended that the customer ask for help from the financial services intraprise. The partnership relieved the bank of "tedious" work and provided a steady base of referrals to the financial services intraprise. As is true in all good partnerships, both parties won.

The many partnerships that resulted from what we call "the free intraprise system" provided a significant competitive advantage. Instead of bureaucratic complacency, internal customers received enthusiastic customer service. New products could be shipped months earlier because the "intraprise" teams treated their customers as partners and did what their customer-partners needed when they needed it. The result was marketplace success in a world in which a delay of just a few months could mean late entry to market and financial losses.

This blossoming of innovation, efficiency, and speed would never have happened without leaders in high places who decided to support the creation of a self-organizing system within a formally hierarchical organization. The free intraprise system described previously liberates service-providing *intra*preneurs from the chain of command and gives them the freedom, motivation, and resources to create partnership networks across the entire company.

In nations, at the core of the free *enter*prise system is a series of rights and responsibilities granted to every citizen. In democratic market economies, all individuals have the right to form a business by themselves or with others of their choice, the right to seek and choose their customers and vendors, the right to keep the money they earn (except for taxes), and so on. The institutions of economic freedom, properly balanced and constrained by community interest, create the conditions for productive partnerships. Similar rights and community constraints define the free *intra*prise system—the opportunity for the creation of internal intraprises that can buy, sell, and partner across the boundaries of a bureaucratic organization. Building these rights into the system limits the command-and-control system in the same way that our Bill of Rights limits the role of government in our lives. The result of these freedoms in the United States has been centuries of productivity growth, an economy of networked partners, and a community spirit that supports the world's strongest not-for-profit sector. Corporations will see similar gains from freeing their employees.

REPLACING DOMINATION AND
SUBMISSION WITH FREEDOM

The human capacity for partnership, teamwork, and community contributions and their positive effects has been greatly underrated. The chain-of-command system for bringing order is rooted in a part of human nature quite distinct from partnership, which is the capacity to engage in relationships based on dominance and submission. The chain-of-command system grants the right of dominance to those higher in the chain of command. Those at the top bring order by figuring out what needs to be done and then cascading orders down the chain of command for execution.

In theory this might work well, if the right people were in charge. Yet, even with goodwill and good intentions, certain behaviors that may not be in the best interest of organizational performance are triggered in relationships of dominance and submission. For example, the dominant person will be more interested in telling than in listening. In fact, knowing the answers and not needing to ask is an innate signal of dominance (which may explain why so many people refuse to ask for directions). A dominant person will tend to be suspicious of meaningful lateral communications between submissive parties, unless fully informed of the content with the right to approve or disapprove the communication. The dominant person will believe that he or she knows more than the submissive people and will tend to issue advice and broad-based commands based on a limited understanding of the challenges the submissive people face. The result can be an organization that acts foolishly and wastefully.

The submissive member of a relationship defined by dominance and submission has a complementary set of innate responses. The submissive one tends to be fearful, and tries to please the dominant one by saying whatever he or she believes the dominant one wants to hear. He or she tries to appease the dominant one by shading the truth to appear to have met the dominant one's expectations. For this reason, as well as the classic degradation of information when passed from person to person in the game of telephone, information that is passed up the chain of command through several levels of review and "refinement" usually ends up seriously misrepresenting the facts.

To make matters worse, the submissive one may harbor a covert hostility toward those who make him or her feel submissive and low status. In some cases, this leads to finding clever ways to frustrate the intentions of those above, perhaps by literal-minded interpretation of the orders given. By producing bad results while doing exactly what they were told, the submissive ones prove that their superior is not so smart after all.

The result of too many submissive behaviors is an organization that is out of touch with reality and unable to coordinate its activities except in the simplest ways. Such an organization clearly does not encourage partnership, nor will such an organization produce good results when addressing complex challenges in a rapidly changing market with rapidly evolving technology. Yet, that is the challenge most medium- to large-sized organizations face today, and many do succeed. How can we explain this discrepancy?

Fortunately, the hooks exist in human character for the more productive partnership relationships based on cooperation, equality, exchange, and mutual contributions, and not just for the relationships of dominance and submission. Indeed, in every effective workplace, the negative effects of hierarchy are softened and humanized by the friendships and caring between employees. It is the responsibility of those of us with the privilege of leadership to create an environment to bring out the best, not the worst, of what it is to be human.

THE WIDER CHALLENGE OF PARTNERSHIP

Leaders of great courage will establish institutions that foster the development of partnerships throughout the organization. One can begin by building an organization that, at its base, is made up of teams, rather than foreman and workers caught in over-reliance on the chain of command. A culture of partnership requires a conscious attempt to build community and to establish choice and the free intraprise system. An organization integrated by partnership relationships requires the creation of new institutions. It requires education in partnership subjects such as participation, teamwork, community, and free intraprise. This is not to say that leaders stuck in a bureaucracy at too low a level to effect formal institutional change can do nothing. They can be good partners and encourage their people to be so as well. But we are reaching the limits of goodwill as a force for organizational change. As long as we leave hierarchy as the unchallenged master of order creation, partnership will take a backseat to politics and jockeying for position. The next decades will see the emergence of partnership organizations that diminish the grip of the chain of command and bring order by developing the forces of partnership, community, and freedom of choice.

PART TWO

*Partnerships and Teambuilding:
Emerging Dimensions for
the Leader as Partner*

CHAPTER 6

LEADERSHIP PARTNERING
FOR PERFORMANCE

Using Situational Leadership®II to
Bring Out the Magnificence in People

KEN BLANCHARD

I think people want to be magnificent. It is the job of the leader, through Partnering for Performance, to bring out that magnificence in people and to create an environment in which they feel safe and supported and ready to do the best job possible in accomplishing key goals. This responsibility to guide and help others to their fullest potential should not be taken lightly. As leaders, we hold the lives of others in our hands. These hands need to be gentle and caring and always available for support.

THE NEW ROLE OF THE LEADER

The leader's role has shifted dramatically in recent years. In the past, the emphasis was more on the leader as "boss." Today, leaders must be partners with their people; they can no longer lead with positional power alone. Leaders must move from the "command-and-control" role of judging and evaluating to a role of ensuring accountability through supporting, coaching, and cheerleading.

Situational Leadership® II has endured as an effective approach to managing and motivating people because it fosters a partnership between the leader and the people that leader supports and depends on. In other words, Situational Leadership® II is not something you do *to* people; it is something you do *with* them. The purpose of

Situational Leadership® II is to open up communication and to increase the quality and frequency of conversations about performance and development.[1]

Situational Leadership® II is a process for developing people by providing effective leadership, over time, so that they can reach their highest level of performance. It is based on a relationship between an individual's development level (various combinations of competence and commitment) on a specific goal or task and the leadership style (various combinations of directive and supportive behavior) that the leader provides. (See Figure 6-1.)

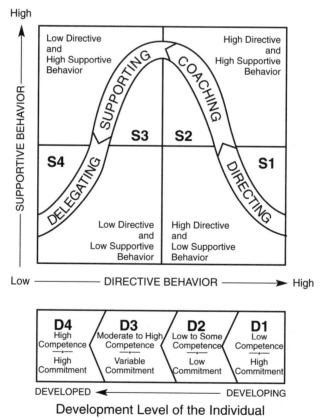

FIGURE 6-1. THE SITUATIONAL LEADERSHIP® II MODEL

There are four leadership styles and four development levels in the Situational Leadership® II Model. The top of the model illustrates the four leadership styles—Style 1 (Directing), Style 2 (Coaching), Style 3 (Supporting), and Style 4 (Delegating). These leadership styles correspond with the four development levels—D1, D2, D3, and D4—shown on the development level continuum at the bottom of the model.

The goal of Situational Leadership® II is to match the leadership style that is appropriate to an individual's development level at each stage of development *on a specific goal or task.* The leader provides the direction and support that an individual needs to move along the development continuum—through the development cycle—from D1 (developing) to D4 (developed). As development level changes, the leader's style should change.

This means that there is no *best* leadership style, because development level varies from person to person, from goal to goal, and from task to task.

THE THREE SKILLS OF AN EFFECTIVE SITUATIONAL LEADER

An effective situational leader is able to use three skills:

1. Diagnosis: assessing an individual's competence and commitment

2. Flexibility: using a variety of leadership styles comfortably

3. Partnering for Performance: reaching agreements with individuals about their development level and the leadership style they need to help them achieve individual and organization goals

Diagnosis

Situational Leadership® II is a partnership model. As that partnership begins with understanding the needs of the individual with whom the leader is working, development level is addressed first.

While there are many variables that can affect an individual's ability to accomplish a goal or complete a task, Situational Leadership® II focuses on one situational variable more than others—the development level of a person on a specific goal or task. Development level is a combination of two factors—competence and commitment.

Competence is the knowledge and skills an individual brings to a goal or task. Competence is best determined by demonstrated performance. It can, however, be developed over time with appropriate direction and support. Competence is gained through formal education, on-the-job training, coaching, and experience. Experience includes certain skills that are transferable from a previous job: for example, the ability to plan, organize, problem-solve, and communicate well. These skills are generic by nature and are transferable from one goal or task to another.

Commitment is a combination of an individual's motivation and confidence on a goal or task. Motivation is the level of interest and enthusiasm a person has for doing a particular job. Interest and enthusiasm are exhibited behaviorally through animation, energy levels, and verbal cues. Confidence is characterized by a person's self-assuredness. It is the extent to which a person trusts his or her own ability to do the goal or task. If either motivation or confidence is low or lacking, commitment as a whole is considered low.

Combinations of varying amounts of competence and commitment characterize the four development levels. (See Figure 6-2.)

The development of an individual to his or her highest level of performance can be seen as a journey. Although the goal is self-reliance (being able to perform independently), the individual at each level of development has distinctive needs along the way.

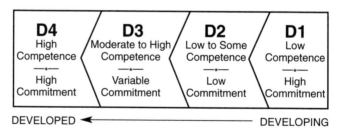

DEVELOPED ◄——————————————— DEVELOPING

Development Level of the Individual

FIGURE 6-2. THE FOUR DEVELOPMENT LEVELS

As the development level of an individual increases from D1 to D4, his or her competence and commitment fluctuates. On new tasks with which they have little, if any, prior experience, most individuals are *Enthusiastic Beginners* (D1).

Soon after beginning a new task, an individual commonly becomes a *Disillusioned Learner*. A letdown occurs when a job is more difficult or is, perhaps, different than expected. This disillusionment causes a decrease in commitment (D2).

If individuals overcome the disillusionment stage and acquire the skills they need, most will then go through the *Capable but Cautious Performer* stage when they question whether they can perform the task well *on their own*. Their leader may say they are competent, but they are not so sure. In other words, they lack the confidence in their own competence. These alternating feelings of competence and self-doubt cause the variable commitment associated with D3—commitment that fluctuates from excitement to insecurity.

With proper support, an individual can eventually become a *Self-Reliant Achiever*—a D4, who demonstrates a high level of competence and commitment on a specific goal or task. In other words, given the appropriate amounts of direction and support, an individual moves from one level of development to another, from being an *Enthusiastic Beginner* to a *Disillusioned Learner* to a *Capable, but Cautious, Performer* to a *Self-Reliant Achiever*.

Development level does not apply to the person, but rather to the person's competence and commitment to a specific goal or task. An individual is not at any one development level overall. Development level varies from goal to goal and task to task. In other words, an individual can be at one level of development on one goal or task and a different level of development on another goal or task.

For instance, Casey may be a marketing genius when it comes to rolling out new products and opening new markets—clearly a D4 as demonstrated by the success of her past marketing plans. However, when it comes to setting up a database to track demographics and buying patterns, Casey has little computer expertise beyond E-mail and word processing on her laptop. Depending on her motivation for the task, she could be a D1 or a D2.

By diagnosing development level, a leader can determine which leadership style to use.

Flexibility

Once diagnosis of competence and commitment (development level) has been completed, a leader has to be flexible enough to use the appropriate leadership style.

Leadership style is the pattern of behavior leaders use, over time, to influence others, as perceived by those being influenced. A leader's self-perception of leadership style is only an indication of his or her intentions and is not necessarily how that leadership style is perceived by others. Studies have shown that this pattern of behavior falls into two basic categories, which are defined in Situational Leadership® II as Directive Behavior and Supportive Behavior.[2] Leaders use some combination of these two behaviors.

Directive Behavior concentrates on *what* and *how*. It involves telling and showing people what to do, how to do it, when to do it; monitoring performance; and providing frequent feedback on results. Directive Behavior develops competence in others.

Supportive Behavior focuses on developing an individual's commitment and initiative. It also focuses on developing positive attitudes and feelings toward the goal or task. Good examples of Supportive Behavior are listening, facilitating self-reliant problem solving, encouraging, and involving others in decision-making. Supportive Behavior builds commitment in others.

When Directive and Supportive Behaviors are placed on the horizontal and vertical axes of the Situational Leadership® II Model, there are four combinations of these two behaviors. These four combinations of Directive and Supportive Behaviors are the four leadership styles in the Situational Leadership® II Model. (See Figure 6-3.)

The four styles vary in the amount of direction and support the leader gives and in the individual's involvement in decision-making.

Style 1, Directing, consists of high Directive Behavior and low Supportive Behavior. In the Directing style, the leader provides specific

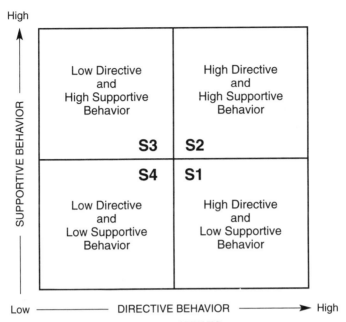

FIGURE 6-3. THE FOUR LEADERSHIP STYLES

instructions about what and how goals or tasks will be accomplished. The leader also closely supervises the individual's performance. Most decisions in Style 1 are made by the leader.

Style 2, Coaching, is characterized by high Directive Behavior and high Supportive Behavior. The leader explains decisions, solicits suggestions from the individual, praises progress, and continues to direct task accomplishment. Input from the individual is considered, although final decisions are made by the leader.

Style 3, Supporting, provides low Directive Behavior and high Supportive Behavior. A leader using Style 3 listens, encourages, and facilitates self-reliant decision-making and problem solving.

Style 4, Delegating, is a combination of low Directive Behavior and low Supportive Behavior. The leader empowers the individual to act independently and provides the appropriate resources to get the job done. Most decisions are made by the individual.

In all four styles, the leader (1) clarifies expectations and goals, (2) observes and monitors performance, and (3) gives feedback to the individual.

To determine the appropriate leadership style to use with each of the four development levels, draw a vertical line up from a diagnosed development level to the leadership style curve running through the four-quadrant model. The appropriate leadership style—the *match*— is the quadrant in which the vertical line intersects the curved line. (See Figure 6-4.)

As a result, Development Level 1 (D1) would get a Directing (S1) leadership style. Development Level 2 (D2) would get a Coaching (S2) leadership style, etc.

Since D1s have commitment but lack competence, the leader needs to provide high direction (S1—Directing). D2s, who lack both

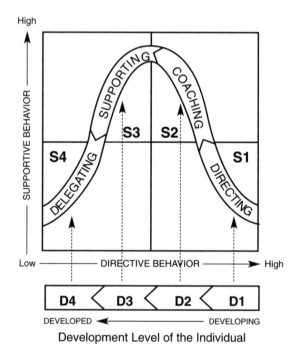

FIGURE 6-4. MATCHING LEADERSHIP STYLE TO DEVELOPMENT LEVEL

competence and commitment, need the leader to provide both high direction and high support (S2—Coaching). D3s have competence, but variable commitment, and therefore need high support (S3—Supporting) from the leader. Since D4s have both competence and commitment, leaders need to provide little direction or support (S4—Delegating).

Directing is for Development Level 1. Style 1 is effective with an individual at D1, because the high direction builds the task knowledge and skills that the individual needs. There is less need for support at this level, as the individual is eager to get started and learn.

Coaching is for Development Level 2. The individual at D2 needs Style 2, with continued high direction to develop competence and increased support to counter the drop in commitment.

Supporting is for Development Level 3. An individual at D3 has variable commitment and therefore benefits from the high Supportive Behavior of Style 3 to reinforce shaky confidence and overcome motivational problems. Because competence is moderate to high at this level, little direction is needed.

Delegating is for Development Level 4. At D4, an individual is highly competent and highly committed. The low direction and low support of Style 4 are appropriate, as this individual is able to provide his or her own direction and support.

Leadership style needs to be matched to the individual's development level to ensure that competence and commitment will increase. When people are oversupervised or undersupervised, that is, given too much or too little direction, there is a negative impact on their development. As the individual moves from one development level to the next, from D1 to D2, D3, and D4, the leader's style should change accordingly. Yet, research shows that most leaders have a preferred leadership style. Research data on the Leader Behavior Analysis II® (LBAII®)[3] indicates that 54 percent of leaders tend to use only one style; 35 percent tend to use two styles; 10 percent tend to use three styles; only 1 percent use four styles.

To be effective, leaders must be able to use all four leadership styles. They must learn to be *flexible.*

Partnering for Performance

One of the important new roles of the leader is that of creating partnerships with people as they strive to achieve their personal and their organization's goals. That involves reaching agreements about each other's role in goal accomplishment. A main objective of Partnering for Performance is gaining the individual's permission to use the leadership style that is a match for the individual's development level. In partnering, the leader and the individual agree on goals, development level, leadership style, future leadership behaviors, how to stay in touch, and how often to stay in touch. Teaching Situational Leadership® II to individuals helps them understand their role in the partnership.

Once goals have been agreed to and both the leader and the individual know Situational Leadership® II, they can mutually diagnose the individual's development level and agree on an appropriate leadership style. Communication should continue as the leader manages the individual's performance, using the agreed-on leadership style. New goals, priorities, and changes in development level should trigger more dialogue and changes in leadership style.

THE DEVELOPMENT CYCLE

An individual on a new goal or task will go through four predictable and sequential development levels. The progress of an individual through the four levels of development is called the development cycle.

In developing Self-Reliant Achievers, the factor that triggers a change in leadership style is performance. Improvements in performance prompt forward shifts in leadership style along the bell-shaped curve from S1 to S2 to S3 to S4, one style at a time. (See Figure 6-5.)

Usually, an individual undertakes a new task as a D1. In some cases, however, an individual may enter the development cycle as a D2. This situation can be the result of an involuntary transfer or other job-related or personal issues. Because both competence and commitment are low, Style 2, with an emphasis on active listening, would be appropriate.

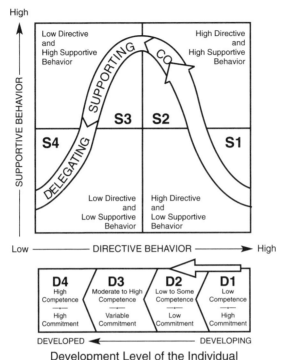

FIGURE 6-5. THE DEVELOPMENT CYCLE

The Regressive Cycle

Just as improvements in performance call for forward shifts in leadership style along the bell-shaped curve, decreases in performance require backward shifts in leadership style. This is called the regressive cycle. In other words, whenever an individual performs at a lower level than previously demonstrated, the leader should adjust his or her behavior to respond to the individual's current development level. (See Figure 6-6.)

For example, a highly experienced individual might start missing deadlines or the quality of his or her work may decrease. Rumors of a buyout or perhaps a family crisis may be affecting this individual's performance. In this situation, shifting from a Delegating style to a Supporting style would be appropriate.

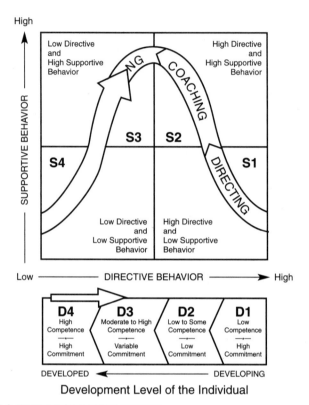

High

SUPPORTIVE BEHAVIOR

Low Directive and High Supportive Behavior		High Directive and High Supportive Behavior
	S3	S2	
S4			S1
	Low Directive and Low Supportive Behavior	High Directive and Low Supportive Behavior

COACHING

DIRECTING

Low ——————— DIRECTIVE BEHAVIOR ——————▶ High

D4	D3	D2	D1
High Competence	Moderate to High Competence	Low to Some Competence	Low Competence
—+—	—+—	—+—	—+—
High Commitment	Variable Commitment	Low Commitment	High Commitment

DEVELOPED ◀——————————— DEVELOPING

Development Level of the Individual

FIGURE 6-6. THE REGRESSIVE CYCLE

Imagine the curve going through the four leadership styles on the Situational Leadership® II Model as a railroad track. Each of the four styles is a station along the way. If you want to go to S4 (Delegating) from S1 (Directing), you have to stop at S2 (Coaching) and S3 (Supporting).

The same is true for the regressive cycle. If a leader is at S4 (Delegating) with someone and his or her performance begins to slip, the leader must move back one stop to S3 (Supporting) to determine the performance problem. Once the problem is identified, if the leader feels the individual can get his or her performance back on track, a return to S4 is appropriate. If, however, it is obvious that the individual needs some help, the leader can move back one more stop to S2 (Coaching).

Furthermore, when leaders bypass a station along the railroad track, performance and development get "off-track" and people get hurt. A common example is the "leave-alone-zap" leadership style, which occurs when a leader tells an inexperienced person what to do (S1) and then jumps to an inappropriate Delegating style (S4), only to return to S1, yelling and screaming, when performance doesn't meet expectations.

In both the development cycle and regressive cycles, changes in leadership style should be made, either forward or backward, one style at a time.

SUMMARY

Situational Leadership® II is more than a model for leading and developing people. It encourages ongoing conversation in a spirit of partnership as individuals learn to take responsibility for their own decision-making and problem solving. Leaders realize their role is to provide individuals with whatever it takes—clear goals, direction, support, training, feedback, and recognition—to help the people they work with become more self-directed, self-motivated, and self-reliant.

Conversely, individuals begin to realize that their *own* behavior determines the leadership style used with them. Thus, Situational Leadership® II becomes a vehicle for individuals to use when asking for the help they need to develop.

Through Situational Leadership® II, the frequency and quality of conversations about performance and development increase, and the organization develops and retains its most talented people.

FURTHER READING

Blanchard, K., Zigarmi, D., and Nelson, B., "Situational Leadership® after 25 Years: A Retrospective." *The Journal of Leadership Studies* (November 1993).

Blanchard, K., Zigarmi, P., and Zigarmi, D., *Leadership and the One Minute Manager.* Morrow, New York, 1985.

Fiedler, F., *A Theory of Leadership Effectiveness.* McGraw-Hill, New York, 1967.

Hersey, P., and Blanchard, K., "Life Cycle Theory of Leadership." *Training and Development Journal* (May 1969).

Hersey, P., Blanchard, K., and Johnson, D., *Management of Organizational Behavior,* 8th edit. Prentice-Hall, Englewood Cliffs, NJ, 2001.

Stodgill, R., *Handbook of Leadership.* Free Press, New York, 1974.

Stodgill, R. and Coons, A., eds. *Leader Behavior: Its Description and Measurement.* Research Monograph 88, Ohio State University, 1957.

Zigarmi, D., Blanchard, K., O'Connor, M., and Edeburn, C., *Developing Leadership and Character: Learning Enough About Yourself to Influence Others.* Wharton Press, Del Mar, CA, 2000.

CHAPTER 7

LEADERSHIP-AS-PARTNERSHIP

RUSS S. MOXLEY AND JOHN R. ALEXANDER

Leaders lead. They provide a compelling vision, they motivate and inspire, and help their organizations navigate change and handle adaptive challenges.

This is the typical way of understanding and practicing leadership. We usually think of leadership as the province of an individual. We have identified this individual with a role in the organization, and thus we often use the terms *leader* and *executive* interchangeably.

Not only have we understood leadership as the province of an individual, but we have also wanted that individual to be extraordinary. We want leaders who are intellectually gifted, who are visionaries, who are charismatic, and who are out front and in charge. In a word, we want our leaders to be *heroic*.

Viewed across history, we have even agreed on the tasks we want our leaders to accomplish. We want them to create a vision (or, in the language of other writers, a mission, a sense of purpose, an agenda for the organization), we want them to be able to articulate this vision in a compelling way so that we will be motivated to accomplish it, and

This chapter is based on an article that originally appeared in *Leadership in Action*, volume 19, number 3 (Copyright © 1999 Jossey-Bass/Wiley) and is adapted from Russ Moxley's book *Leadership and Spirit: Breathing New Vitality and Energy into Individuals and Organizations* (San Francisco: Jossey-Bass, 2000).

we want our leaders to be able to help us navigate the "permanent whitewater" without getting pulled under by an eddy.

This view of leadership has worked reasonably well, particularly in industrial settings, and remains the dominant means by which leadership is understood and practiced.

THE LIMITATIONS OF THE TYPICAL VIEW OF LEADERSHIP

This understanding and practice of individual-as-leader has its limitations. First, with the increasing diversity of the workforce, it is difficult for any one person to create and articulate a vision that will be shared by all. Today, a shared vision is possible when the diverse interests and different agendas of many stakeholders are combined. Second, the resources—the gifts, skills, and energies—of a single person will invariably run out. The mantle of leadership is too heavy for one person to bear alone. To be successful over the long haul, organizations need systems, structures, and practices of leadership that call forth the gifts and skills and energies of all employees. Third, the increasing complexity of tasks and technologies and the resulting need for intellectual capital call for a new understanding and practice of leadership. Today, for work to be effectively accomplished, there must be integration across specialized functions. Expertise and leadership must be widely shared. Warren Bennis puts it this way, "To a large degree our growing recognition for the need for a new and more collaborative form of leadership results from the emergence of intellectual capital as the most important element of organizational success."[1] Finally, the changing needs and expectations of workers are nudging us toward a different way of practicing leadership. Peter Drucker suggests that, "Altogether, an increasing number of people who are full-time employees have to be managed as if they are *volunteers*. They are paid, to be sure. But knowledge workers have mobility. They can leave. They own their 'means of production,' which is their knowledge."[2]

With all the changes in the workforce and changes in the employment contract, Peter Drucker has suggested that workers today have to be treated as if they are volunteers, and volunteers must be managed and led differently.

AN ALTERNATIVE: LEADERSHIP-AS-PARTNERSHIP

We would like to suggest an alternative to individual leadership: *leadership-as-partnership*. In this view, leadership is not what one person provides another, but rather it is what emerges from the reciprocity of relationships, from the quality of interaction of at least two people, sometimes more. It is the understanding that leadership is an activity that happens in and comes from a collective. Rather than seeing leadership as the expression of a single extraordinary individual, this understanding suggests that it is a process shared by many ordinary people.

We like the name *partnership*. It suggests the basic idea: men and women coming together to accomplish the leadership tasks—*they* create a shared vision, *they* work together to build commitment to and maintain alignment with the vision, and *they* use the skills and energies of all partners to handle change and deal with adaptive challenges.

The primary difference in executive-as-leader and partnership is simply this: the source of leadership is different. Our typical view suggests that leadership comes from within a person—so, for example, vision comes from the head and heart of the "leader." In partnerships, the source of a vision is the relationship; vision emerges from the reciprocity, from the give-and-take, of a relationship. An organization must have a vision or a sense of direction if we are to say that leadership is happening in that organization. The source of that vision has typically come from the person at the top; we are proposing that the source can be a relationship—a pair, a team, a workgroup, or an entire organization. Understanding this difference in the source of leadership is crucial.

Perhaps the best way to understand how a partnership is different from individual leadership is to look at how it works in three different settings: a one-to-one relationship, a team, and an organization. These examples are taken from our personal experiences with individuals and organizations.

Partnership in a One-to-One Relationship

Robbie is a brand manager in a large manufacturing organization. He is knowledgeable, hard working, focused, optimistic, considerate, and a quick study. He has recently had a series of conversations with his boss about problems they were having with the final development and launch of an important new product. The boss not only expressed appropriate concern about the delay, but also then told him exactly what needed to be done to get the product back on the fast track. There was no shared agreement on the direction that needed to be taken, and Robbie felt no commitment to the proposed solution. In fact, Robbie knew from experience that what the boss told him to do would not work, but he did it anyway—an act of sabotage.

Robbie wanted the boss to do things differently, not just in this one instance, but also in all their work together. First, he wanted the boss, before he gave an order, to ask what Robbie thought needed to be done; then Robbie wanted the boss to ask if there was anything that he, the boss, could do to help. Instead, by being high-handed, the boss left Robbie feeling not only that he was responsible for the delay, but also that he had no power to correct it.

In this case, Robbie and the boss had a shared goal; so one of the requirements of partnership was in place (see sidebar). However, the boss sidelined Robbie—he assumed that he knew what needed to be done, though he didn't have time to discuss it, and saw his role as being directive. Robbie, however, wanted dialogue, not direction. He wanted to be a partner, not to be overpowered. He wanted to be a person, not a puppet. What the boss needed to do here was to engage Robbie as a full participant in getting the task accomplished, and Robbie needed to have sufficient courage to speak his truth to the boss.

In the book *Co-leaders,* David A. Heenan and Warren Bennis tell stories of executives who have worked as partners to accomplish the leadership tasks in their respective organizations.[3] The authors suggest that we cannot fully appreciate the genius that is Bill Gates unless we understand and appreciate the quality of interaction Gates has with Steve Ballmer, the president of Microsoft. Leadership emerges from the quality of their interaction, from the give-and-take of their relationship. Leadership is not, we repeat, what one of them provides, but rather it comes out of their relationship.

Partnership in a Team

Business was good for a major consumer products company, but the young president knew that the executive team could be stronger. Relationships among the six members of the team were cordial on the surface, but underneath that surface lay unresolved conflicts and tensions. Individuals had built fiefdoms and now worked hard to protect them. They avoided interdependence. Conflicts were pushed up to the president to resolve. Responsibility and accountability were not shared. In fact, there was more finger pointing than working together toward accomplishment of the leadership tasks. There was no shared understanding of the company's mission or direction, and the team members obviously were not in alignment and pulling together. Differences in style and personality were not honored; indeed, there was no appreciation that diversity might be a strength upon which team members could build.

When the executives finally admitted this gap between the appearance of harmony and the reality, it was time to take steps to create a team that represented true partnership. They worked on different ways of being and acting together, on acknowledging conflict, on spelling out assumptions, on engaging in real dialogue, on solving problems rather than passing them on, and on dealing with the adaptive challenges faced by the organization.

Changes came slowly but perceptibly. Over time, the executive team members became more open, less guarded, more collaborative, and less competitive—more willing to put issues on the table and less likely to engage in sabotage after a meeting. They developed new understandings of their roles and how they could accomplish the leadership tasks collaboratively, and over time they developed the capacities to act on this new understanding.

In this case, once the executive team adopted the partnership approach, it improved the company's performance, and it also improved the work climate for the executives. Backbiting became a thing of the past, and shared commitment to company goals was held up as the highest value.

In talking about the importance of "great groups," Warren Bennis and Patricia Ward Biederman have said, "In a global society, in which timely information is the most important commodity, collaboration is not simply desirable, it is inevitable. In all but the rarest of cases, one is too small a number to produce greatness."[4] The emergence and use of self-managed work teams—of groups that are great and groups that are not so great—may be one of the best indications that our understanding and practice of leadership is changing. Even though we kid that a "camel is a horse designed by a committee," we also know that "one is too small a number to produce greatness," and we have learned from experience that work teams that learn to utilize the skills and gifts and energies of all team members fully can creatively and effectively accomplish the leadership tasks. Leadership can and does emerge from a team when differences are honored, assumptions suspended, and the quality of interaction is good. Synergy does produce better results than what any individual can accomplish alone.

Partnership in Organizations

Executives of a major airline, operating under the authoritarian style of its first president, realized that this style would not allow them to develop the esprit de corps that they thought critical to long-term success. The president's attitude fostered compliance, not commitment. The top-down, command-and-control style did not elicit the inspired performance or alignment with company goals that this growing company needed.

A new president developed and implemented a different approach to leadership: partnerships. In this company today, leadership happens in collaborative relationships. Pilots work with ramp agents and customer-service agents assist skycaps. The culture focuses on the organization as family, as a group of individuals who are in this venture together, not as individuals out for themselves.

The employees of this airline understand that collaboration and partnership require new ways of understanding accountability and authority. In this company, employees understand that they are accountable for performance and accomplishment of organizational goals, and they are accountable even in areas for which they don't have authority.

Yet, individuality is honored, especially through creative enterprises such as storytelling and making humorous videos about working at the airline. The employees also focus on fundamentals: on-time arrivals, quick turnarounds, and low-cost fares. They take their work, if not themselves, seriously.

But, what about the bottom line? Can an organization that practices leadership as collaborative relationship be profitable? The simple answer is an unqualified "Yes." The profitability of this airline has been among the best in this industry, and, as you might expect, it has become a highly prized place to work.

This airline is one of many organizations that have implemented a new way of understanding and practicing leadership. Another organization we know has fostered collaboration and partnerships by organizing itself so that no more than 200 people work in one place. Titles are eschewed, there is minimal bureaucracy, and employees are energized and inspired.

A Swedish manufacturing company we know is organized in peer communities—it is here that the leadership tasks are accomplished and work is done. Rather than leading to anarchy as some might fear, it has lead to a responsive and flexible company, with employees motivated to use all their skills and energies in service of their work.

A well known furniture manufacturer is a company with outstanding leadership and enduring principles: the importance of covenantal relationships (relationships based on shared commitment rather than fear), a core belief that the company must have a redemptive purpose, and a conviction that executives must be willing to "abandon themselves to the strengths of others." Although the term isn't used, in this company leadership-as-partnership is practiced.

OBJECTIONS TO LEADERSHIP-AS-PARTNERSHIP

Significant questions are often raised about leadership-as-partnership. Without assuming that we know or can adequately answer all question or concerns, we want to address the issues most often raised.

The objection we hear most often is that leadership-as-partnership diminishes the role of the individual, especially the role of the "great leader." We think the opposite is true. It doesn't diminish the importance of a single individual as much as it enhances the importance of all individuals. Instead of leadership being the province of a single individual, in the partnership approach, the gifts, skills, and energies of each person in the relationship are honored and used. There is no more than or less than; no one is up or down; no one person has power with others feeling powerless. In partnership, leadership is cocreated as people work collaboratively. Furthermore, it is often an individual who is the catalyst for starting the leadership process, who suggests a vision or an important new direction, or who advocates a new way of responding to an adaptive challenge.

Another concern we hear is that partnerships have embedded in them a naïve view of power. Too many times to count, we have heard the lament from people with whom we have been privileged to work that they need more power, not less, and the power they need, they think, is the power to control. To them, the idea of leadership-as-partnership seems quaint, even wrong-headed.

This lament is based on the belief that the only real source of power is the power to coerce—that if we take away their carrot and stick, we will render them powerless. What we have too often have failed to realize is that the carrot and stick are not sources of real power. Coercive power held by managers and executives is only on loan from subordinates, and subordinates can call the note on a moment's notice. For those who need a method of coercion to feel powerful, the hard truth is that it is the subordinate who decides if the manager has power.

In partnerships, power has a different source. It comes from within the person. It is based on a sense of competence and expertise, and it is rooted in self-confidence and feelings of self-worth. Personal power cannot be given to us or taken from us; it is ours to claim. It may sound quaint, but in the long run personal power is the only real source of power we have.

One last objection we want to mention briefly is that leadership-as-partnership undercuts personal responsibility and accountability. If we are all accountable, the skeptic suggests, no one is. The buck must stop somewhere; a partnership cannot be accountable.

To be sure, throughout history individual accountability has been part and parcel of managerial and executive roles. As hierarchies are created, accountability is built in, the level of accountability corresponding to the level in the organization, with the buck finally stopping at the CEO's door. Accountability and authority have been linked. We cannot (it has long been argued) have accountability unless we have authority, and someone else must give this authority to us. This is how the system works.

The problem is that if accountability is linked to authority, and thus belongs to those in positions of authority, then "they" are responsible and "we" are not. Organizations can no longer afford for the few to be accountable for the many. Partnerships require that all people engaged in the partnership be responsible and accountable for what happens. Now, we are they. We must accept responsibility and accountability for the accomplishment of the leadership tasks, even if we don't have the authority we thought we always needed. For leadership-as-partnership to work, ownership, authority, and accountability must be felt at every level, by every person.

CHAPTER 8

WHERE TEAM PERFORMANCE FITS IN A BALANCED LEADERSHIP APPROACH

JON KATZENBACH

Of the several ways that leaders can function as partners, one of the most versatile configurations for increasing organizational performance is the team. Building team performance among leadership groups, however, is a somewhat different challenge from achieving team performance on the frontline. The time demands on senior leaders invariably work against effective teaming. Leadership at the top of most line or staff organizational units demands insight, wisdom, and versatility. In fact, most chief executive officers find that they have to learn the CEO game "on-the-job." The road to that coveted role seldom prepares one for all aspects of the job, and there are no realistic training courses for CEOs. At the same time, emerging leaders who learn to balance multiple elements of leadership and organization within their own personal style are more likely to master the CEO challenge when they get there.

Even though personal leadership styles at the top are unlikely to change, most CEOs can learn to accommodate different styles within their overall leadership approach. The strong, decisive leader can enable team performance within his or her leadership group just as the more natural team leader can inject more natural decisive leadership when that style is more appropriate than teaming. For example, during the tenure of Andrew Sigler as CEO, Champion International became a widely recognized pioneer in team performance at the plant levels. Sigler was also able to elevate team disciplines effectively among his senior leaders; however, his personal style was clearly that of a strong, single leader who made all the key decisions. He could not change that style to function as a real team leader, nor could his colleagues supplant his leadership when he was in the room. His natural style as well as his physical stature and strong personality precluded real team leadership on his part; however, he was able to instill real team performance among his senior leaders by taking himself out of the picture—and when he retired, he convinced his board that his successor should be a more natural team leader. A complex company today requires more than one style of leadership at the top, and usually that implies an integration of several executive styles within the senior leadership group.

Certainly, an important element of a balanced leadership approach is team performance. Yet, it is only one element. Overall organizational performance requires the alignment of the decisions and actions of people at all levels. Leaders of organizations that consistently outperform the competition usually rely on all four of the basic alignment mechanisms:

1. *Formal structures* that clarify roles and responsibilities; it is important to know who reports to whom for what. Yet no formal structure in and of itself creates organizational alignment in high performance enterprises.

2. *Formal processes* that create action flows across formal structures; it is important to move information, services, and products efficiently and effectively from the originating sources to the end users. Although some have argued to extend this approach into a "horizontal organization" concept, even this more extensive kind of process cannot create or explain high performance institutions.

3. *Informal networks* that provide critical connections to supplement formal structures and processes; no formal construct of organization (structure and process) works without an effective informal construct. The informal networks and flexible units are the organizational elements that enable any formal structure or process configuration to adapt to rapidly changing market place dynamics.

4. *Flexible units* (effective working groups, real teams, and single-leader units) are small groups that can enhance performance within any formal or informal organizational construct. Because of their inherent flexibility, such units are essential in any rapidly changing enterprise.

The purpose of this chapter is to reflect on the flexible units and describe where and how team performance fits in an overall leadership approach. As commonplace as the terms "team" and "teamwork" have become in our business lexicon, most leadership groups do not differentiate between performance situations that warrant a real team effort, compared with those that are better addressed with effective groups or single-leader units. Teamwork is a "value" that can produce admirable and valuable cooperation and support across an entire organization. A team, however, is a small, tightly focused performance unit that yields a higher performance result when applied to the right kind of performance challenge. Such team efforts require adherence to a very specific discipline to achieve their potential; they are *not* a natural byproduct of broad-based teamwork values.

Realistically speaking, most "teams at the top" seldom function as real teams, even though senior leadership groups like to refer to themselves as a team. Moreover, when they do actually function as a real team, their behavior change stems from an unexpected problem or an urgent performance shortfall, the resultant teaming takes place behind closed doors, and the group strives to return to their normal pattern of behavior as soon as possible. Thus, most of their real team effort is unnecessarily limited to extreme situations. Yet, no self-respecting CEO—and very few business analysts or journalists—would argue that it is not important to have his or her own "team at the top." This common terminology leads us to overlook the fact that real teams at the top are oten not the best way to address particular performance challenges. The terminology also obscures the fact that most real team efforts at the top are of short duration rather than an ongoing configuration.

When you define a team as a performance unit rather than an effective group, its characteristics are simple to describe: a *small group* of people (typically fewer than 10) with *complementary skills* (working skills rather than organizational position) who are *equally committed* to the following:

➤A clear, compelling *performance purpose*

➤A set of *specific goals*

➤A *common working approach*

The members hold one another *mutually accountable* for each of the above, rather than being individually accountable to the leader. In a real team effort, the collective or joint work products are more important than individual ones, and the leadership role shifts back and forth among the members to match the skills and experience with specific performance needs, even though the formal leadership mantle remains in place.

This simple definition of a real team also describes the disciplined behaviors that must be rigorously followed if team performance is expected at any level of the organization. Team performance is more about peer- and self-discipline, as well as mutual respect among the members, than it is about strong leadership, personal chemistry, bonding, or togetherness. Moreover, team discipline differs from executive leadership discipline, which relies more on role clarity, single-leader direction, and individual accountability. Unfortunately, learning to apply team discipline to the right issues in the right way usually requires more time than applying the more common executive leadership discipline. Hence, senior leadership groups instinctively gravitate toward the latter and often miss opportunities to apply team discipline.

The balanced-leadership approach accommodates both disciplines and therefore integrates team efforts and single-leader unit efforts. Teams are not always better than single-leader performance units, and the best leaders know when and how to apply each to advantage. The single-leader unit can be faster and more effective when the leader knows best, and the work required can easily be disaggregated and assigned to each member, who then becomes individually accountable to the leader. The real team unit works best when important aspects of the work require multiple skills and cannot be disaggregated for assignment to individuals; members need to work cohesively together to achieve desired results. Mastering both kinds of performance discipline (team and single-leader) requires flexibility from a leader who understands and appreciates the difference, as well as a group that can perform within both modes. Leaders who are disciplined about when and how to perform as a team, and when and how to perform as a single-leader unit, expand the leadership capacity of the group. They also increase the performance results that the group can deliver, because it is able to divide itself into subgroups in ways that enable both disciplines to be applied in the right places.

A few years ago, I was working with Jim Rogers, then CEO of General Electric's Motors and Industrial Systems business in Fort Wayne, Indiana. Jim was an excellent CEO who made very appropriate use of both team and single-leader unit disciplines within his company. For example, he had developed the team skills of his managers to the point where he would establish the leadership groups for each of his five business units without officially designating a "General Manager" for the unit. When I asked Jim if this approach always worked well, he admitted that it did not—but on those occasions it was simple enough to return to the more normal General Manager "single-leader unit" model. Both models have their place.

The specfic issue that Jim and I were working on was how to create a "real team" effort within his senior leadership group of 12 executives from both line and staff positions. We were initially frustrated, because we could not find practical ways for that entire group to function as a real team. Yet, it was often possible for subgroupings to apply the real team discipline successfully. Of course, the insight from this example is that within formal leadership structures, smaller subgroupings (when properly constituted with respect to skills) are more likely to adhere to the real team discipline than larger diverse groups of senior executives each of whose individual capabilities may neither fit nor be required for specific team tasks at a hand.

In short, teams—or more precisely team performance—have an essential place in any leadership system that seeks to optimize leadership capacity and performance contribution. Like naval gunnery, you can miss this target on either side, and thereby suboptimize the performance of your group. If a performance challenge requires speed and individual accountability among members whose tasks are not interdependent, the single-leader discipline works unit is typically more effective than the real team performance unit. Whenever the challenge requires synergistic, collective work products, and multiple-leader contributions, then real team discipline is likely to be more effective than the single-leader discipline. Using one or the other in the wrong place is both frustrating to the members and wasteful of valuable executive resources. The power of partnering suffers when team performance is not an appropriate part of the equation.

Interestingly, the U.S. Marine Corps is one of the best institutions that I have researched with respect to getting real teams in the right places, and integrating the real team discipline with the single-leader unit discipline. To begin with, Marine rifle teams are masters of the team discipline. These basic four-person units are trained so that any one of the group can lead as the battle situation dictates, and the leadership role shifts as conditions change. In addition, the Leadership Recognition Course at OCS in Quantico, VA, challenges groups of four officer candidates with different physical "puzzles" that they must solve as a group—sometimes working as a real team, and sometimes as a single-leader unit. The course enables the instructors to help each candidate to recognize these different leadership disciplines and approaches, and apply them accordingly.

Most companies, however, have neither the luxury nor the urgency of this kind of training for their executive leaders. Many executives, however, can learn how to recognize when a team approach is required, and when a single-leader performance unit is best—and they can develop a balanced leadership process that will integrate the two over time.

‹○›

CHAPTER 9

LEADERS MUST BUILD
CULTURES OF COLLABORATION

JAMES M. KOUZES AND BARRY Z. POSNER

If the goal is superior performance, the winning bet will be on cooperation over competition and individualistic achievement every time. Competition almost never results in the best performance; neither does going it alone. Pursuing excellence is a collaborator's game.[1]

Collaboration is *the* critical competency for achieving and sustaining high performance in the Internet Age. It won't be the ability to fiercely compete, but the ability to lovingly cooperate, that will determine success.[2] In fact, the Internet was created so that people could more effectively collaborate![3]

Rather than focusing on stomping the competition into the ground, exemplary leaders focus on creating value for their customers, intelligence and skill in their students, wellness in their patients, and pride in their citizens. World-class performances aren't possible unless there's a strong sense of shared creation and shared responsibility. And, as paradoxical as it might seem, leadership is *more* essential—not less—when collaboration is required.

This chapter is excerpted from *The Leadership Challenge* by James M. Kouzes and Barry Z. Posner. (San Francisco: Jossey-Bass. Revised edition, August 2002.) This material is used by permission of John Wiley & Sons, Inc.

This was made glaringly obvious when one of us (Jim) first had DSL (Digital Subscriber Line) service installed in his home office. Here's a brief glimpse at the experience:

> It took at least six different vendors before the service was actually functioning, and those were just the ones with whom I was in direct contact. There was my ISP, the DSL provider, the supplier of the router, the local phone company for the outside wiring, the company that connected the phone line to the router, and a tech-support person I hired to help manage these relationships once it got too weird, too technical, and too time-consuming for me to coordinate all the parties. At one point, with three of us on a conference line trying to figure out why the router wouldn't route, I overheard one vendor scold another. "And these folks," I thought to myself, "are supposed to make my life easier? If that's going to happen, first they need to learn how to get along."
>
> Then after less than a year, my DSL provider declared bankruptcy, sold its assets to another company, and disconnected 100,000 customers. I waited three weeks for the new DSL provider to install the service—a short time if you ask my friends—and it didn't work. It took at least six separate visits from the voice people and the data people—who, by the way are in different divisions in the same company and don't talk to each other—before it worked properly. This time the problem wasn't several different vendors unable to collaborate; it was two departments within the same vendor!

Broadband may be key to speed and performance on the Internet, but unless high-tech—or low-tech companies, for that matter—get their acts together, a lot more will go broke. It won't be because of a failure of technology. It'll be a failure of relationships. In the old, the new, or the next economy, success comes to those who can out-collaborate their competition.

To succeed at collaboration, a leader must be able to skillfully

➤Create a climate of trust.

➤Facilitate positive interdependence.

➤Support face-to-face interactions.

Collaboration is a social imperative. Without it we can't get extraordinary things done in organizations. By building a culture of collaboration, leaders can enable multiple constituencies to sustain high performance over the long term.

CREATE A CLIMATE OF TRUST

At the heart of collaboration is trust. It's *the* central issue in human relationships within and outside organizations. Without trust in each other, people cannot work together, and without the capacity to trust others you cannot lead. Individuals who are unable to trust cannot lead precisely because they can't bear to be dependent on the words and work of others. They either end up doing all the work themselves or they supervise work so closely that they become overcontrolling. Their obvious lack of trust in others results in others' lack of trust in them.

Carolyn Borne is unit director at the Clinical Research Center, in the Department of Nursing, University of California, Los Angeles (UCLA) Medical Center. She's also program director of UCLA's Women's Health Initiative (WHI) in the Department of Medicine at the same institution. The WHI is the largest and most ambitious longitudinal study of women's health concerns ever undertaken, involving 40 centers across the country and 167,000 women. It requires careful planning, analytical ability, and meticulous attention to detail, and, because of the sensitivity, significance, and collaborative nature of the study, it also requires a high degree of trust. Yet, that wasn't how Carolyn Borne found it when she started her job as program director. Instead, as she put it:

> The WHI group lacked collaboration, respect, and trust for each other. People did not socialize; there was a lack of trust and support. The emphasis seemed to be competition rather than cooperation. Hard as they were working, they were not at the expected national study goal for recruitment. Productivity and morale were low.

She had to immediately take some steps to change the situation and create a different kind of climate, a climate of trust and respect.

I did a needs assessment, which consisted of an interview with each staff member in which I asked what they liked about the job and what the barriers were to getting the job done. I found the group was enthusiastic about the study but frustrated because of a lack of systems, organization, and teamwork. Each member of the team was a talented professional, but ready to quit. They all liked their jobs, but did not feel supported.

We started creating a team environment with a daylong retreat in which we began to identify our values, philosophy, and mission. We shared stories about families and loved ones and began to feel a sense of trust and respect for each other.

Having identified internal and external sources of frustration, which were barriers to creating a productive team, my goal became increasing group cohesion through improved communication among each other. We developed a staff communication pad that everyone was encouraged to use to share ideas or anything that was important for other staff members to know on a daily basis.

Creating a climate of trust, by determining what the group needed and by building a team around purpose and respect, are among the many things that we can all do to begin creating a climate of trust. The important message in Borne's example—and in the thousands of other personal best cases that we examined—is that leaders must put trust on the agenda. You can't leave it to chance. As a leader, you have to make a conscious effort to create trust and to sustain it.

FACILITATE POSITIVE INTERDEPENDENCE

At the beginning of the new millennium a British television import became a ratings hit in the United States. *Survivor* topped the charts week after week, as millions tuned in to watch the latest rage in "reality TV." With its competitive games, petty rivalries, backstabbing betrayals, tribal councils, a modest tease of sex and romance, and cliffhanger endings, *Survivor* was a hit.

On more than one occasion during the peak weeks of the show, we'd find some of our clients using *Survivor* as a case study in how to be successful in the world of business. A carefully staged and edited production had not only become an entertainment phenomenon; it had become a classroom for the corporate world. This was, to us, a very troubling turn of events. *Survivor* may be riveting entertainment, but it teaches all the wrong lessons about how to survive in the "real world." In the real world, if people were to behave as these players on television did, we'd all be dead. As the acclaimed anthropologist Lionel Tiger put it when commenting on the first *Survivor* series, "The contest format distorted savagely what would have otherwise been a very different outcome involving ongoing cooperation. The behavior on the island is also not a reflection of corporate America, as has been suggested. It is a reflection of the nature of the prize and what winning it demanded. The goal of human survival has always been to endure for another day, and in the group."[4]

Survivor lacked all the elements of a cooperative effort. While the alliance building on the show gave an appearance of working together, these alliances were nothing more than a transparent means of beating the other players. Everything was structured to support the victory of only one person in the end. Even though some in corporations may see this as the way it's supposed to be—only one of us gets the raise, only one of us gets the promotion, only one of us gets the biggest bonus—those folks make lousy leaders. Exemplary leaders recognize that self-serving behavior is the path to organizational suicide, and that successful leaders and team members subordinate their own goals to the service of a greater good.

One of the most significant ingredients to cooperation and collaboration missing from *Survivor* was a sense of interdependence, a condition in which everyone knows that they cannot succeed unless everyone else succeeds, or at least that they can't succeed unless they coordinate their efforts. If there's no sense that we have to, and can, rely on each other, that "we're all in this together," that the success of one depends on the success of the other, then it's virtually impossible to create the conditions for positive teamwork.

Director Sidney Lumet, whose films include such cinematic greats as *Twelve Angry Men* and *Network,* tells a very different story about what it takes to be successful as a leader of a group of highly talented and very demanding people. In talking about his role as a director he says[5]:

But how much in charge am I? *Is* the movie *un Film de Sidney Lumet?* I'm dependent on weather, budget, what the leading lady had for breakfast, who the leading man is in love with. I'm dependent on the talents and idiosyncrasies, the moods and egos, the politics and personalities, of more than a hundred different people. And that's just in the making of the movie . . .

So how independent am I? Like all bosses—and on the set, I'm the boss—I'm the boss only up to a point. And to me that's what's so exciting. I'm in charge of a community that I need desperately and that needs me just as badly. That's where the joy lies, in the shared experience. Anyone in the community can help me or hurt me.

Lumet has captured the essence of the second condition for cooperation and collaboration. There has to be a sense of mutual dependence—a community of people each of whom knows that they need the other to be successful.

Cooperation may be in everyone's best interests, but leaders have to take an active role in creating a positive context and structure for collaboration. Among the most important actions a leader can undertake to create conditions in which people know they can count on each other are to develop cooperative goals and roles, support norms of reciprocity, and reward joint effort. Help begets help just as trust begets trust. Focusing on what's to be gained fosters agreement in what might otherwise be divisive issues.

SUPPORT FACE-TO-FACE INTERACTIONS

Trust and mutual dependence are essential for collaboration to occur, but it's positive face-to-face interaction that has the most powerful influence on whether group goals are achieved.[6] Empirical studies point out that as the complexity of issues increases, greater face-to-face communication is required to integrate differences.[7] While we increasingly have more and more access to virtual tools that make staying in touch much simpler and quicker, there's no substitute for positive face-to-face interactions.

We're social animals, after all, and we need to connect with each other. Leaders must make sure that key constituents are able to make human contact. To interact, people must be close together. Leaders must provide team members with frequent and lasting opportunities to associate and intermingle. Leaders must help to break down barriers between people by encouraging interactions across disciplines and between departments.

People who expect durable and frequent future interactions are likely to cooperate in the present. The knowledge that we'll have to deal with someone in the future ensures that we won't easily forget how we've treated, and been treated by, others. And when durable interactions are frequent as well, the consequences of today's actions on tomorrow's dealings are that much more pronounced. In addition, frequent interactions between people promote more positive feelings for each other.[8]

Of course, we recognize that in this global economic environment—where speed is a comparative advantage and loyalty is no longer a strong virtue—durable interaction may seem quaint and anachronistic. But that doesn't change the facts. It may be difficult to achieve, but sustaining durable face-to-face interactions increases your effectiveness. You just have to make it one of your leadership imperatives.

Dick Nettell, corporate services executive for the Bank of America, knows all about the importance of human networks and face-to-face interaction. When we were talking to him about how he gets things done, he said: "I'm the epitome of the old operating guy. The operating guy gets stuff done through the network. It makes no difference what level in the organization it is, it's how you grease it to get it done." When San Francisco–based Bank of America merged with Charlotte-based NationsBank, "My network basically got blown to bits," said Nettell. So he had to go about rebuilding his network before he could get on with his new job.

For family reasons, Nettell needed to remain in the San Francisco Bay Area, but in order to reconstruct his network, he needed close relationships with people at the Charlotte headquarters. That meant spending 1 week per month in North Carolina, as well as constant talking on the phone. It took him about 1 year to develop the relationships with the 35 or so key individuals whom he relies upon to make things happen. "It's nurturing those relationships," says Nettell, "and once you've started to build them, it's making a conscious effort to continue them and make sure that you're always doing the right things and people want to deal with you." Without personally investing time and effort in building his web of relationships, Nettell knows he would be unable to do his job.

"You can't do it alone" is the mantra of exemplary leaders. You simply can't get extraordinary things done by yourself. Collaboration has become the master skill of this age. Our ability to work together will determine mutual failure or mutual success. It may seem para-doxical, but the more high technology we add to our lives, the more dependent we become on the quality of human relationships to make it work to our benefit.

CHAPTER 10

THE LEARNING LEADER AS PARTNER

JUDY ROSENBLUM AND CHERYL OATES

Webster defines a *partner* as "one who shares; one associated with another in action; two persons who dance or play together against an opposing side." When interviewed, partners in professional-service firms describe a partner as "an individual who works with others toward common goals, deriving strength from others, doing things that they couldn't do alone and sharing in the results." They go on to say that community, caring, trust, and transparency are all essential elements of a successful partnership. It seems that the requirements of professional partnerships are not that different from those of the personal partnerships in our lives.

WHY LEADER AS PARTNER?

"Leader as partner" is an intriguing concept. Think about it. It was not too many years ago when the notion of a leader needing to partner was a sign of weakness or at best something dealt with privately. The image of the leader as commander, as the all-knowing top of the pyramid is one that stayed with us through the 1980s. Why did it change? We would advocate that industry consolidation, globalization, technology, and learning are at the heart of the change. These four trends led to an imperative to work across all sorts of boundaries, to reach a goal and to form collaborative relationships where once only authoritarian or adversarial relationships existed. Traditional expressions of power and control were no longer as effective with customers, suppliers, governments, or employees. Language changed to reflect the shift. Knowledge workers would not "report" to supervisors, and companies sought to "partner" with their customers. Competition required that value chains be pulled closer together. If you didn't get closer to your customers and employees, someone else would.

THE LEARNING LEADER AS PARTNER

This change leaves the leader with an even more difficult job. Not only must leaders see new opportunities and capitalize on them, but they must also do so with a clear understanding of the partners needed along the way. Not only must leaders be able to create new meaning in their own community, but they must also successfully negotiate that meaning with others. Leaders need to be effective partners if they are to be the architects and orchestrators of a disconnected, but aligned, collaboration of entities and individuals with common interests. They also need to be effective learners, if they are to understand deeply the assumptions and beliefs of their partners, appreciate the nature of the joint opportunity, and have a systemic perspective of the facts and data behind the opportunity. Mastery of learning disciplines and skills is required to deal with the organizational complexity, scope, and distance often found in joint ventures, collaborations, and community partnerships. On the basis of those disciplines, the dynamics of a successful partnership can be defined.

DYNAMICS OF SUCCESSFUL PARTNERSHIPS

Our work with both corporations and not-for-profit organizations has shown that the goals for a partnership cannot be met without success in subjective areas, such as trust and transparency. The learning orientation of the leader facilitates these outcomes. In support of this, we offer a framework that incorporates learning as a driver toward the objective and subjective aspects of successful partnerships.[1]

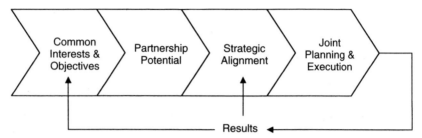

FIGURE 10-1. FRAMEWORK OF A SUCCESSFUL PARTNERSHIP

Common Interests and Objectives

A successful partnership starts with common interests and objectives. These common objectives represent the reasons that the partnership exists—the mutual benefit that can be attained via the relationship. Once common interests and objectives are established, then optimizing what we call "partnership potential" and attaining strategic alignment are critical next steps. These factors, which are unique to our framework, are explored in more detail later in this chapter. Once strategic alignment is attained, the partners are able to engage in joint planning and execution. This produces mutually beneficial results that reinforce the strategic alignment between the partners, as well as the common interests and objectives. Figure 10-1 illustrates this framework.

Partnership Potential

Partnership potential involves starting a "virtuous cycle" of interaction among the partners. Better, more appreciative relationships lead to more fact-based insights among the partners, which promotes a shared view of the opportunity for the partnership and reinforces the appreciative relationships. This dynamic is depicted in Figure 10-2.

Appreciative Relationships

We define *appreciative relationships* as those in which each partner values the knowledge, experience, and contribution of the other partner(s). This is manifested through interactions among the partners with the following behaviors/qualities:

➤Mutual respect and trust

➤Good advocacy, inquiry, and listening (key "learning skills")

➤Following through on commitments

➤Seeking to understand others' points of view

In an appreciative relationship, processes, structures, and routines are coordinated so that each partner can be appropriately involved in key discussions and decisions that impact the partnership. At the very least, the partners meet frequently enough to develop the relationship and discuss relevant issues and decisions.

Appreciative relationships make the partners open and willing to share relevant information, such as market data or trade knowledge, with each other. As more information is shared the degree of interconnections between the partners and their resulting interdependence becomes apparent. This open sharing of information and discovery of interconnections becomes the basis for fact-based insights about the market and the partnership prospect. As a result of these new insights

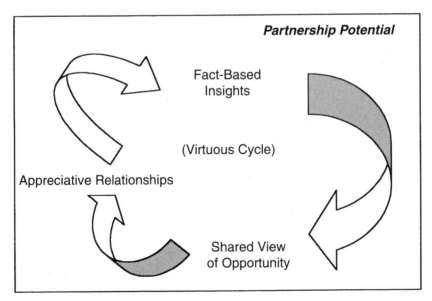

FIGURE 10-2. PARTNERSHIP POTENTIAL

and the appreciative relationship between the partners, a shared view of the opportunity develops and initiates the virtuous cycle. Activating partnership potential supports common interests and objectives, and paves the way for strategic alignment among the partners.

Strategic Alignment

Strategic alignment is an ongoing management process of establishing mutual commitment to shared goals, directed toward fully leveraging the resources of the partners for their mutual benefit. Strategic alignment requires partners to share a common

➤View of market opportunity

➤Destination (i.e., a time-bound picture of success with desired results described)

➤Commitment to goals and strategies for reaching those goals

➤Accountability to deliver on the destination

This is an ongoing management process, because it is manifested through management routines, such as integrated strategic plans. From strategic alignment comes the ability to jointly design and execute the necessary plans to gain the benefits (results) of the partnership. As shown in the framework, the results reinforce the strategic alignment, as well as the common interests and objectives of the partners.

SUCCESSFUL PARTNERSHIP: THE ALLIANCE FOR A HEALTHY NEW ENGLAND

An example that illustrates the successful working of this framework involves the American Cancer Society's (ACS) spearheading of the Alliance for a Healthy New England. The goal of the alliance is to greatly reduce tobacco consumption and increase access to healthcare by significantly and simultaneously raising the cigarette excise tax in all six New England states. The leading partners in the alliance include ACS, the Medical Societies of New England, and a health access advocacy group, Community Catalyst. Since its inception in early 2000, the alliance has seen cigarette excise tax increases of 26 and 29 cents per package in Maine and Rhode Island. In 2002 the other four states, Massachusetts, Connecticut, New Hampshire, and Vermont, are also expected to enact significant increases. No other region in the United States has effectively orchestrated such an increase across multiple states.

The success of the alliance partnership in not only raising the taxes, but also in getting the funds used for tobacco education and healthcare is remarkable for several reasons.

➤New England–area states have a history of strong individuality and of "border wars"—strategizing to maintain lower cigarette prices in one state to lure purchasers across the border.

➤Many states desire to use tobacco-settlement funds to supplement waning budgets and for nontobacco-oriented purposes, such as road repair.

➤The ACS and some of its alliance partners previously viewed themselves as competitors, because they often advocated for limited state-budget funds for their own specific issues of concern.

With the aforementioned challenges, how and why did the alliance partnership work? Peg Camp, ACS New England Division COO says,

> We saw a unique window of opportunity at the end of 1999 with the environment ripe for a concentrated effort in tobacco control. The Tobacco Master Settlement funds coming into the states, the general public's annoyance with tobacco companies and an all-time high level of support for increasing tobacco excise taxes existed, but there was the realization that no one organization alone would be powerful enough to make the desired impact. Using tobacco excise taxes for increased access to healthcare was seen as a good "mission" match as well for all the partners. We needed to partner with groups of like interest and focus our energy on the "prize." This involved valuing the differences and strengths that we all brought to the table, using facts and figures to support our focus, and making a long-term commitment to the cause. We knew that we'd never be able to do this independently, and we had to trust each other not to break off and pursue our own interests in this area.

Peg's description of their efforts demonstrates the importance of the first two areas of the framework, developing common objectives and activating partnership potential.

Once the partners were on board, they used a steering committee structure to ensure strategic alignment and sustain the broader relationship. The steering committee meets on a monthly basis to develop strategies to be used across the states and to coordinate and maintain overall focus for the alliance partnership in the region. It also provides assistance, such as drafting bills and conducting research, to the state-level alliance groups. The steering committee operation described illustrates a pragmatic approach to the ongoing management process required to maintain strategic alignment and facilitates joint planning and execution at the local level. In the state-level alliance groups, the three primary partner organizations work with up to 75 local collaborating groups and leverage the steering committee strategies to design and execute plans that help fulfill the goals of the alliance for the particular state. Two of the state-level groups (Maine and Rhode Island) have already seen the fruit of their effort. This success has helped bolster the resolve of the partners to pursue their common goals and keep their long-term commitment to the Alliance for a Healthy New England.

PITFALLS TO SUCCESSFUL PARTNERSHIPS

Smoke-free New England is just one of many examples of successfully leveraging a partnership and its resources for a common cause. Following the framework as a learning leader, however, is not as simple or easy as it may seem. In our work, we have encountered some recurring pitfalls that erode partnership potential and strategic alignment and threaten the success of partnerships. These pitfalls are described later.

"The Pressure Cooker"

Sometimes, profit, business, or personal pressure causes one party in the partnership to break commitments made to the other. While the "promise breaker" gets relief from his or her pressure, the broken commitments cause mistrust and a desire to plan and act separately. This desire can lead to independent and conflicting actions by the partners and a focus on self-interest versus the common goals. Self-interest then reinforces the belief that commitments made to the other party can be broken when the pressure is on.

How "real" is the Pressure Cooker? In a marriage partnership, the spouse who allows work pressures to constantly interfere with family plans may find that he or she is growing apart from his or her mate and family. In a business partnership, constantly breaking commitments—no matter how urgent the pressure—can lead to "divorce." In like manner, the Pressure Cooker compromises appreciative relationships by damaging the trust and integrity of the association, and it can cause promising partnerships to dissolve. Common objectives are no longer common. Learning leaders must find constructive ways to relieve the pressure, which can lead to parochial self-interest and conflict in a partnership. If they don't, the partnership can fall victim to the "boiled frog" syndrome. A pattern of broken commitments, while relieving the short-term pressure on one partner can, over time, cook the relationship to death—in the same way that a frog is boiled by slowly increasing the water temperature so that the change is undetected. The Pressure Cooker can live within the structure of partner potential and erode it over time. Learning leaders must have the capacity to see the systemic implications of their actions, organize teams to honor commitments, and skillfully communicate pressures to the partners so that joint plans can be revised.

"The Pygmalion Effect"

The belief that one partner is "difficult" can become a self-fulfilling prophecy. Because of this perceived difficulty, one partner may think that he or she needs to have fully formed ideas before engaging with the other. This results in less time dedicated to co-creating plans and ideas. This can cause the partner to whom the idea is being "sold" to believe that his or her opinion is not valued, and thus increases resistance to the ideas being presented. The "seller" then views this resistance as an example of the other's difficult behavior; the original belief is reinforced and starts a vicious cycle—a negative Pygmalion Effect. (See Figure 10-3.)

This scene is enacted daily in interactions between labor and management, teachers and students, and parents and children, just to name a few. In a partnership negative beliefs about the motives, intelligence, intentions, or aspirations of the other party can prove deadly. Appreciative relationships and the virtuous cycle of partnership potential are stopped cold by negative beliefs. While such toxic beliefs may seem unlikely and illogical, experience has shown that they do exist in many partnerships and are usually deeply held. Learning leaders are aware of the impact of their beliefs on the results they see in the partnership, and that their expectations will in many cases determine outcomes. Self-awareness and reflection are critical attributes of learning leaders that allow them to suspend judgment long enough to inquire about the views of the partner and to understand what is really behind the difficulty.

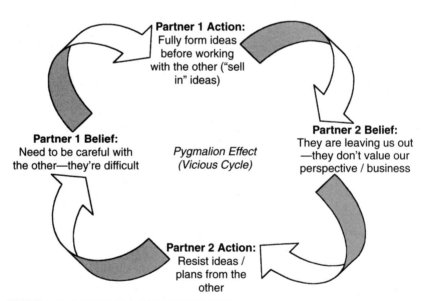

Partner 1 Action:
Fully form ideas before working with the other ("sell in" ideas)

Partner 2 Belief:
They are leaving us out —they don't value our perspective / business

Partner 1 Belief:
Need to be careful with the other—they're difficult

Pygmalion Effect (Vicious Cycle)

Partner 2 Action:
Resist ideas / plans from the other

FIGURE 10-3. THE PYGMALION EFFECT

"Spoon-Feeding"

A partnership requires mutual disclosure and a great deal of openness. When one partner shares minimal information or communicates just enough for the other to execute tactics, then the quality of the interaction is low. This can lead to feelings of being uninvolved and the perception of being "used," and can thus create conflict in the relationship. These issues can further reduce information sharing, result in less understanding of each other's business, and reduce the partner's desire to communicate and interact.

Spoon-feeding reflects a lack of trust and respect between the partners. In some cases, one partner has perceived "power" or leverage over the other and spoon-feeds as a control mechanism. Although this tactic may prove effective in some cases, today's competitive environment calls for partnerships to which each party gives 110 percent. Power plays such as spoon-feeding take away from the commitment required for performing at the 110 percent level. Not only does the learning leader need to be willing to reveal facts and data, but he or she also needs to help create an environment in which data and facts are available and can be shared throughout the team.

"Living Single"

In an ideal partnership, each party will do whatever is necessary to achieve its shared goals. In the real world, people need to understand their roles and responsibilities to be accountable for results. Many organizations resort to "role sorting" to prevent duplicative effort and reduce inefficiency in the system. In partnerships, role definition can be a two-edged sword: providing clarity on the one hand and terms of separation on the other. When role sorting results in "silo-ed" activities and reduces the quality of communication among the partners, the ability to resolve issues decreases and results in greater inefficiency. "Living single" via role sorting is a common fix for inefficiencies in a partnership, but often worsens the problem in the end.

The learning leader knows that at the heart of role sorting is a desire to avoid overlap and a reluctance to deal with the assumptions and work processes of the partner. Instead of rushing to slice the pie in a way that allows the partners to operate independently, he or she works to understand assumptions, processes, and overlaps, focusing on the common objective and building common processes and routines that coordinate and build on the strength of each partner.

COMPETENCIES OF THE LEARNING LEADER AS PARTNER

What does all this mean the learning leader must do? For each key area of the framework, we have listed learning oriented approaches for developing successful partnerships.

To drive toward common objectives and appreciative relationships, the leader must:

➤Have the interpersonal skills to engage in productive conversations with partners. She or he must have the discipline to suspend judgment, understand assumptions, and avoid driving to personal conclusions.

➤Utilize both power levers (e.g., board presence, influence) and value levers (e.g., relationships, expertise) to facilitate alignment.

➤Organize his or her internal team as a coordinated, aligned unit, so that the partner faces one organization, not many.

➤Bring a level of personal authenticity and reliability to the endeavor and a sincere commitment to a good outcome for the partner.

To facilitate fact-based insights, the leader must:

➤Be willing to reveal facts and data behind conclusions.

➤Create an environment in which data and facts are available and can be shared.

➤Build the capability and willingness of the group to think analytically and systemically about issues and opportunities.

In reaching for a shared view of opportunity and strategic alignment, a leader must:

➤Be willing to coach other members of the partnership and his or her internal team.

➤Bring knowledge to the table.

➤Recognize and value the capabilities of all partners.

➤Lead a dialog that encourages inquiry, stretches thinking, and results in clarity of goals and responsibilities.

➤Demonstrate mutual, senior-level commitment to common goals.

➤Lead a team toward integration of plans and strategies.

In facilitating joint execution of plans and strategies, a leader must:

➤Ensure that alignment around goals reaches both the translator and implementer levels of partnering organizations.

➤Focus the team on the critical factors behind effective execution.

➤Put in place shared systems, processes, and coordinating structures.

➤Put in place milestones and measures of progress.

➤Drive routines that encourage continuing dialog amongst the partners.

THE DIMENSIONS OF THE LEARNING LEADER AS PARTNER

Taken together, the skills and behaviors of leader as partner clearly fall into two key dimensions:

1. A *social dimension,* including building relationships, engaging in productive conversations, forming effective teams, communicating well, authenticity as a leader, and an orientation toward the good of other partners.

2. An *analytical dimension* focusing on the use of data and facts in developing conclusions, systems thinking, knowledge sharing, and the development of systems and processes that drive toward results.

Figure 10-4 demonstrates the implications of the presence or absence of either dimension on the ability of the leader to function as an effective partner.

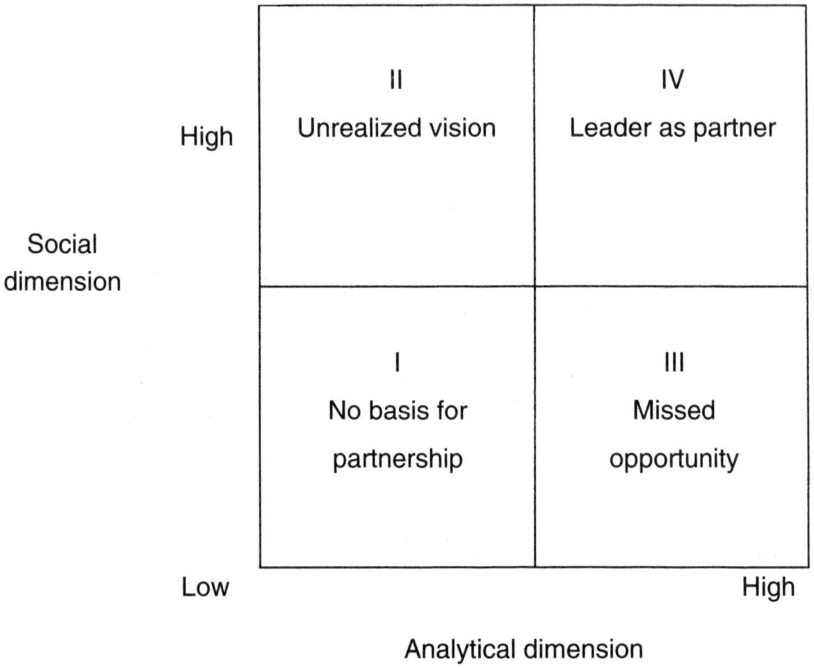

FIGURE 10-4. PRESENCE OR ABSENCE OF SOCIAL AND/OR
ANALYTICAL DIMENSIONS

Cell I: No basis for partnership—characterizes a leader who may have a belief or idea that he or she feels strongly about, but who does not have the ability to bring people along or develop the necessary relationships to form an effective partnership. Further, he or she has not developed the factual context that makes the idea believable. This leader usually must resort to a command structure to move ideas forward in the organization and gets limited compliance.

Cell II: Unrealized vision—characterizes a charismatic leader who is able to bring people effectively into his or her dream and build strong personal relationships with potential partners. The difficulty here is that the leader does not have the systemic view, facts, or data to build an effective business case, so the vision or dream is never realized.

Cell III: Missed opportunity—is just the opposite of cell II. This is a leader who has the knowledge, data, and systemic perspective to support his or her idea, but not the communication skills, relationships, or authenticity as a leader to attract effective partners. The opportunity might be real, but it will never be pursued.

Cell IV: "Leader as partner"—here the leader has both the social and analytical skills to maneuver through the maze of differing contexts and assumptions and to build an effective partnership that can execute ideas. Mastery of learning disciplines and skills helps the leader effectively work in both dimensions.

CONCLUSION

In today's environment, the leader cannot stand alone. The complexity of markets, issues, and opportunities requires collaboration across boundaries both external and internal to the leader's organization. This collaboration is critical for expanding the competencies and access of the organization. Working effectively with partners requires both the social and analytical skill sets that are present only in a "learning leader." These skill sets form the basis of aligned, appreciative partnerships that can effectively execute toward common goals.

CHAPTER 11

THE MULTIPLICITY OF ROLES AND DEMANDS FOR THE LEADER AS PARTNER

DEBRA A. NOUMAIR AND W. WARNER BURKE

Partnering, by definition, assumes a relationship. One cannot partner alone. Leadership is likewise a relationship. If there is no follower, there is no leader. The executive leader at the top of an organization, however, experiences multiple relationships and multiple partnerships that go up, down, and sideways. Our purpose in this chapter is to explore these multiple relationships and to discuss the inherent complexities embedded in simultaneously multidirectional partnering for the leader.

To illustrate the complexities of concurrent multiple partnerships, we begin with the case of Carmen. Carmen is the executive director of a not-for-profit service agency in a large northeastern city in the United States. The first author began executive coaching with Carmen when she had been in the position of executive director for about 18 months in her 2-year contract. At this time, the co-chairs of the board of directors were discussing with her the possibility of negotiating a second two-year contract.

To provide a flavor of the multidirectional nature of leadership in this kind of organization, three vignettes regarding Carmen's executive leadership and partnering with a variety of constituents follow.

VIGNETTE 1

Initially, Carmen hired the first author to provide coaching concerning her partnership with the board of directors. While Carmen had a strong working alliance with the co-chairs of the board, she was anticipating some upheaval in the near future, because for personal reasons both co-chairs would be resigning. Thus, it was imperative that both the co-chairs and the executive director address succession, or more accurately, address the fact that no succession plan was in place. Carmen was concerned that the departure of these co-chairs left her in a more vulnerable position, as her relationships with other board members were quite different from her associations with the co-chairs. The co-chairs viewed her as a superb leader who was in the process of turning around an agency that had been at risk when she was hired. As co-chairs, they viewed their role as providing the executive director with the necessary support and guidance for her to effectively represent the agency to its stakeholders in the external environment and for her to provide leadership to her senior management team, and thus to the agency as a whole. The clarity of role boundaries on the part of the co-chairs contributed positively to Carmen's ability to function well as executive director. The dyadic and triadic partnerships forged by the three of them served the board, the agency, and each of them in their roles.

By contrast, other board members were not as clear about their roles and responsibilities and, consequently, were confused about what to expect of Carmen in her role as executive director. Moreover, not knowing what was expected of them, they often overstepped the boundaries of their role and authority or, alternatively, misrepresented what responsibility they did have. Thus, wittingly or unwittingly these other board members seemed ready to undermine Carmen's authority at any given moment.

Carmen's request for coaching came as a result of this struggle to manage the boundaries of her role as executive director and facilitate clarity of role boundaries for the board. She worried that without providing board members with training and development, poor boundary management would weaken her leadership and, ultimately, threaten the work of the agency.

VIGNETTE 2

Carmen had a senior management team of five directors, each of whom headed a department: human resources, finance, development, and programs (for which there were two directors). In addition to supervising each of them individually, she held a management team meeting each week. It is not surprising that simultaneous partnering with each director individually as well as with all of them as a team presented Carmen with some of her greatest challenges. Even though one of her strengths as a supervisor was being able to differentiate them and provide each of them with development opportunities and regular feedback, they were invested in using social comparison as a means of evaluating their own performance. These comparisons, along with their reactions to the comparisons, interfered with their task-related work and undermined Carmen's partnerships with them as individuals as well as with them as a team.

This situation was made more complex by the relationship between the board of directors and the senior management team. The formal structure was such that senior managers reported to the executive director and the executive director reported to the board. This board often overstepped its boundaries in relation to senior staff, however, by attempting to influence them directly regarding the operations of the agency. This boundary spanning issue was, yet again, a way of undermining Carmen's role as executive director.

However, it was not only board members who contributed to poor boundary management; senior staff also played a role in helping to derail the work of the agency. Knowing that the board of directors was responsible for selecting the next executive director, they were eager for opportunities to "audition" for them and therefore welcomed invitations from board members to "collaborate" on operations.

For Carmen, these auditions and duplicitous collaborations between the board of directors and the senior management team demanded that she behave as a traffic cop, policing violations of role and task. Having to allocate resources for monitoring boundaries when she could have been building alliances and nurturing partnerships interfered with Carmen's primary focus.

VIGNETTE 3

A major role of any executive leader is to scan the external environment for information regarding the organization's customers, so that appropriate decisions can be made on behalf of the organization. In this case, customer demographics had changed since the inception of the agency and services needed to be tailored to respond more appropriately to the needs of this new constituency. At the same time, however, the agency continued to receive generous financial backing from representatives of the original clients. Thus, Carmen's challenge was to maintain a stance of "both/and" rather than "either/or."

An example of this stance was when the only person of color among the senior managers acted as if he were considering leaving the agency, because he had not been selected as executive director. Carmen directed her attention toward getting him to stay. Having done her homework on the external environment, Carmen recognized that it was important to the organization that he remained with the agency. She realized that instead of avoiding him because she got the job he desired, she could work toward bringing his goals and the agency's goals into alignment. Her efforts resulted in an action plan that allowed him to achieve the recognition and advancement that he wanted, and that served the organization's goals as well.

These three vignettes have provided snapshots of the multiple demands and roles that exemplify executive leadership today. This is only one case, of course, but we believe that it illustrates the complexities of both real life as a leader and theory about leadership.

THEORY

One of the purposes of providing this example of a leader struggling with multiple demands on her time and priorities is to ground our chapter in reality regarding leadership in the early days of the twenty-first century. Another purpose, and the objective of this section, is to ground reality within theory. Stephen Zaccaro's work is helpful here.[1] His book on executive leadership covers four primary theories. Central to Zaccaro's premise is that all four of these approaches address two leadership responsibilities that are critical to understanding executive leadership: boundary management and organization-wide coordination. *Boundary management* involves managing the organization's relationship with its external environment; *organization-wide coordination* involves overseeing the day-to-day running of the organization itself.

In brief, the four sets of theories that Zaccaro summarizes are the following:

1. *Conceptual complexity theories:* These theories assume that the executive leader operates within highly complicated environments and that being able to conceptualize these complexities in a way that followers can understand and manage them is a hallmark of effectiveness for the leader. Moreover, the ability and need to think long-range is key to ultimate organizational survival. Elliott Jaques's work is illustrative of this set of theories.[2] Referred to as stratified systems theory Jaques and colleagues assume that people differ with respect to their ability to conceptualize environmental complexities and to think long-term, that is, to visualize the future. Hierarchy therefore is important and executives at the top of organizations must have these abilities.

2. *Strategic decision-making theories:* These theories stress the importance of the executive's ability to establish a strategic direction for the organization. Strategy must be in response to the external environment, that is, properly aligned, and serves as the guide for how the organization is structured and managed. Thus, the effective executive leader constantly scans the organization's external environment, analyzes this information in order to form strategy and policies for the organization, implements the strategy and policies, and then evaluates the consequences of these actions. Examples of this set of theories include the work of L. J. Bourgeosis, Donald Hambrick, and Max Wortman.[3]

3. *Visionary and inspirational theories:* There are a number of different theories in this set, but what they have in common is that the primary role and responsibility of the executive leader is to develop a vision that structures the implementation process and motivates followers for collective action. A good example is Marshall Sashkin's visionary theory/model.[4] Also in this set of theories is the emphasis on empowerment and development of followers; see, for example, Bernard Bass.[5] Other related concepts include charismatic and transformational theories that stress the importance of aligning followers' motives with established purposes and direction for the organization (e.g., Robert House).[6]

4. *Behavioral complexity theories:* These theories emphasize the need for executive leaders to respond effectively to the demands and requirements from multiple constituencies, yet manage these multiple processes in such a way that they remain consistent with the organization's purpose, mission, and strategy. The main idea of these theories is that executive leaders must enact multiple roles for a variety of constituencies and that different leadership behaviors are required to be effective in these multiple situations. Leaders must constantly balance their behavior with competing demands, and from time to time, conflicting values. Robert Quinn's work in particular addresses this latter demand regarding values.[7] Other examples of behavioral complexity theories include the work of Henry Mintzberg and Anne Tsui.[8]

With respect to applying the first theory (conceptual complexity) to the case study, Carmen's need to be diligent concerning fundraising meant that she had to conceptualize this organizational survival need on a daily basis. Conceptualizing the alignment of the organization with the changing external environment to make the agency attractive for funds was a continuing executive leadership task.

Regarding the second theory (strategic decision-making), Carmen's action of reading the changing characteristics of her customers and then working hard to retain the individual (person of color) who had been a potential candidate for her job illustrated a highly important strategic decision. By partnering with this individual, her action reflected alignment with the environmental changes and a commitment to represent the diversity of the stakeholders in the authority structure of the agency.

Concerning the third theory (visionary and inspirational), in spite of the duplicitous nature of the interaction between board members and senior staff, Carmen empowered her senior staff by establishing opportunities for them to make formal presentations to the board. In advance of these meetings, she would conduct dress rehearsals and coach them. Following one of these meetings, one board member stated that the presentations by the senior staff had been "like velvet."

The fourth theory (behavioral complexity) fits best with Carmen's situation. It is clear from the case that she had to deal with multiple and conflicting demands. For example, she handled the board when it overstepped its boundaries with the senior staff, yet created opportunities for the senior staff to perform and "show their stuff" at board meetings.

Another example of behavioral complexity was Carmen's ability to manage upward and partner effectively with the co-chairs, and yet manage the boundary problem with the other board members as if she were their boss. Managing this tension was stressful for Carmen, because she had to differentiate her role as executive director as a function of whom she was attempting to partner with on the board.

Albeit selective, the examples provided are demonstrative of the linkage between theory and practice. Some suggestions for effective executive leadership practice are as follows:

➤To respond to the boundary management issue with both board members as well as senior staff, one approach to transforming this problem into an opportunity for learning is for Carmen to focus on the interdependence of their roles in service of the task and the importance of the executive director as a boundary manager. Rather than positioning Carmen as a police person and the board members and senior staff as partnering illegitimately, Carmen could develop, with them, ways of collaboration that make their differentiated yet complementary roles and responsibilities explicit and that include her appropriately as the executive director.

➤As the leader of this agency, it is Carmen's responsibility to hold on to the big picture, stay connected to the external environment, and provide an overview of the organization and its component parts. One means for accomplishing this task is to use an organizational model, such as the Burke–Litwin model,[9] to present a conceptual framework for the agency and to depict the interrelatedness among various parts of the organization (mission, strategy, culture, structure, etc.) and between the organization and its external environment, that is, conforming to open systems theory. Familiarity with how the model works could provide a roadmap for leadership, followership, and partnership.

➤Although the senior managers use social comparison as one form of performance evaluation, Carmen's job is simultaneously to promote differentiation and integration among them. That is to say, she must balance the need for effective teamwork and the need for each manager to make a unique contribution. Moreover, Carmen's commitment to rewarding practices that represent a commitment to both individual and team excellence is essential.

➤As a leader, Carmen must continue to learn that while it is important to plan and do her political homework, especially with board members, she must also be prepared to take the heat for unanticipated consequences. One cannot expect plans to be implemented precisely as planned. With board members who act as if each of them individually is her boss, Carmen needs to pay attention to when she unduly delays taking action as a result of overpreparing a political case, such as firing a senior staff member, rather than being decisive and dealing with the consequences.

CONCLUSION

Leadership today and in the foreseeable future consists of multiple relationships, a variety of partnering with each having its distinct characteristics: unique demands, values, and tensions. Our case of Carmen, the executive director of a nonprofit community service organization, illustrates the reality of these multiple demands of partnering she had to manage.

To conclude, let us consider a major quality of leadership now and in the future: the leader's need and ability to manage tensions and paradoxes and partnerships with followers and other constituents. Here are some conflicting or paradoxical instances of what followers as the primary leader constituent simultaneously demand:

➤To provide direction for the organization, *yet* respect followers' needs for autonomy and therefore avoid telling them what to do

➤Another way of stating the previous point is: To inspire followers through sharing a vision for the organization, *yet* allowing them the freedom to find their own way of executing the vision

➤To remain optimistic, energetic, and enthusiastic regardless of circumstances, *yet* be open and tell followers the truth

➤To keep followers informed about what is going on in the organization, *yet* buffer them from frequent illogical and senseless actions of senior management

➤To respect followers' needs for autonomy (again) and leave them alone to conduct their work as they see fit, *yet* respond to their requests for feedback regarding their performance

Perhaps the major quality of leadership today and in the future is to balance these conflicting demands. It is not as if the leader has a choice; both sets of demands must be served. Leadership is therefore about paradox, balancing tensions, and serving multiple and complex partners.

CHAPTER 12

THE ACCIDENTAL PARTNER

HARVEY ROBBINS

At the time of this writing, the economy has stalled. Smaller companies are either being gobbled up or cobbled down. Larger companies are undergoing the largest merger-fest in US. history in order to stay globally competitive. Business strategies have been painfully twisted and squeezed to bolster the bottom lines of too many companies with too few customers. The result of all this chaos is a shifting of resources. Hundreds of thousands of people are finding themselves in new roles with new responsibilities in new or reorganized organizations. Those who have managed to survive the draining of human resources often find little time to grieve for lost co-workers. For now, there is as much (or more) work to get done with fewer people.

If you have found yourself a member of this next generation of leaders, you're probably scrambling. Because you have the title, or seem to know what you're doing, or you've been there 30 days longer than the next person, people are looking to you for leadership. Asking you questions. Asking you for directions. Whether by choice or circumstance, you've been given the ball, you're a leader, and people are looking to you for the next play.

What do you do? You look for partnering opportunities. You don't have the time or inclination to worry about learning all the theories on leadership. You may have attended a few classes on leadership in the past, but probably can't remember much of what was discussed. The class binder may look impressive, but it's not very useful. What you really need is a quick guide to help you through these changing times. Here are some areas that you need to look at, both in terms of leadership advice and partnering opportunities.

GET A GRIP (DON'T PANIC, PLAN)

The anxiety you are experiencing as a new leader is normal and natural. The fear comes from not knowing what you don't know. It is driven by a concept known as "closure." This idea says that if there is something that you don't know, you tend to fill in the blanks with negatives (worst-case scenarios). Ghosts of past failures come back to haunt and taunt you into believing that you will most likely fail again. These thoughts tend to prevent you from moving forward, to protect you with inaction. Not only are these fears irrational, but also they will most likely lead you to self-destruct as a leader. The best advice is to plan your actions. Find someone you trust who is already in a leadership position and ask him or her to be your mentor for a period of time, to be someone you can turn to for advice and counsel. Choose more than one person if you feel insecure. Then, you can begin by measuring what you have to work with, both your capital (budget) and human resources. Choose your direction, prioritize your goals, divide up your roles, and move forward. When in doubt, check with your partner, your mentor, who can provide the business advice and morale building you will need.

SET THE DIRECTION (VISION, MISSION, VALUES)

You may hear the terms "vision, mission, values" bantered about frequently. You may even feel the need to get these quickly or lose the right to lead, but don't be in such a rush. Vision is important in that it sets the direction for the company and what it would like to be known for in the future. Many companies fail, however, when they don't align the "little visions" of the separate departments with the vision of the bigger organization. Can you imagine what it's like working in an organization in which the separate visions of the different departments all go in different directions? Some are in alignment with the overall corporate vision, and others are askew because of some burning mission of a maniacal team leader.

You can develop a vision of your own (just for your department), but only after you have coordinated it with the individual visions of the other departments with whom you interact. Your department's vision can't step on the toes (or steal the resources) of another department with whom you must partner.

Like a vision, a department mission must also be created in coordination with your partners. A *mission* tells your department why it exists and how it plans on accomplishing the vision. If you don't have a clear idea of how and with whom you and your team plan on partnering, you will miss the boat.

Value statements tend to measure the correctness of your vision. A *value statement* is a set of behavioral guidelines or expectations on how people plan to interact with each other while accomplishing the mission and vision. Most value statements include some recognition of the need to partner with others within the organization, both in terms of sharing information and coordination of activities. These become markers that can later be used for both personal evaluation/feedback and measurement of progress toward outcomes.

SET SOME GOALS (THE WHAT AND WHEN)

You will never know if and when you are successful until you first identify what success looks like. You'll need to identify success targets for people to try to attain, so they're all aiming in the same direction. You don't, however, want people shooting themselves in the foot, so coordination is critical. Take, for example, the goals of two separate departments within the same organization. One hopes to increase production by 15 percent, while the other wishes to reduce equipment downtime. On the surface, everything seems aligned, until the second department has to take the equipment off-line to maintain it at peak efficiency. If these two departments do not work in partnership to create coordinated goals, it is quite possible for conflict to ensue if the first department feels like the second department is interfering with its ability to increase production by taking the equipment down. Partnering is therefore crucial when creating department goals and objectives, if you want peace and harmony in the workplace.

DEFINE SOME ROLES (THE WHO)

One of the worst things for a new leader to experience is seeing his or her people running hard, uncoordinated, in all directions, with wheels spinning purposelessly. You can avoid this by asking the question, "Who is responsible for what, by when, and how are we going to check with each other to make sure we're on track?" You intentionally look for overlaps and gaps in responsibilities and put in concerted efforts to reduce them. Cross training is fine as long as everyone is crystal clear about what he or she is responsible for at the moment, from whom he or she gets information, and who uses the information and output. Everyone's job has a purpose and that purpose is usually to meet the needs of someone else. That someone else can be considered your partner, someone with whom you coordinate your activities. If you are doing activities that meet no one's needs, stop doing them.

GET SOME TEAMS (THE WE)

Almost nothing good is ever achieved by a person acting in isolation. Teams often, but not always, get outcomes accomplished with greater speed and quality. It has often been said that there is no "I" in "team." I disagree. People are not willing to work effectively in a team, until, and unless, their personal needs are met somewhere along the way. It's the equilibrium theory that won John Nash the Nobel Prize in Economics in 1994. The best teams are comprised of people working both for the good of the group and for their own self-interests. They coordinate their activities both with people inside the team (core team members) and with those outside the team (resource team members), whom they consider partners in the achievement of successful outcomes.

GIVE SOME FEEDBACK (THE HOW)

One of the hardest tasks you will experience is giving feedback to others, because people, in general, and leaders in particular, feel uncomfortable about "evaluating" others. Yet, giving feedback is necessary if you want your people to remain on target or adjust their activities to meet changing priorities. Quite often, your people are involved in projects under the direction or supervision of others, out of sight. Therefore, it becomes impossible to give accurate feedback to these employees without getting input from the people closest to their work. The most effective leaders are continuously checking with their peer partners to receive input that they can then use to improve and reward the performance of their team members.

GET SOME FEEDBACK (BLIND MAN'S BLUFF)

Ken Blanchard once said that feedback is the breakfast of champions. He was referring to the fact that competitive athletes improve their performance by getting feedback from others. The same can be said for leaders. To improve your performance as a leader, you need to ask for feedback from people with whom you have created partnering relationships, such as your boss, your peers in other departments, and your direct reports. Create a partnering network of people who are aware of both the technical and interpersonal sides of your job: people you trust to give you fair and accurate feedback. Set up a process for obtaining regular input from your partners. Help each other out, and cheer each other on.

GET A PERSONALITY

Among the many ways to lead, the best is to try to lead in a way that takes advantage of your natural personality. In other words, don't be what you aren't. Learning how others behave, how they think, what they focus on and find important, however, will make you a better leader. Let's face it; most of us are self-centered to a certain extent. We really don't care how others think or behave as long as they don't get in our way. To be a better leader, it is important to understand and be able to work with the behavioral patterns of others, especially those with whom you must interact to achieve your outcomes. Partner up with individuals who see the world differently than you do. Have some discussions over coffee. Try to find value in their points of view. Some of the best discussion groups are comprised of people with opposing views, who learn to understand, value, and respect the opinions of others.

It is important that you find out which leadership personality is most suited to your situation. One hopes that it is one that aligns with your own personality. If you are seen as changing your personality often, however, people won't know how to relate to you as a leader and they probably won't trust you.

FIND A CULTURE YOU LIKE AND COPY IT
(GAINING CONSISTENCY)

There are generally four different cultures that you can create within your organization: pummel, push, pull, and pamper. A *pummel culture* is one that is terribly threatening, with a high level of stress and people constantly looking over their shoulders. It is usually created by a boss who is heard shouting, "My way or the highway" with blood-curdling regularity. A *push culture* is also threatening, but the threat is perceived as situation-based, not boss-based. The threat comes from outside the company, from the competition taking food off your plate. A *pull culture* is one driven by a vision of the future, accompanied by a pathway of activities designed to get you there. A *pamper culture* is one in which people are not held accountable for outcomes. It is very laissez-faire.

The ideal situation created by effective leaders is a combination of push and pull, a sort of one–two punch. The threat posed by the stark reality of a somber situation (e.g., constant reminding of the gaining competition) is combined with a way out of the stress via a pathway toward future success, a light at the end of the tunnel. But this works only if you, as leader, are consistent across your activities. You cannot be considered a good leader, for example, if you pummel when handing out assignments, but pamper when it comes to giving feedback.

Partnering is also a large part of an effective culture. If you set the expectation upfront that one of the values important to you is the concept of coordination and collaboration within and between departments (and levels), and if you bolster this belief through the use of effective performance feedback systems, then partnering will become engrained.

SPREAD SOME JOY (REWARDS)

One of the consistently high-ranking items on the list of how people want to be led is to be recognized and rewarded for good work. At the heart of all of the various reasons for working is the desire to have some personal needs met. It could be fame, fortune, positive affirmation, or good-looking colleagues that drives people's desires.

As mentioned earlier, people don't work in isolation. They need partners to help them achieve both their personal and professional outcomes. Therefore, reward and recognition systems should be consistent with the needs and values of your people. Create reward and recognition systems that include input from partners and customers. Some of the most coveted rewards are those given by, say, group one to group two in recognition of group two's support for group one's partnering efforts.

GET A LIFE (DON'T WORK YOURSELF INTO AN EARLY GRAVE: WORK/LIFE BALANCE)

I do not subscribe to the tenet, "Work hard, play hard, die young, and leave a good-looking corpse." The tendency for a new leader is to want to do everything for everyone all the time. This is a bad idea. First, you don't know everything. Second, you just don't have the time. That's where good delegation techniques and good partners come in.

Those organizations that have been successful in creating collaborative working environments—where people back each other up, partner with colleagues and mentors, and put the "we" in team—consistently outperform their competition.

All work and no play, however, can lead to schizophrenia and interpersonally challenged behaviors. The best partner ultimately is the person with whom you can talk one-on-one outside of work. No, it is not the face in the mirror, but someone you can confide in and with whom trust is reciprocated. It could be your significant other or just a really good friend, someone who helps you wind down at the end of a hard day, a stress reliever.

GET PARTNERS (NO ONE LEADS ALONE)

"No man is an island." "Pride goeth before the fall." A slew of guilt-inspiring phrases can be used, but the fact is that no leader leads alone. You will never be successful as a leader if you do not take advantage of the help and advice that others naturally provide. If you keep your ears open, you'll be surprised at the variety of sources offering input to your success. People like to partner with others. Seek them out.

CHAPTER 13

RUB SOMEBODY THE RIGHT WAY

BOB NELSON

"We realized that our largest asset was our work force and that our growth would come from asset appreciation."

Larry Colin, President, Colin Service Systems

"Why do people do what they do?" This question has baffled humankind since the dawn of time. In general, it is thought that our actions are driven by our unmet needs. That is, if we are hungry, we eat; thirsty, we drink; tired, we sleep; and so forth. Once our physical needs are met, our attention turns to meeting higher level needs such as a sense of belonging, achievement, and partnerships. Many of these needs are achieved in the workplace in the course of our careers.

Although we all have the same basic needs, we are each motivated differently over time and at any given time. One person might be motivated to spend more time with family; another might want a raise; a third might want more responsibility. For this reason, when it comes to motivation, it is safest to say that what motivates people, motivates people, and the best way to gain understanding of what motivates people is to establish a relationship, or partnership, with them.

Motivation is also thought to come from within, that is, to be *intrinsic* in nature. It's believed that you can't motivate others; you can only motivate yourself. True, at times you can force others to do what you want, but such coercion is apt to be short-lived, lasting only as long

[127]

as the direct force or threat exists. As the joke goes, if you tell some-one what you'll give her for doing something, that's called an *incentive;* if you tell someone to do something or else he'll get fired, that's called *motivation.*

The use of coercion, fear, and the threat of punishment doesn't work that well in most organizations today. This is in part due to a change in societal norms in which it is politically incorrect to force anyone to do anything. However, more importantly, such a style of management does not get the best results with today's employees, who have the most to say about the work they do, how they use their discretionary energy, or even if they will stay in their present jobs. In other words, whether you get the best effort and performance from an employee will always be his or her choice. Add to this the fact that today's employees are increasingly expected to use their own judgment to act in the best interests of the organization, and it is easy to see why motivating people is such a challenge today.

> *You get the best effort from others not by lighting a fire beneath them, but by building a fire within them.*

The most effective role of managing has thus shifted from an authoritative, command-and-control, "my-way-or-the-highway" style, which has served as the predominant style of management since the Industrial Revolution, to a style in which the most effective managers act as partners to their employees.

You can create an environment in which individuals can be motivated. In fact, doing so is perhaps the most important role of managing today. The key element in shaping a motivating work environment is the management of consequences, the most important of which are the positive ones.

Most employees want to be magnificent, and start new jobs excited about doing their best. Yet, somehow, for many employees the excitement of the job quickly wears off. I believe this is due more than anything else to how employees are treated by their managers on a daily basis. An unmotivated employee in most instances reflects more on that person's manager than his or her own potential in the workplace.

As Bill Hewlett, co-founder of Hewlett-Packard has said, "Men and women want to do a good job, a creative job, and if they are provided the proper environment, they will do so." Today's managers need to establish a supportive environment in which people can be their best. They need to create a new partnership with employees to help them reach their full potential in obtaining both the employees' goals as well as the goals of the organization. The use of recognition and rewards is a primary way of creating a supportive work environment in which employees can be—and are—highly motivated.

YOU GET WHAT YOU REWARD

We know from more than 100 years of research that human behavior is shaped by its consequences. If you recognize and reward behavior, it will tend to be repeated. If you ignore or punish behavior, it will tend to stop. In short, you get what you reward. Sometimes referred to as the Greatest Management Principle in the World, "You get what you reward" is probably the most validated principle of human behavior that we know.

Although the notion of rewarding desired behavior is common sense, it is far from common practice in business today. Yet, it needs to become common practice if your organization is to thrive, let alone survive.

Everyone likes to be recognized and appreciated. How many managers, however, consider appreciating others to be a major function of their job today? It should be. At a time in which employees are being asked to do more than ever before, to make suggestions for continuous improvement, to handle complex problems quickly, and to act independently in the best interests of the company, the resources and support for helping them are at an all-time low. Budgets are tight; salaries are frozen. Layoffs are rampant; promotional opportunities are on the decline.

In today's business environment, what used to be common courtesies have been overcome by speed and technology. Managers tend to be too busy or too removed from their employees to notice when they have done exceptional work and thank them for it. Technology has replaced personal interaction with one's manager with constant interfacing with one's terminal. And all this is happening at a time in which employees are looking to have greater meaning in their lives, and especially in their jobs.

IS MONEY THE TOP MOTIVATOR?

You might ask, "But isn't money the primary reward for work?" It's easy to think so. Most people, however, don't work just for money. In fact, money is seldom the top or only motivator of employees.

I'm not saying money isn't important. Clearly it is. We all need money to pay our bills and maintain the standard of living to which we are accustomed. I'm also not saying money has no motivational value. Clearly it does, and the strength of that motivation will vary over one's life. If you are about to buy a new home, have some unexpected medical bills, or have children in college, you will be more keenly aware of your monetary needs.

Yet, for most of us, most of the time, once we are able to make our monthly bill payments, our attention turns to other factors that have much greater significance in our work lives: feeling we are making a difference and a contribution. This includes having a manager who tells us when we do a good job, having the respect of our peers and colleagues, being involved and informed about what is going on in the company, or having meaningful, interesting work.

The point is, the money that employees are paid for the job they are hired to do is *compensation,* which should be a function of your company's compensation philosophy and its market and geographic considerations. *Recognition* is what you do above and beyond compensation to get the best effort from employees. Every employee who works is paid, but every employee does not get recognition. As management expert Rosabeth Moss Kanter says, "Compensation is a right, recognition is a gift." Adds management guru Peter Drucker:

> Economic incentives are becoming rights rather than rewards. Merit raises are always introduced as rewards for exceptional performance. In no time at all they become a right. To deny a merit raise or to grant only a small one becomes punishment.

The increasing demand for material rewards is rapidly destroying their usefulness as incentives and managerial tools.

You might ask, "Why isn't what I pay people good enough to get them to do their job? Why do I have to do more?" People will do their job for what they are paid, but it will do little to get them to do their best job or to go above and beyond what you expect of them. That extra effort is more a function of how they are treated, the softer side of management, not what they are paid. In the work of management theorist Frederick Herzberg, a fair salary is considered a *hygiene factor:* something everyone needs in order to do the job they are hired to do. Like adequate workspace, light, heat, and a telephone, if you do not have any of these items you will be demotivated and unable to do the job you are hired to do. If you have all of these items, you will be able to do your job, but it will do nothing to help you to do the best job possible. Getting people to do their best job is more a function of what Herzberg calls *motivators,* which include praise and recognition, challenging work, and growth and development opportunities.

There is a big difference between getting people to come to work and getting them to do their best work.

Another question I am asked is, "If money isn't a top motivator, then why is it all I seem to hear about from my employees?" I've had a chance to examine this question firsthand in several companies and have found several explanations: (1) In some working environments, in which people are doing jobs they don't enjoy for managers who don't show their appreciation, employees conclude, "If this is what it's like to work here, at least they better pay me well." That is, money becomes a psychological exchange for enduring a miserable job. (2) In other companies, I've found that managers use *only* money to thank people. For example, they use bonuses, on-the-spot cash, or an extra percentage in the employees' annual salary increase for completing projects and for desired behavior. Without intending it, these managers implicitly send the message to employees that unless you get cash, your contribution to the company is not important. Essentially, they *train* employees to expect cash as the only true form of thanks.

It's true some people directly correlate the amount of money they earn with their perceived worth to the organization. You need to be careful, however, that you do not just respond to those individuals who constantly ask for more money, as you want to reinforce results, not requests. Also, realize that you will never get the best effort from employees just by paying them more. Employees who just want more money will never be satisfied with what they are paid. Their expectations will always rise with each salary increase.

Another manager might ask: "Since money is a basic need, don't you have to pay people well first before the other factors you're discussing are motivating?" That question came up at a conference keynote I was giving, and I was delighted to have a business owner in the audience stand and interject: "Not necessarily! I found that by using positive reinforcement, I was able to increase the level of performance of my employees, which led to increased sales revenues, which ultimately made it possible to pay people better." In other words, nonmonetary incentives can allow the boat to rise financially for everyone.

Another way to look at the relationship between money and motivation is that most of us cannot influence that much what we earn, but many things can influence how excited and motivated we are about our jobs on a daily basis. How managers treat employees is paramount to whether or not they will come to work energized and committed to bringing their best thinking and initiative to their jobs. The daily interactions of management with employees either build and develop partnerships with employees or hinders and erodes them.

In the past, the focus of work was on renting employee behavior. In fact, in some work environments people were even referred to as "hired hands." Today, it's not good enough simply to rent the behavior you want from employees. You need to find a way to elicit their best effort. You have to make employees feel valued, so that they *want* to do their best work on a daily basis, to consistently act in the best interests of the organization. You have to build partnerships with people if the company is to obtain the extraordinary results from ordinary people that are necessary for the business to be truly competitive today. You can get such results from your employees by focusing more on how you treat them. For the best results, pay them fairly, but treat them superbly.

The irony of the situation is that what motivates people the most takes so relatively little effort—just a little time and thoughtfulness—starting with a simple "thanks."

ASAP CUBED: GUIDELINES FOR EFFECTIVE PRAISINGS

The best way to start appreciating others is with simple praisings. In the workplace, praise is priceless, yet it costs nothing. Although giving effective praise may seem like common sense, many people have never learned how to do it. I suggest an acronym, ASAP-cubed, to remember the essential elements of good praising. That is, praise should be done *as soon, as sincerely, as specifically, as personally, as positively, and as proactively as possible.*

As Soon

Timing is very important when praising. To be the most effective, the "thank you" should come as soon as possible after the achievement or desired activity has occurred. If you wait too long to thank a person, the gesture will lose its significance. Implicitly, the employee will conclude that other things were more important to you than taking a few minutes with him or her.

As Sincere

Words alone can seem hollow if you are not sincere in why you are praising. You need to praise because you are truly appreciative and excited about the other person's success, otherwise it may come across as a manipulative tactic—something you are doing only when you want an employee to work late, for example. As the saying goes, "People don't care how much you know, until they know how much you care."

As Specific

Avoid generalities in favor of details of the achievement. Specifics give credibility to your praising and also serve a practical purpose of stating exactly what was good about the behavior or achievement. Praisings that are too broad tend to seem insincere. However, saying, "Thanks for staying late to finish those calculations I needed. It was critical for my meeting this morning," says specifically what and why an employee's effort was of value.

As Personal

A key to conveying your message is praising in person. This shows that the activity is important enough to you to put aside everything else you have to do and just focus on the other person. Because we all have limited time, those things you do personally indicate that they have a higher value to you.

As Positive

Too many managers undercut praise with a concluding note of criticism. When you say something like, "You did a great job on this report, but there were quite a few typos," the "but" becomes a verbal erasure of all that came before. Save the corrective feedback for the next similar assignment.

As Proactive

Praise progress toward desired goals or you will tend to be reactive—typically about mistakes—in your interactions with others. Don't wait for perfect performance: praise improvements and approximately right behavior and you will get the results you want faster. In other words, the essence of a good praising communicates:

➤I saw what you did. (Others don't know what you see.)

➤I appreciate it. (Place value on the behavior or achievement.)

➤Here's why it's important. (Always provide a context.)

➤Here's how it makes me feel. (Give an emotional charge.)

Make the extra effort to appreciate employees, and they'll reciprocate in a thousand ways.

GETTING STARTED WITH EMPLOYEE RECOGNITION

You need to go beyond simple praising, however, to create a motivating workplace. Here are some additional guidelines that I have found useful.

➤*Start in your immediate sphere of influence.* To be successful with motivation you need to operate at a very immediate, personal, one-on-one level. One of the great aspects of this is that you don't need anyone's permission to start using the principles involved. You can immediately use partnering tools, such as positive recognition, praise, and encouragement, toward performance goals with those individuals with whom you work. Simple praisings, gestures of thanks, and public acknowledgments of achievement are the high-leverage actions that will motivate employees in your workplace.

➤*Do one thing differently.* The best goals are attainable, reasonable goals, so it may be best to suggest to managers that they focus on doing just one thing differently. It is far better if managers focus on one thing that is then consistently done than on a dozen things that all fall to the wayside once people step back into their old routines. For example, start each staff meeting with good news and praisings for individuals who deserve it, perhaps reading thank you letters from satisfied customers or employees from other parts of the organization. It's estimated that 90 percent (or more) of our daily behavior is routine; so don't underestimate the power of selective focus.

➤*Involve those individuals you are trying to motivate.* Bring up the topic of recognition and ask the question: "Does anyone think we need to do more recognition around here?" I've never heard of any employee saying, "I just get too much recognition where I work," so this is almost a rhetorical question. Take the initial interest you receive in having more recognition and ask if anyone in the group would be willing to help come up with a program for the group. Volunteers drive some of the best recognition programs! After initially helping them establish goals, have them develop the criteria and mechanics for the program. From the outset, it can be *their* program, not management's, and thus be more likely to succeed. Remember, the best management is what you do *with* people, not what you do *to* them. Make employees partners in their own success.

➤*Ask employees what motivates them.* Whether you have them jot down items that they find motivating on their first day of work, or complete a simple recognition survey of items they find motivating, start with employee preferences for recognition. What motivates us differs from person to person and for the same person over time. Make time to spend with each employee, finding out where they want to go with their careers, personal hobbies, and to the extent they wish to share this, their family situations. All of this information is fodder for motivation. By helping them to reach their goals, you can unleash their excitement and commitment to do their absolute best to help you and the organization succeed.

➤*Focus on what you can do, not what you can't do.* In almost every work environment, there are constraints that can keep you from implementing recognition activities. For example, many organizations are unionized, which restricts some recognition practices; public organizations must be careful how they use public funds for recognition activities; nonprofits and smaller companies may not have any financial resources to devote to recognition programs; older companies may be slow to change from noneffective paternalistic incentives; and larger companies may feel hypocritical conducting motivational activities during or after times of layoffs and downsizing. Instead of dwelling on what you can't do, focus on the hundreds of things you can do. For example, everyone wants to know what's going on, especially as it affects the person individually, and just providing this information can be motivating.

➤*Don't expect to do recognition perfectly.* Some managers attempt recognition activities, and then abandon their efforts because they didn't feel they were initially successful. Remember, any new behavior or change will be awkward at first. There is no perfectly right way of doing recognition. Instead, try things, learn from what worked, and seek to improve. Seek the help and feedback from others in your work group as you try some new behaviors. Have fun in the process and you will seldom go wrong!

SIMPLE GESTURES COUNT THE MOST

Recognition does not have to be fancy. In fact, the simpler and more direct it is, the better. The more I work with recognition and rewards, the more I continue to be intrigued with the simple, sincere ways employees use to appreciate each other with a minimum of cost, paperwork, and administration.

Tektronix, Inc. instituted a simple way for managers and employees alike to focus on recognizing others for doing something right. Simple memo pads were printed that had a cartoon and the heading "You Done Good Award," which could be given to anybody in the company from anybody else in the company. On it, individuals stated what was done, who did it and when, and then gave the memo to the person. By providing such a vehicle for employees to thank one another, praisings happened much more often. The idea has caught on and is now part of life at Tektronix. Says Joe Floren, former communications manager for Tektronix, "Even though people say nice things to you, it means something more when people take the time to write their name on a piece of paper and say it."

Another simple, yet effective, approach is to put notes on business cards. Hohn Plunkett, director of employment and training for Cobb Electric Membership Corporation, says, "People love to collect others' business cards. Simply carry a supply of your cards with you and as you 'catch people doing something right,' immediately write 'Thanks,' 'Good job,' 'Keep it up,' and what they did in two to three words. Put the person's name on the card and sign it."

Following are some more simple, yet powerful, recognition items that have been done with little, if any, budget.

Appreciation Days

ARAMARK, the food-services company headquartered in Philadelphia, PA, organizes a day of appreciation for worthy employees. They send out a proclamation announcing Bob Jones Day, for example, with the reason for the honor. The honoree enjoys all sorts of frills, such as computer banners and a free lunch.

The Spirit of Fred Award

At Walt Disney World in Orlando, FL, one of their 180 recognition programs is called The Spirit of Fred Award, named for an employee named Fred. When Fred first went from an hourly to a salaried position, five people taught him the values necessary for success at Disney. This help inspired the award, in which the name Fred became an acronym for friendly, resourceful, enthusiastic, and dependable. First given as a lark, the award has come to be highly coveted in the organization. Fred makes each award—a certificate mounted on a plaque, which he then varnishes—as well as The Lifetime Fred Award—a bronze statuette of Mickey Mouse given to multiple recipients of the Spirit of Fred Award.

Thanks a Bunch

Maritz Performance Improvement Company in Fenton, MO, has a "Thanks a Bunch" program, in which a bouquet of flowers is given to an employee in appreciation for special favors or jobs well done. That employee then passes the flowers onto someone else who has been helpful, with the intent of seeing how many people can be given the bouquet throughout the day. With the flowers goes a written thank you card. At certain intervals, the cards are entered into a drawing for awards such as binoculars or jackets with logos. The program is used during especially heavy workloads or stressful times.

World of Thanks

A division of AT&T in Jacksonville, FL, uses the World of Thanks award as one of more than 40 recognition and reward programs. It's a pad of colored paper shaped like a globe with "Thank You" written all over it in different languages. Anyone in the company can write a message of thanks to someone else and send it to that person. The program is extremely popular. In four years, they have used more than 130,000 such notes.

The Wingspread Award

The Office of Personnel Management in Washington, DC, uses a "pass around" award that was first given to the division's "special performer." Later that person passed the award to another person who, he believed, truly deserved it. The award came to take on great value and prestige, because it came from one's peers. A recipient can keep the award as long as he or she wants, or until another special performer is discovered. When the award is to be passed on, a luncheon ceremony is scheduled.

The Golden Banana Award

A Hewlett-Packard engineer burst into his manager's office in Palo Alto, CA, to announce that he'd just found the solution to a problem the group had been struggling with for many weeks. His manager quickly groped around his desk for some item to acknowledge the accomplishment and ended up handing the employee a banana from his lunch with the words, "Well done. Congratulations!" The employee was at first puzzled, but over time the Golden Banana Award became one of the most prestigious honors bestowed on an inventive employee.

MAKING TIME FOR EMPLOYEE RECOGNITION

One of the biggest obstacles to having more recognition in the workplace is time, especially on the part of managers. Managers are often too busy focusing on what's urgent, such as dealing with daily crises in their jobs, and as a result don't have any time left to focus on what's important—namely, the people they manage.

The situation is made worse by the false perception on the part of many managers that they are in fact already providing employees with plenty of praise and recognition. According to Aubrey Daniels, president of Aubrey Daniels & Associates, Inc., and a leading authority on the topic of performance management, "Those managers who feel they do it (positive reinforcement) the most, in my experience, actually do it the least."

Managers may have learned somewhere that they need to reinforce their employees positively and they may feel they are doing so, but on a day-to-day basis they often do very little to catch their employees doing something right. Worse yet, often the positive reinforcement they show is incorrect; for example, providing individual feedback that is nonspecific or insincere, praising some employees while overlooking others who have contributed equally to a given success, or having their facts wrong about specific behavior or performance when it is acknowledged.

How can managers recognize their employees more? Like any behavioral change, you have to find a way to make it habit—a natural part of your daily routine. Hyler Bracey, president of The Atlanta Consulting Group, knew he wanted to praise employees more, but found his good intentions did not often translate to daily behavior. To correct this situation, he started putting five coins in his jacket pocket each morning and transferring a coin to another pocket each time during the day that he gave positive feedback to an employee. Within a few weeks, the new habit took hold and praising employees became second nature to him. Says Bracey, "Praising employees truly works. There is so much more energy and enthusiasm in a workplace where praise has become ingrained in the manager."

For managers who are too busy or for some other reason cannot bring themselves personally to praise employees, try to find out what recognition activities they are willing and able to do. For example, you may get a manager to sanction a department celebration, even if he or she can't personally attend the celebration.

Following are some additional techniques reported by successful managers for making recognition of others a priority in their workday.

▶ *Write thank-you notes at day's end.* Managers who are too busy throughout the day may well be able to take a few minutes before they go home to jot some personal notes to individuals who made a difference that day. Get some personalized note cards made up and keep a stack of thank-you cards next to your telephone on your desk so as to be a constant reminder.

➤*Be visible and observant.* Take different paths to your office to get a chance to mingle with your employees. Enter your facility at different entrances from time to time to get a chance to greet others and ask them about their work. Learn employees' names. Take breaks with groups of employees. If you become pressed for time, ask an employee you are speaking with to schedule a meeting with you for more focused attention on your part.

➤*Be accessible and quick to respond.* Alternatively, if you have an "open door" policy, make sure you are actually around for employees to use it. Be accessible when your employees need you to be, not just when it is convenient for you. Take time to listen to them. Then, as important, is responding to employee needs and questions to the best of your ability.

As simple and as relatively easy as these activities and techniques may seem, they can have a significant impact on the morale, productivity, and performance of your employees and can result in a competitive advantage for your organization. Try one or more of these techniques and stick with those that work for you. The power of positive reinforcement can occur only as managers find time to put the principle into practice on a daily basis with each of their employees. "People are our most important asset" is a saying that can be heard in the corridors of most every organization, yet, unless managers walk that talk, no employee will ever believe it.

TECHNIQUES FOR MAINTAINING COMMITMENT

I'm increasingly intrigued by what keeps managers from acting on their best intentions to recognize employees more frequently. It seems that you can raise their level of awareness as to the importance of recognizing employees and you can have them practice their interpersonal skills so that they have the ability and comfort level to recognize others, yet for more managers than not, the desired behavior will fall short of their intentions once they get back on the job. I'm convinced that the ratio of success could increase if we can find ways to help managers keep their commitment to their commitment, that is, to develop an individualized strategy and support plan that increases the likelihood that they will do something different. Following are some tactics that I've seen work for managers in various organizations. Try them, adapt them, and combine them as you see fit for your circumstances and the managers you are trying to influence.

➤*Link the activity to your day planner.* For many managers, the key to impacting their routine is tying the new behavior into their current planning and organizing system. I've been successful at getting analytical, task-oriented managers to start praising employees more by getting them to think of their people as things to do. I have such managers list the names of each person who reports to them on their weekly "to do" list and cross each person off the list once they have given him or her praise based on that person's performance. For some managers, such a specific technique helps change a general, intangible activity to a specific, finite action item, and thus much easier to complete. The manager can also write reminders in his or her calendar for future dates, for example, employees' anniversary dates of hire with the organization.

➤*Elicit the help of others.* Many managers get inspired to start a new behavior and feel it's a personal quest they have to do all on their own. Not true! In fact, they are likely to have better results if they discuss what they are trying to do and involve others with whom they work. For example, have managers partner with someone else that they work with for recognition activities. Perhaps this is a colleague they met in a training session or someone from a different area of the company with whom they want to have a reason to keep in touch. Have them exchange action plans with specific times for follow-up and discussion of progress made. This person thus acts as a designated monitor, counselor, and enforcer all in one—essentially, a soul mate for acting on the new behaviors. Another option for the manager is to say at the next staff meeting, "I'm going to be trying some new behaviors and I would appreciate feedback from people about it. Specifically, I'm going to be acknowledging people when I see them doing a good job. I'm trying to do this in a timely, specific way. Let me know when I do it right and if you value me doing it."

►*Harness the power of technology.* If it is available to you, you can also use technology to leave voicemail or E-mail messages. These simple gestures indicate that you are not too busy to miss the fact that an employee has done something special. Instead of just using voicemail to assign tasks to employees, try leaving employees praisings. This can be done from your car phone as you commute home after work and reflect on the day's events and those individuals who were especially helpful to you. Create an "applause" bulletin board on your company's E-mail system in which anyone can post a note of thanks to another member of the organization. Have the electronic bulletin board pop up when individuals first log onto the system.

►*Hold one-on-one meetings.* One systematic approach for making more time for your people (a top motivator) is to start holding one-on-one meetings. The idea is to set a minimum acceptable standard for face time with each employee. This can be a 15- to 30-minute meeting with each direct report at least once every two weeks. This is the employees' time to use as they desire; thus the meetings may start with the manager asking, "What's on your agenda?" One employee might want feedback on a project she recently completed, another may be looking for advice on how he might improve a working relationship with another employee (possibly through role playing), and yet another might want to discuss career options and skills she'd like to learn on the job. By meeting employees where they are, a manager can increase the likelihood that they'll be motivated.

►*Schedule time for recognition.* You can also provide structure or systems in your work environment that will encourage praisings to take place. For example, a general manager at the Xerox Corporation told me he always saves some time at the end of every meeting with his managers to ask everyone to share one thing they've done to recognize someone on their staff since the group was last together. Other managers conduct a "praise barrage" in which the group focuses on positive feedback for a deserving team member. Other companies have scheduled "bragging sessions" with upper management in which they update (and celebrate) the progress of major projects.

DEVELOPING A RECOGNITION CULTURE

By using the principles and ideas that are discussed in this chapter, you will be well on your way to shaping a motivating workplace. Experiment, learn, and build on your successes. Stop what is not working and try something different. If you keep at it, one day soon you will have a work environment in which people are excited about their jobs, enjoy others with whom they work, and want to do the best job possible each and every day. You will have partners in the goal of making your business a success. As Ron Zemke, senior editor for *Training* magazine puts it: "Recognition is something a manager should be doing all the time. It's a running dialogue with people." Making recognition a priority will not only make you a better manager and give your organization a competitive advantage, but also it will be a source of personal pride knowing that you have had a role in shaping such a work environment.

To sustain the results you will obtain from the use of positive reinforcement techniques and programs, over time you will need to align desired behaviors and performance with organizational systems of hiring, orientation, and training practices and the use of traditional incentives, such as raises and promotions. When this happens you will have truly developed a culture of recognition and performance that systematically reinforces desired behavior and performance in a self-sustaining way. You will have created an environment in which every employee will want to work.

◄○►

CHAPTER 14

LEADERSHIP, MANAGEMENT, PARTNERSHIP, AND DIVERSITY

R. ROOSEVELT THOMAS, JR.

As a context for my comments on the leader as partner, I wish to use "The Giraffe and Elephant" fable.[1] After presenting the tale, I'll look at reasons for establishing a partnership, barriers to effective partnerships, and finally, the lessons that can be gleaned from the fable about effective leadership as a partner.

"THE GIRAFFE AND ELEPHANT" FABLE

In a small suburban community, just outside the city of Artiodact, a giraffe had a new home built to his family's specifications. It was a wonderful house for giraffes, with soaring ceilings and tall doorways. High windows ensured maximum light and good views while protecting the family's privacy. Narrow hallways saved valuable space without compromising convenience. So well done was the house that it won the National Giraffe Home of the Year Award. The home's owners were understandably proud.

The home worked so well for the giraffe, he decided to put his woodworking business in the basement. One day the giraffe, who was working in his state-of-the-art woodshop in the basement, happened to look out the window. Coming down the street was an elephant. "I know him," he thought. "We worked together on a PTA committee. He's an excellent woodworker too. I think I'll ask him in to see my

[145]

new shop. Maybe we can even work together on some projects. I'll need some help, if I am going to keep up with the orders I am receiving." So, the giraffe reached his head out the window and invited the elephant in.

The elephant was delighted; he had liked working with the giraffe and looked forward to knowing him better. Besides, he knew about the woodshop and wanted to see it. So, he walked up to the basement door and waited for it to open.

"Come in; come in," the giraffe said. But immediately they encountered a problem. While the elephant could get his head in the door, he could go no further.

"It's a good thing we made this door expandable to accommodate my woodshop equipment," the giraffe said. "Give me a minute while I take care of our problem." He removed some bolts and panels to allow the elephant in.

Soon, the giraffe and elephant were happily exchanging woodworking stories, as their appreciation for each other's skills grew by leaps and bounds. They got along so well that the giraffe offered the elephant a partnership on the spot, and the elephant quickly accepted. Work with the giraffe would not only elevate his status in the industry, but would also increase his income.

Immediately after the new partners signed their agreement, the giraffe's wife leaned her head down the basement stairs and called to her husband: "Telephone, dear."

"I'd better take that upstairs in the den," the giraffe told the elephant. "Please make yourself at home; this may take a while."

The elephant looked around, saw a half-finished project on the lathe table in the far corner, and decided to explore it further. As he moved through the doorway that led to that area of the shop, however, he heard an ominous scrunch. He backed out, scratching his head. "Maybe I'll join the giraffe upstairs," he thought. But, as he started up the stairs, he heard them begin to crack. He jumped off and fell back against the wall. It too began to crumble. As he sat there disheveled and dismayed, the giraffe came down the stairs.

"What on earth is happening here?" the giraffe asked in amazement.

"I was trying to make myself at home," the elephant said.

The giraffe looked around. "Okay, I see the problem. The doorway is too narrow. We'll have to make you smaller. There's an aerobics studio near here. If you'd take some classes there, we could get you down to size."

"Maybe," the elephant said, looking unconvinced.

"And the stairs are too weak to carry your weight," the giraffe continued. "If you'd go to ballet class at night, I'm sure we could get you light on your feet. They also do a lot of stretching and exercising in ballet. If we can get you in that stretching part, maybe we can elongate your body."

Before allowing the elephant to respond, the giraffe made a closing pitch for the elephant's participation in the aerobics and ballet activities: "Oh, I know you'll like the classes, because I like you and really need you here."

"Perhaps," the elephant said, "but to tell you the truth, I'm not sure that a house designed for a giraffe will ever really work for an elephant, not unless there are some major changes."

REASONS FOR A PARTNERSHIP RELATIONSHIP

Why would a leader wish to establish a partnership relationship, as opposed to the traditional hierarchical arrangement? Does the partnership structure bring special benefits? Several factors can motivate giraffes to establish a partnership relationship.

A common rationale for partnerships is respect for what individuals bring to the table. In the fable, the giraffe not only possesses first-hand knowledge of the elephant's skills, but also affirms in their conversation that this is a quality craftsman. So much so, that to offer mere employment would be beneath his stature. This individual requires a position of greater standing—that of partner.

Another motivation for partnerships is to extend an invitation for the individual to contribute beyond simply "doing" the work. Partner candidates are invited to participate in a special relationship that calls for sharing in the leadership and management functions of the entity. They are expected not to just associate with the company, but also to commit. To take advantage of what partner-caliber people can offer fully, space must be created for them to engage beyond "doing" the work.

To say that a partner participates in the leadership function means that he or she is part of the process of assuring that an appropriate macro framework is in place to facilitate the firm's success. Key leadership questions include the following:

➤Do we have an appropriate mission? Are we clear as to why we exist, why we are here? Is the mission congruent with our external environment?

➤Do we have an appropriate vision? Do we have a clear picture of what would constitute successful achievement of our mission?

➤Do we have a viable strategy for achieving our mission and vision? Do we have a plan that will give us competitive advantage in pursuit of our mission and vision?

➤Do we have a culture (driving, fundamental assumptions) that is congruent with the organization's mission, vision, and strategy?

Partners together accept responsibility for determining and institutionalizing mission, vision, strategy, and culture throughout the entity.

To say that a partner participates in the managerial process indicates that he or she shares in the decision-making about day-to-day operational issues. The leadership function focuses on creating a macro-context for the conduct of business, while the managerial process assures that bottom-line requirements are achieved on a day-to-day, month-to-month, and quarter-to-quarter basis. While these two dynamics, leadership and management, must ultimately complement each other, they can differ significantly. Further, at a given point in time, they may generate contradictory implications.[2]

Each partner therefore has a threefold role: *individual contributor* (I), *leader in the leadership function* (L), and *manager in the managerial process* (M). Depending on where the partner is in the hierarchy, the relative importance of each role option will vary.

At the executive levels, the allocation of the three roles for a partner is likely to be *iLm*. This reflects a primary focus on leadership and secondary emphases on the individual contributor and managerial roles. On the other hand, at the manager/supervisor level, the distribution likely would be *ilM*, which, of course, conveys the greater stress on managerial concerns. Finally, at the individual contributor level, the positioning of the roles' importance would be *Ilm* with the greatest emphasis on "doing" the work. (See Figure 14-1.)

Despite the differing allocations, each participant would be a partner with a special relationship to the organization. All partners would share the three roles; indeed, this sharing would be a requisite for membership in the partnership.

Another point about the partnership is in order. While hierarchical relationships exist, they reflect role differentiation more so than value to the organization or positional status. Regardless of where an individual serves, he or she is more of a colleague than a superior or subordinate. Each participant places a priority on developing and sustaining this sense of spirit of collegiality.

A final reason for establishing partnership arrangements is to secure commitment, in terms of both the intensity and the duration of the engagement. Leaders of the organization want partners really

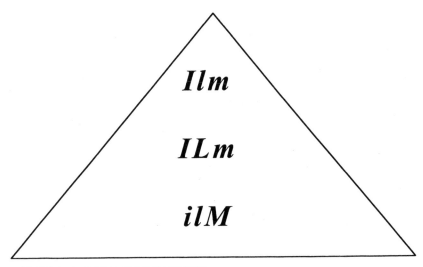

FIGURE 14-1. ROLE ALLOCATIONS

to become involved and to stay on board for a while. In partnership settings, leaders seek more than casual or at-will employment relationships.

In sum, the notion of partnerships implies a special relationship characterized by intense, broad involvement over a significant period of time. Establishment and acceptance of partnership parameters makes sense only when all parties feel excitement about the potential of the relationship. Because both the giraffe and the elephant saw benefits in being associated with each other, they readily agreed to a partnership.

BARRIERS TO EFFECTIVE PARTNERSHIPS

What are obstacles that can hinder the efforts of individuals who wish to lead as partners? "The Giraffe and Elephant" Fable provides examples of some common barriers that can compromise a leader as partner.

➤ *Too much emphasis on similarities:* The giraffe was attracted to the elephant because of their similarities. From his experience with the elephant on the PTA project, the giraffe knew that they shared a love for woodworking, a commitment to high professional standards, and a willingness to serve as a volunteer in the community. These similarities made the elephant a great partner prospect.

➤ *Not enough awareness of differences:* So enthused was the giraffe about the commonalities he shared with the elephant, he failed to focus on significant differences, especially with respect to size and shape. As a consequence, the elephant experienced difficulty entering the house, damaged doorframes, and cracked steps and walls. Not being conscious of physical differences and their implications meant that the giraffe was not prepared for the diversity he and the elephant generated.

I define *diversity* as any collective mixture characterized by differences and similarities. *Attribute diversity* refers to differences and similarities with respect to the characteristics of the mixture components, while *behavior diversity* relates to the activities of the mixture participants.

The giraffe and elephant constituted a diversity mixture with at-tribute differences and similarities that generated behavioral diversity. They can be described as diverse with respect to size and shape, and they can also be viewed as diverse in terms of behavior within the giraffe's house. The giraffe navigates easily from one room to another without difficulty, while the elephant, because of his size and shape, inflicts substantial damage as he explores the house.

The giraffe appeared comfortable with the elephant's attributes, but uncomfortable with their behavioral consequences. He was so uncom-fortable that he suggested that the elephant go away to aerobics and ballet classes, and return less of an elephant and therefore less likely to behave in ways harmful to the house. If the giraffe had been more conscious of the differences between him and the elephant, he might have been better prepared for the subsequent behavioral diversity.

➤ *Too much emphasis on friendship and relationships:* Partnerships revolve around relationships and contextual variables, such as mission, vision, strategy, culture, systems, and organizational patterns. The giraffe–elephant partnership is in trouble, not because of difficulty between the giraffe and the elephant, but because of a poor fit between the elephant and the giraffe's house.

In the fable, the house symbolizes contextual variables, such as the organization's culture, system, and behavior patterns. If the giraffe had not been so enthralled with the budding friendship with the elephant, he would have had a greater appreciation for the "fit" issue between the elephant and the house. Now, he appears to trivialize it. In part, he does so because he assumes the elephant will adjust as neccssary, and also because they have such a great friendship. At the end of the fable, he expresses confidence that the elephant will go to the classes because of their friendship. The giraffe places too great an importance on friendship.

➤*Desire to avoid diversity tension:* Given the giraffe's emphasis on friendships and relationships, one might infer that he wishes to min-imize, if not avoid, diversity tension (the stress and strain that can ac-company the presence of differences and similarities). Leaders often assume that the hiring of friends can work to contain diversity tension.

Increasingly, I find that if you have significant diversity, you will have significant diversity tension. This will be true even among friends.

The leadership task is to create an environment in which, in the midst of similarities, differences, and tensions, individuals can successfully pursue individual and collective goals. Effective partnerships of diverse individuals must possess this capability.

➤ *Inadequate scoping of partnership:* Given both parties' elation about their embryonic friendship, professional respect for each other, and the potential of the business, it is not surprising that they would fail to define the partnership sufficiently. Neither appears to have any awareness of the multiple roles partners can be asked to play. While both talk of a "partnership," they act as if they are in a traditional, hierarchical, superior–subordinate, employer–employee relationship. Even if the elephant stays, without explicit exploration and definition of role options, the chances of their developing a true partnership relationship will be slim.

➤ *Too much focus on self:* Even though the giraffe talks partnership, he places the greatest emphasis on self. He needs to preserve his award-winning house; he needs a skilled colleague; and he needs to work with someone he likes. His needs take precedence.

At no time does the giraffe focus on the elephant's needs. Because he and the elephant consider each other to be a friend, he assumes the elephant will go to the aerobics and ballet classes. Also, because he believes the elephant shares his fondness for the giraffe's house, the giraffe assumes the elephant will agree to adapt. He never seeks information from the elephant about his needs, nor does he foster an awareness and delineation of the partnership's requirements. His drive is to assure that his needs will be met, as if his needs are equivalent to those of the elephant and the partnership.

If a leader wishes to lead as a partner, these examples of obstacles suggest that more than good intentions will be required. They also portray partnering as more than a "good feeling" or a quality relationship.

CHARACTERISTICS OF THE
EFFECTIVE PARTNERSHIP LEADER

The preceding discussions prompt some thoughts about requirements for success. If a leader wishes to lead as if he or she and other organizational participants are partners, what characteristics would facilitate fulfillment of this aspiration? The effective partnership leader would do the following three things:

1. Develop a well-defined set of partnership expectations and requirements. At a minimum, the following questions will be addressed:
   ➤What does each partner expect and require from the partnership?
   ➤What requirements must be met if the partnership is to be viable?
   ➤What roles will each partner be expected to play?
   ➤What will be the benefits of the partnership? The challenges?
   These questions suggest that individuals should not rush into partnership. At a minimum, they should take time to scope the proposed relationship in detail, and avoid acting on "good feelings" only.

2. *Expect and prepare for diversity.* Potential partners can look forward with certainty to diversity. If nothing else, they individually and collectively must respond to the diversity mixture of partnership roles (individual contributor, leader, and manager). The quality of their response to this mixture will determine in large part the effectiveness of the partnership. To the extent that all partners do not engage in the three roles, they will compromise the concept of partnership.

   In addition, partners will have to respond to the attribute and behavioral diversity their similarities and differences generate. They must recognize the implications of the reality that their partnership constitutes a diversity mixture. They must be fundamentally aware of the significant differences and similarities that characterize this mixture.

   Beyond recognizing differences and similarities, they must also anticipate the diversity tension that can surface. Regardless of the good feelings and friendships they may share, they must expect that their diversity will generate tension. The partners-to-be should give some thought to the likely nature of the potential tension and how they might and should respond. If not, they risk being blindsided by the tension and, like the giraffe and elephant, having to respond on the run.

3. *Empower individuals for the partnership.* The giraffe did nothing to ready himself or the elephant to perform as partners. He acted as if they were prepared or could acquire the necessary capabilities as needed and in a timely fashion. As the troubles plaguing the giraffe–elephant partnership indicate, this can be a dangerous approach.

Another option would be to consciously and deliberately empower individuals for partnership. For starters, steps can be taken to acquaint potential partners with the role options of the partnership. This would include educating them around the "content" of the roles. For example, with respect to leadership, the empowerment efforts might focus on the nature of mission, vision, strategy, and culture, and also on the process of developing and institutionalizing these parameters in a partnership.

Attention should also be given to developing individual and collective capabilities for responding to diversity mixtures effectively. Partners-to-be should become skilled at recognizing diversity mixtures, analyzing them, and selecting appropriate responses. Once again, as "The Giraffe and Elephant" Fable suggests, one cannot take for granted that these skills exist.

The characteristics noted here will greatly mitigate barriers that can challenge individuals desiring to lead as partners. Pursuit of these attributes will enhance a leader's capability to establish and lead effective partnerships.

PART THREE

Becoming a Global Leader
Through Partnerships

CHAPTER 15

LEADERSHIP AND ALLIANCES

LARRAINE SEGIL

Nothing will ruin a good alliance faster than a lack of leadership. Whether the leadership is in the senior executive who sponsors or supports the alliance or the team leader who drives its implementation, favorable results from alliances are a direct outcome of strong, focused, and communicative leadership. Nowhere is this more clearly evident than in alliances between companies in different countries.

It is rare that leadership becomes a metric in alliances. Most metrics focus on the strategic, financial, customer, internal, learning, and growth perspectives. However, leadership is often elusive and difficult to measure.

Yet all alliances that succeed manifest directed leadership—not just the "cheerleader" type of motivational leadership, but rather what I call *dynamic leadership*[1] that is measurable, quantifiable, and multi-leveled. It must not only emanate from the individual, but must also resonate from and be supported by the organization. This means that organizational processes must encourage and direct the outcomes that the individual characteristic of the dynamic leader creates.

THE DYNAMIC LEADER

Dynamic leaders manifest the following ten essential traits: to create an adaptive organization: fearlessness, completion, commitment, inspiration, assuredness, penetration, intelligence, integrity, energy,

[157]

and being in the customer's head. The Larraine Segil Matrix describes these ten essential traits and explains how leaders can use these qualities to further partnerships and alliances. The matrix includes three categories of analysis: (1) the individual or personal characteristic of a dynamic leader; (2) the organizational characteristic that will support and grow such a leader; and (3) the management process that facilitates it. In this article, I will discuss just one of the ten essential traits, penetration, which is a good illustration of how the whole matrix can be valuable in alliances. (See Table 15-1.)

"PENETRATION"

Penetration is particularly important in alliances. The bureaucracy and "silo" nature of large organizations can result in technology, knowledge, and expertise being created within the organization in one group or division, while another group is outsourcing and purchasing that very same know-how, with the impression that it is not available within their own corporate "family." However, internal alliances between employees of the same company can add value, longevity, and cost efficiency to internally generated knowledge, as well as enable the amortization of development capital. The managerial and leadership quality of "penetration" is an essential trait for that organization. Alliance managers are particularly well positioned to take the initiative in this regard.

A person who is "of the people" can communicate with those who are considered to be competitors; with people of diverse backgrounds; with individuals senior or junior to themselves; colleagues who are more knowledgeable; or those who are far less knowledgeable, educated, or powerful. It is the ability to cross all barriers, facilitate discussion with those who hold opposite points of view, and most importantly, to listen and hear the positions of others.

This characteristic is of particular value to those creating and managing alliances, who often have inherent conflicts. At the same time that they create an atmosphere of respect and mutuality of benefit for all the partners to the alliance, they must carefully manage the expectations of everyone in the alliance whether inside or outside of the organization. The credibility that alliance managers create for them-

Personal Characteristic	Organizational Environment Needed	Example of a Management Process for Implementation
1. Fearlessness	Permits failure	Shared learning and shared power
2. Completion—ability to complete; has patience and is flexible	Results-oriented with process freedom	Horizontal, project-oriented management processes with cross-functional and multi-locational teams
3. Commitment—emotionally vested	Encourages individual contributions	Small work groups and flexible work behavior; fun
4. Inspiration—inspires and communicates vision, motivates	Access to internal and external people networks	Constant visibility and accessibility
5. Assuredness—knows what he/she wants	Opportunities for advancement and reward	Career progression process
6. Penetration—"of the people" and builds personal equity; listens with respect; empowers with dignity; confident; good mediator	Flexible organizational structure	Free information exchange, communication and benchmarking across groups and divisions
7. Intelligence—talent to place right people in right place	Resource commitment to learning	Training and education
8. Energy—opportunistic optimism and sense of urgency	A "why not" (not "why?") culture; open to new ideas and resistance to bureaucracy	Continuous improvement and innovation processes and rewards and quick decisionmaking
9. Integrity—trust and credibility	Values honesty	360° feedback
10. Being in the customer's head	Customer-focused, both internal/external and domestic/international	Creates and values alliances

© 2002, Larraine Segil
For a full explanation of each characteristic, please refer to *Dynamic Leader, Adaptive Organization,* by Larraine Segil (New York: John Wiley & Sons, Inc., 2002). Reprinted by permission of John Wiley & Sons, Inc.

TABLE 15-1. THE LARRAINE SEGIL MATRIX OF TEN ESSENTIAL TRAITS OF MANAGERS

selves as individuals will stand them in good stead as they move through an organization. Often, they have to marshal resources from finance, marketing, research and development, and manufacturing, all to serve the common goal of the external alliance partner.

Case Illustration: Fortune 500 Alliance
with New Technology Company

The challenge for a Fortune 500 company in the electronics industry was its size. Its partner was an Australian software company with interesting technology and an online financial services business model that was a breakthrough in its area. The smaller company faced the challenge of learning who the appropriate people were at the larger company, and with whom they needed to partner, even though the alliance contract and equity investment was signed and sealed. Potential partners within the larger company were in the research and design group, the consumer products and services group, and marketing and sales across the whole company. The smaller company's executive sponsor was in the office of the CEO of the Fortune 500 partner. However, as is often surprising to many who are new to the alliance field, even the highest level of sponsorship in the company did not ensure success for this alliance. The implementation of the relationship depended on the individuals in each group who would understand, buy in, and then take the time to understand the connection between their organizations. That was hard enough. The next step meant changing the behavior and management processes, the choices and metrics that were already in place. Even more, then, in the implementation stage, the success of the alliance would sit squarely on the shoulders of small teams within the larger company.

How did this work? The senior executive sponsor, who was in the office of the CEO, was an individual who had spent many years in the company, and embodied the characteristics of "penetration." He had taken the time to create relationships—what I call building personal equity. This is an investment of time, energy, and trust as targeted as a financial investment in stock equity would be. He had taught himself to be a good listener and to hear differing opinions with respect. As a result, he knew where the strong and influential people were in each of the departments of the organization and had built a personal network, which was far stronger than any corporate organizational chart could have been in endowing him with the power of persuasion and influence. He also knew, most of the time, whom to avoid—the "big talkers" who were all talk and no results.

Both companies had to navigate through the nondynamic managers to select the dynamic managers in each nook and cranny of the organization; to create a series of metrics, which were agreed on and realistic for both partners; and to advise on the team selection and alliance reporting processes, so that the alliance could be implemented as negotiated.

Leadership is too often perceived as a quality of hierarchy. In internal relationships with others in the same organization but different groups and functions, lateral relationship development is often more challenging than external relationship creation and management. Internal politics, territoriality, and the "NIH" (Not Invented Here) factor all play a role in clouding a clear and collaborative definition of success. The ability to take the leadership quality of a dynamic leader (any one of the characteristics in the ten essential traits in the Larraine Segil Matrix) and apply it to increase productivity in both internal and external alliances is a key to delivering results.

However, the individual characteristic of "penetration: being of the people" must be supported by the organizational environment if it is to survive. Otherwise, those who are able to create the internal relationships will be frustrated as they try to make change happen, but are thwarted by internal bureaucratic management processes that make busywork with no substance or validity. This will be seen in flexible organizational structures.

Organizational Structures that Support the Characteristics of "Penetration"

There should not be a single organizational structure that fits all circumstances. Some organizations function well in a hierarchical structure with firmly accepted processes and project management, for example, most missile manufacturers. A stringent set of circumstances, a set date for performance, a series of intersecting deadlines, and a rigid set of quality and safety standards were some of the characteristics that I observed in a number of the customers we served when I was CEO of a distributor of aerospace products. Companies such as TRW and Northrop Grumman were hotbeds of project management, PERT and GANTT charts, and were hierarchical and structured in their style and approach to management. Yet within one of the most structured organizations, Hughes Communications, part of the former Hughes Aerospace, a stealth organization of "out-of-the-box" thinkers evolved that went on to become DIRECTV. This internal island of consumer services and product innovation was run as a virtual organization of multiple alliances and outsourcing arrangements with partners, each of whom contributed his or her core competencies to the enterprise. This group eventually became the shining star of Hughes Communications and a hotly sought-after acquisition target.

What were the success factors that drove this phenomenon? Many will say it was the personalities of those individuals within Hughes Communications who saw the opportunity. However, many other fundamentals contributed to the success of this venture—the convergence of a great idea, a business opportunity with a market demand and need, along with the willingness of a large and structured organization to take risk and bet on the creativity of a few individuals. James Ramo, one of the founders (and also the son of Cy Ramo who founded TRW), explained how it happened in my recent interview with him.[2]

> I was working for Hughes Communications, in charge of the C-Ban Satellite sales group, selling to the Cable Television Broadcast Industry. Hughes Communications was a leader in that business. There was a gap in the market, but filling that gap meant going directly to the customer and we at Hughes were certainly not in the consumer products or services industry, nor were we in the entertainment field. It meant taking a huge leap of faith, and we were fortunate that our organization gave us enough rope to hang there over the cliff and make it happen. (Of course, the rope could just as easily have been the one we hanged ourselves on!)

James and his colleagues at Hughes saw an opportunity to join forces with a number of other companies to offer content directly to consumers. This meant creating a series of alliances with companies such as MCI (now WorldCom), Warner, Thompson in France for the "black box" used for the DIRECTV product—in short, the supply chain pieces that would take content, via satellite, to consumers. It was a bold idea that was completely different from the kind of business in which Hughes Aerospace was active. They were in the satellite transponder business, not the business of providing mass entertainment. Nevertheless, with the support of management (especially Michael Armstrong who had become CEO of that part of General Motors that owned Hughes), they forged ahead, showing fearlessness, innovation, creativity, and perseverance. Now DIRECTV is one of the jewels of the Hughes organization and James has moved on to other projects. He now runs an innovative joint venture with a number of movie companies committed to the digital world of movies on demand—beyond even what TIVO can offer. The idea was groundbreaking, but the implementation depended squarely on one main competency: partnering.

Partnering was the critical success factor of the idea and the leadership that supported the concept development was the catalyst. Managing the intricate relationships that made up the value chain of the DIRECTV product, content, delivery, customer service, and installation became the core competency of the organization. James Ramo shared some thoughts on his years at DIRECTV.

> Many of our resources were focused on the value-increase of those critical relationships. The explosive growth of the company and acceptance of the concept meant we were successful, but the relationships had to expand and flex along with the market opportunity. That was the real challenge for the company and for us as individuals over past years. There are so many stakeholders in complex alliances, often it feels as if you have to embody the wisdom of a Solomon in order to resolve the many contradictory interests that change constantly over time.[3]

How did the organizational structure and management processes support this enterprise?

What the *intra*praneurs at DIRECTV achieved was the creation of an entirely new business for themselves and the organization. Hughes was open to the change and supported the risk-taking of these few managers. Fortunately the risks created unimagined rewards. The outcome forever changed Hughes and the individuals involved.

In this way, if the organization is open to it, dynamic leaders who are good alliance managers can spot market opportunities and bring innovation and motivation as well as culture change to all kinds of organizations. Again, this means identifying and moving out the elephants that are in the room, bringing value in their place.

THE ELEPHANTS IN THE ROOM

"Sometimes if people don't adapt to change, you have to move them along, either into a different position in the same company, or possibly move them out of the company altogether," said George Fisher, former chairman and CEO of Eastman Kodak and Motorola.[4]

It's hard enough for individuals to change, but organizations are like aircraft carriers—a steady hand, a clear direction, and a sustainable approach will finally move them in a different direction, but it takes time, focus, and strength of purpose. Certain difficulties stand in the way, like elephants in a room. These are the issues that no one wants to face, but everyone admits are the real problems to address. Elephants are too large for rooms and can make a rather unpleasant mess; unless someone deals with them, they will gradually overtake the environment.

Examples in the arena of alliances and leadership include the following:

➤Dysfunctional alliances: These include alliances that are not working but are not terminated. The dysfunction goes unrecognized or unacknowledged and the alliance is left to become one of the "living dead" that drains corporate resources.

➤Territoriality issues: These can manifest in corporate managers as well as those in the business unit. This is especially troublesome when the business unit manager has profit-and-loss responsibility, but the corporate manager is responsible for the oversight of the alliance. If they don't see eye to eye, the company and the alliance suffer. Often that territoriality is the real elephant in the room, not the alliance!

➤Cross business unit competition: This is particularly troublesome when, in alliance development, different teams from the same organization bump into each other in the lobby of a potential alliance partner. This shows a lack of coordination and collaboration and gives the potential partner a strategic negotiating advantage.

➤Bureaucracy: An excess of bureaucracy in the creation and management of alliances or its opposite, a lax approach that means each alliance must be redesigned without repeatable processes. A delicate balance of not too little or too much management must be maintained if alliances are to be successful. Unfortunately, large organizations have realized the need for process and have created substantial alliance organizations, sometimes with hundreds of alliance managers. This creates a need for "busy work" in excess of that required to run an alliance. Thus, this valuable process can become another elephant that is too large, unwieldy, and inflexible to change and adapt to the needs of the partnership.

The following are a few common elephants that we have seen:

"We created this industry. How could they possibly have designed something that is better/smarter/higher quality and lower in cost than we did?"

"We can't do that here. We never have and we never will. It's not our way. We do it differently. (And we are right . . .)"

"Creating an alliance with them is a bad idea. We are not good at alliances and don't want to create them anyway. We do better on our own."

Alliance managers have to be good leaders, facilitators, and also good elephant spotters. They see what is in front of them (and behind them too!) and are unafraid to tell the truth. In alliances, they are willing to advocate the position of a partner, even one who is potentially or actually a competitor, while still remaining loyal to their own company. They are the ones who can see the benefits, measure the mutuality, and create and continually modify the metrics.

Jerome Adams is a senior executive at Shell, and a flexible, dynamic leader with a true understanding of alliances, leadership, and their interrelationship. He ran the Shell Learning Center for a number of years in Houston and built it into one of the premier corporate learning centers in the world. In working with Jerome for a number of years, I have come to respect his leadership and perception greatly.

> Our center is the place that not only our executives and managers can come to learn and share experiences, but also our partners. We have opened many of our processes and learning techniques to those with whom we both compete and collaborate. There is a huge need for managing relationships that morph from collaborator into competitor and back again, and here at the center we encourage that kind of exchange. It is also a safe place for our people to talk about the challenges they face personally and corporately. Frankly, unless there is a level of safety in discussion, people will not open their minds and share real insights with others. This is a place they can do that.[5]

Jerome personifies a leader who has taken the characteristics of managing internal alliances with his peers and those who work at Shell very seriously. He works hard to make sure that his internal network stays strong and encourages those he comes in contact with to do the same.

"It is up to each person to direct their own career path. Here at Shell, we post job opportunities so that people can decide where they want to make change internally, so that we can keep the corporate memory in the family. We value each individual at Shell as a contributor, an internal alliance partner, if you will, that deserves the nurturing and consideration that we apply to our external partners."[6]

By showing leadership in alliances and applying the ten essential traits, Shell is known within its industry as an excellent partner that is ethical, has integrity, and is the true embodiment of its credo "Count on Shell."

SUMMARY

What are the success factors that surround issues of leadership in the creation, implementation, and outcomes of an organization's alliances?

➤Identifying the challenge: Combine dynamic leadership with effective alliance management skills, which means emphasizing the characteristics in leaders that include developing their networks internally and externally. The goal is to be able to call on resources within multiple functions and units within the organizations of all partners and to encourage those who report to you to do the same. The "penetration" element will stand alliance managers and executives in good stead when they need to call on both the expertise and the political influence that is required to achieve the goals of the alliance. Alliance managers and executives who are weak internally will be poor influencers of those who make critical decisions about alliances and will lack resources when they most need them. Identifying the lack or presence of this characteristic (among others) will give rise to the opportunity for remediation through training, changed reward systems, and heightened awareness.

➤Applying the solution: Create an alliance process that includes leadership expectations as part of the alliance metrics. This is the ability to embody the ten essential traits as part of the learning and expertise required by effective alliance managers, which involves creating a baseline of the characteristics for each manager or executive involved in an alliance. That baseline will serve as the yardstick for improvement, and alliance results and management will be enhanced by these capabilities. Don't let the process overwhelm the people! Keep an eye on it so that it doesn't grow to be an elephant in the room with too much busy work and bureaucracy.

➤Establishing the prerequisite: This means having an organizational structure that includes sufficient flexibility to create an environment for innovation, and where an individual with the ten essential traits who manages alliances can improve those traits and thrive. This will mean rewarding those who spot the elephants in the room and move them out, replacing them with value. No one person can manage an alliance alone; it must be a team effort. Team collaboration often occurs across corporate cultures as well as across global country cultures. The structure of an organization must allow for cultural differences as well as organizational preferences. Even those who score high on the leadership and alliance charts cannot succeed without the organizational environment that nurtures and rewards such behavior. This is the prerequisite for success—making the individual, organizational, and process characteristics work together to support effective leadership and alliances.

◀◉▶

CHAPTER 16

BECOMING A CULTURALLY LITERATE LEADER IN A GLOBAL WORLD

ROBERT ROSEN

On the morning of September 11, I was working in my home office in Virginia when a friend called and told me to turn on the television. From my living room, I watched in horror at the live footage of United Flight 175 exploding into the South Tower of the World Trade Center. Then, I heard news of the attack on the Pentagon, less than one mile from where I live in Arlington, Virginia.

Like so many people, language failed me that day. Words could not convey my shock and sadness. When I could no longer bear to see replays of the crash, I called a friend and together we walked from my house to a grassy hilltop near the Pentagon. In the distance, we could see one side of the mammoth building in black smoke and flames.

I sat on the hill listening to the rising pitch and wail of police and fire engine sirens. Smoke billowed out of the Pentagon, creating ominous dark clouds against a clear, blue sky. At one point, I looked up to see a pair of F-16 fighter jets flying low overhead, an image I never thought I'd see in the nation's capitol.

I sat there contemplating the events of that morning. We were witnessing the dark side of globalism, or "Jihad online," as *The New York*

Portions of this chapter were adapted from *Global Literacies: Lessons on Business Leadership and National Cultures.* New York: Simon & Schuster, 2000.

Times columnist Thomas Friedman described it. The forces of free trade and technology that unite us as one world economy also allowed men to hijack commercial planes and steer them with cruise missile-like precision into civilian targets. Forces that help people spread wisdom and compassion around the world allowed others to fuel hatred and violence. In our new global world, individuals have the power to take on entire nations.

Yet, in the face of this darkness, we are reminded that the paradox works both ways: If individuals can bring a country to its knees, individuals can put it back on its feet. We must believe in these ideas if we are to live harmoniously in a global marketplace and community.

The World Trade Center and Pentagon attacks may be America's single greatest tragedy, but this tragedy can also be the greatest teaching moment for the world. In its wake, we have been forced to ask ourselves: What kind of people do we want to be? What kind of relationships do we want to build? In what kind of world do we want to live?

Life has a mysterious way of renewing itself. We go back to living our lives, altered forever in mind and spirit. We go back to leading work projects, coaching soccer teams, and mobilizing church groups. Government services continue, volunteers share their goodwill, and entrepreneurs recommit to building businesses and creating wealth. Yet, this time something profound changed inside ourselves. We must live locally in a global world; build relationships that make life better, not worse for others; learn new thinking and practices from around the world; and have the courage to lead full, responsible lives—together as one global humanity.

After September 11, the message is more urgent than ever: Leaders must become culturally literate global citizens.

ALL BUSINESS IS GLOBAL BUSINESS

Corporate survival and prosperity increasingly depend on our ability to interact and manage people of different cultures, locally, regionally, nationally, and globally. Increased multicultural connections, driven by technological revolutions, have created new tensions and opportunities among groups. New cultural identities and mixtures are emerging as boundaries between cultures blur and become permeable. We are confronted with greater complexity than we can handle: uncertainty, contradictions, ambiguities, and contrasting interests abound, as do boundless opportunities.

For years, mega-corporations cornered the market on crossing cultural borders. By sending expatriates abroad to search for international customers and suppliers, they experienced the benefits and pitfalls of the multicultural world. Local companies stayed home and through diverse workforces got a taste of internationalism and the challenge of managing across cultures.

Today, everyone is part of the global marketplace, even though many companies don't yet realize that fact. Service firms, law offices, and even taxi services are global companies. Small bookstores in South Africa, independent wine merchants in New Zealand, and even co-op galleries in Finland buy from and sell to the world. The Internet is the great equalizer.

To thrive, all leaders must adopt a global-centric approach to business. They must develop a multicultural perspective, an international knowledge base, and a global imagination—in other words, cultural literacy.

In this globalized world, culture is no longer a soft concept, but an asset to be leveraged. Cultural literacy allows us to understand our own culture and the culture of others deeply, enabling us to mobilize diverse people, serve diverse customers, and operate across cultures around the world.

To be culturally literate, leaders must take on new roles:

➤Proud citizen

➤Inquisitive internationalist

➤Respectful modernizer

➤Culture bridger

➤Global capitalist

To succeed in these roles, we must value our own culture, be literate about others' cultures, and use this knowledge to strengthen our own culture, create connections, and leverage culture for our advantage.

Proud Citizen

Zhu Youlan reveres the stories that are an integral part of her Chinese culture. As CEO of Hong Kong–based China Resources, she adds to that heritage every day, using images of boats and shirt collars to describe her leadership philosophy. Zhu knows that learning how to exchange business cards is superficial; what really counts is a much deeper understanding of her culture. She's proud of the fact that the Chinese do things differently.

Zhu Youlan is a strong leader with a proud legacy, and she is intent on learning from her ancestors. She understands what it means to be a progenitor, to accept the responsibility of "going before," and to pass on the culture from one generation to the next. Zhu understands her cultural roots and how they affect her style of thinking and behaving.

Proud citizens understand the psychology of cultural self-awareness. With a healthy knowledge of their country's history, strengths, and shortcomings, they come to the table willing to share their past. They understand the cultures in which they live and recognize that each of us is the product of more than one culture. We can be German, Bavarian, female, and an accountant simultaneously, wherein each identity provides cultural tendencies and data that inform how we live our lives.

Culturally literate leaders also have an honest sense of themselves in the world. By exercising cultural self-esteem, they value their roots and build confidence in themselves, which enables them to come to the international table as mature adults.

Proud citizens also know that feelings of cultural inferiority create resentment and diffidence. Worse yet, feelings of cultural superiority create arrogance and antagonism. When we believe our values are better than those of others, we are unable to listen cross-culturally. People who try to impose values on others expect others to fall into line with their views of the world.

Inquisitive Internationalist

Istanbul sits squarely at the meeting place of Europe and Asia, with a bridge literally spanning the distance between these two continents and mindsets. Sakip Sabanci, chairman of Turkey's leading global conglomerate, Sabanci Holdings, clearly mirrors that span in his business leadership. He is a proud Turk, balancing his nationalist passion with his keen desire to learn from others. At Sabanci Holdings, he travels abroad incessantly, enters into international joint ventures, and incorporates outside business practices, such as Japan's *kaizan,* into his management toolbox.

Like Sabanci, inquisitive internationalists know they must be literate about other cultures. Insatiably curious and sensitive about people and places, they analyze their own cultural biases and act like polite guests when traveling abroad, always respecting local customs.

Culturally literate leaders look beyond their own culture for business solutions. By seeking markets, competencies, and resources in the farthest corners of the globe, they enlarge their ideas and expertise. Like bees with pollen, they are incessant cross-fertilizers who take the best from one place to another, understanding the need to synthesize multiple perspectives.

Inquisitive internationalists don't shy away from diversity and debate. Instead, they are drawn to it, unafraid of differences. They prefer to talk about, question, and celebrate these differences rather than be paralyzed by them. Because they know that one-size-fits-all leadership doesn't work, they cherish the fact that people differ in ability, background, and personality.

All of these qualities enable Sakip Sabanci and others like him to meet cultures as equals in the global marketplace.

Respectful Modernizer

Keshub Mahindra manufactures vehicles in Mumbai. As CEO of India's Mahindra & Mahindra, the world's largest manufacturer of tractors, he sees himself as much more than a carmaker. He is a trustee of his company and his country. As such, he has a dual responsibility: to both respect India's past and modernize its future. Keeping one foot in his own culture and one foot on the world stage, Mahindra is a respectful modernizer.

Becoming culturally literate requires an honest sense of your own culture, creating a national pride tempered with an awareness of national flaws. You must be aware of your personal biases and prejudices and cultural strengths and shortcomings and be careful not to let these blinders obstruct your vision. You must be confident and clear about whom you are and express the best of your country.

Understanding and valuing others is the natural next step. By developing the capacity to see the world from another perspective, you open yourself to learning what each country has to offer. By looking globally for new ideas and business practices, you expand your worldview and open up the possibility of bringing something of value back into your own country.

The final step is to modernize your own country with the new ideas you learn abroad. By integrating others' worlds into your own, you enlarge and enrich your perspective and become enlightened and elevated in the process. Inevitably, you become a broader person and modernize your country. But, you must be open to change.

Culture Bridger

Leo van Wijk, CEO of KLM Royal Dutch Airlines, literally bridges cultures everyday; flying 13 million people a year from one place to another. "We are culture bridgers, listening and sharing what we learn from around the world," says van Wijk. A culturally literate leader, he is able to bridge other cultures to form alliances and connections, such as KLM's extensive partnership with Northwest Airlines.

Building connections with other cultures doesn't happen just with airplane flights. The opportunities exist for everyone, every day, in the global environment. Being successful requires a special mindset and a commitment to collaborating cross-culturally.

Culture bridgers are true integrators. They get excited seeing similarities and differences among people. Accepting that others may have different values than their own, they look for ways to discover those differences, destroy the walls between them, and celebrate their commonalities. They connect on some things and extract lessons from what's different, always using the differences to build sturdier bridges.

Like civil engineers, culturally literate leaders know that building bridges depends on a strong and solid foundation. You must first like yourself and your national culture; then, you must survey the distant shore to know where you're going. Taking the time to understand another culture is critical to building a permanent bridge. Bridge builders also value balance and rely on the creative tension that holds the arch of the bridge together. By combining the solidity of knowing yourself with the flexibility of being open to others, you too can manage the creative tension.

Bridges are also built brick-by-brick, just as relationships are built one person at a time. It's inevitable that conflicts and miscommunications will arise, but culture bridgers know how to resolve them with grace. When bridges rust or have a loose foundation, they require upkeep and attention. Cultural relationships require the same.

Global Capitalist

Jean-Louis Beffa is French, European, and global. As CEO of Saint-Gobain, one of France's largest industrial conglomerates, which created the windows of Versailles, Beffa embodies the concept of a global/local mindset. With a French appreciation for history and strategic planning, a European love of truth and debate, and a global appreciation for diversity and world markets, Beffa is a true global capitalist.

Like Beffa, global capitalists develop a global/local mindset, use the diversity of their employees to respond to diverse markets, and broaden the definition of business success by focusing on their corporate social responsibility. They understand the global marketplace, see regional opportunities, and are sensitive to local markets—and they recognize, hire, develop, and nurture local managers with global literacy skills.

Culturally literate leaders understand the interconnectedness of the global economy, always looking globally for customers, capital, suppliers, and talent. In so doing, they bring global power to local problems and local solutions to global opportunities. They tap into the world's resources, utilizing them to create new products around the globe. They know how to access new talent, information, and experience from around the world.

Global capitalists leverage a diverse workforce to serve diverse customers. They know that different people bring their own experiences and habits to work and that all these differences are vital for creativity and innovation. By learning multiple languages, building an international board of directors, and creating multicultural teams, these leaders create a sense of wholeness, incorporating all that diversity.

Also, these leaders truly understand their corporate social responsibilities. By broadening the definition of success to incorporate a triple bottom line of financial, social, and environmental measures, they enhance the role of business as global citizens and environmental stewards.

These leaders deeply understand their role in building a healthier, sustainable planet for all our citizens. They use their cultural wisdom to manage the private–public interface between consumers, environmentalists, investors, human rights activists, governments, and societies.

No matter how global they become, they try hard to protect their local communities. With their enlightened self-interest, they know only too well that nothing is worse than alienating a local community of customers.

DEVELOPING A NEW WORLDVIEW

To survive and thrive in the global marketplace, all leaders must expand and enlighten their view of the world. Today's world is interconnected like never before, as free market capitalism and democracy have become the business and government institutions of our time. It's also a borderless, multicultural world in which we are all global citizens, regional traders, national promoters, and local neighbors all in one. Together, we must promote one global marketplace and one global society. By becoming global citizens, we will expand opportunities for all, learn and respect our diversity, and strengthen the bonds of community that bring us together as one global humanity.

CHAPTER 17

THE LEADER AS PARTNER: A CONTRAST OF EUROPEAN AND AMERICAN LEADERSHIP STYLES

STEPHAN A. FRIEDRICH, HANS H. HINTERHUBER, D. QUINN MILLS, AND DIRK SEIFERT

The European model of leadership is different from the American model, because it is based on a more partnership-oriented approach. Jack Welch, former CEO of General Electric, used very different leadership techniques compared with his German counterpart Heinrich von Pierer, CEO of Siemens. Both were successful in modernizing large-scale companies and in preparing their organizations for future challenges. Welch, however, took the "destroy-your-business-approach" and "some-always-have-to-leave-the-company," whereas von Pierer appeared to be more cautious and integrative in his partnership-oriented management style. Another interesting example involves Jürgen Schrempp, CEO of DaimlerChysler. He comes from the European style of leadership and is now adopting his leadership to a more American style. The authors of this chapter, who are both European and American, take a closer look at the partnership tradition in leadership and what the unique features of this model are.

SOME IMPORTANT DIFFERENCES

What are the requirements of a great leader in Europe versus American expectations? In North America, business leaders are often displayed on the cover of business and news magazines, and their importance and corporate relevance is measured to a significant degree by their

[177]

annual compensation package. This is different than in Europe. Many business leaders do not like to be displayed on the covers of business magazines, owing to the history of kidnapping of wealthy executives in some European countries, as, for example, Mr. Oetker and Mr. Reemtsma in Germany. Beside this, it is simply not their style. In Europe, the public and employees of companies in particular view large compensation packages negatively. In America, it seems to be just the opposite. Large salaries appear to prove that the leader is a standout. European leaders do not like this, because they know that in the long run they can be successful only if they gain respect as a member of a group. Because of legislation in most European countries, employees have many more rights within the company. They may vote on management decisions, and it is much more difficult to lay off employees in many European countries than in the United States. Leadership founded on partnership is usually a prerequisite for success in Europe.

> "European civilization is an old civilization, and the citizens of our companies expect their leaders to be civilized people."
> Francois Cornelis, CEO, Petrofina

SOURCES OF LEGITIMATE LEADERSHIP

In the United States, the main source of a company's societal legitimacy is the shareholder's meeting. The shareholders are the source of power; if the shareholders accept the CEO and his or her team, the leadership is legitimate. There is no element of partnership in this, unless one is prepared to imagine a partnership between the CEO and the shareholders in his or her company. However, this would be a fairly distant and formal partnership.

In Europe, a partnership is at the core of leadership legitimacy. If a company's top leader is not accepted by the executive team, by the company's workers and their unions, in some cases by the national politicians, by state and local governments, and by the public, then she or he is not legitimate and may not be effective economically. Corporate leadership must negotiate and harmonize the divergent interests of its stakeholders. Partnership is crucial for major management decisions. The power base of European companies has to be larger than in the United States companies, and therefore leadership is more complex—involving more partnerships—than in American companies.[1]

The following are central to a partnership approach to leadership:

➤The conception of a company as a coalition

➤The desire for a resolution of conflicting interests within the coalition rather than in the courts or in the marketplace

➤The objective of achieving a necessary level of profit rather than profit maximization

In this context, the interest of shareholders loses its primacy and is balanced against those of other stakeholders. This is reflected in the European concept of leadership and its behavior. Two centuries of class struggle have deeply influenced Europe, so that top leaders must be able to convince and to negotiate. Consider, for example, the recent case of Swissair in which bankruptcy has been avoided (or postponed) through a concerted action of large Swiss banks, the Swiss government, and Swiss corporations, because the reputation of Switzerland is at stake. The specific role of business in the European tradition is to create not only economic and technical progress, but also social and political progress.

European leadership is strongly tied to partnering and networking. In the United States, one sometimes gets the impression that competition is more focused on rivalry between leaders than between products and services. Larry Ellison, CEO of Oracle, is a good representative of that attitude. In Europe, leadership tends to be more modest, eschewing the spotlight. Decisions are more likely to be made by numerous members of an organization rather than by individuals.

THE THREE COLUMNS OF LEADERSHIP

"We are responsible not only for what we are doing, but also for what we are not doing."

Marcus Aurelius[2]

The sources of leadership are alertness to opportunity and the imagination and vision to capitalize on it.[3] Leadership means:

➤Identifying opportunities that others might not see and exploiting these opportunities rapidly and fully

➤Inspiring people to achieve more than they think they can achieve and demonstrating to them that they should never be satisfied with where they are now[4]

It is in the second of these aspects of leadership that partnership is crucial. Partner-based leadership is a learned or acquired ability of influencing people to work enthusiastically toward goals identified as essential to the common good.[5] Leadership of this type is not based on power, forcing someone to do one's will, but on *authority*, one's personal influence in getting people to willingly contribute to achieve shared goals.

A partnering leader has to (see Figure 17-1):

➤*Be a visionary:* He or she has to foster the will to win by reaching the hearts and minds of co-workers with a shared vision that indicates a direction and gives meaning to all stakeholders. The vision of Barilla, the Italian food company, is to spread the Italian style of nutrition all over the world. The vision of SOS Kinderdoerfer, an Austrian charitable nonprofit organization operating worldwide is: love, a home, and a family for every child.

➤*Be an example and show courage:* To communicate on a credible basis and to inspire people to act in a positive way, a leader has to be an example and to take risks. A French company, having integrity as one of its core values, is selling its foreign subsidiary, because it views corruption there as not controllable.

➤*Create value for all stakeholders:* First for the customers, second for the employees, and third for the shareholders and the financial community.

Leaders discover and exploit new opportunities through the power of their vision, the example and authenticity of their character, and the values they create for the key stakeholders.

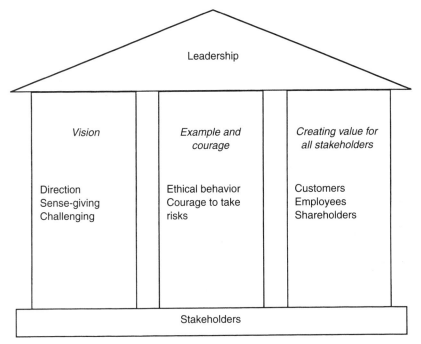

FIGURE 17-1. THE THREE COLUMNS OF LEADERSHIP

LEADERSHIP AS A WAY OF LIFE

"If you serve others, you serve yourself."
Marcus Aurelius

Partnering leadership is a conscious decision to lead a particular type or style of life. This decision is the result of a complex interaction between: (1) a critical reflection on alternative ways of life (e.g., those of a civil servant or of an employee or a professional); (2) an understanding of how a way of life (e.g., as an business leader) fits one's character, and (3) a conviction that corroborates and justifies this way of life.

What is required is a coherent philosophy of life that drives a person's thought and action. The interaction between leadership as a lived example of and a philosophy of life is shown in Figure 17-2.

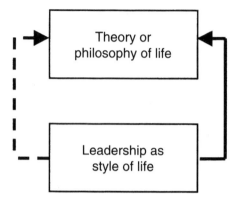

**FIGURE 17-2. LEADERSHIP AS THE RESULT OF CORRESPONDENCE
BETWEEN ONE'S BELIEFS AND ACTIONS**

The conviction built through thinking and reflecting determines
the leader's goals and the meaning he or she attributes to business
life, including day-to-day leadership behavior and style of life. At the
same time, the style of life influences the nature of business thinking
and acting, in other words, her or his conviction. Partnering leadership is nothing else than living according to one's own convictions
and is thus a lived "theory." To lead means to be consistent with one's
self.

THE STOIC THEORY OF LEADERSHIP BEHAVIOR—
CONVICTION-BASED PARTNERING

"The reason shall guide the emotions."
Marcus Aurelius

One of the most influential theories of leadership behavior goes
back to the Roman emperor Marcus Aurelius. He is best known for
his *Meditations* on Stoic philosophy.[6] His personal nobility and dedi-
cation as a statesman are best expressed by his three guiding principles
for the conduct of life (see Figure 17-3):

1. *Control the flow of your thinking,* that is, pay attention to the subjective judgments through which you attribute value to things.

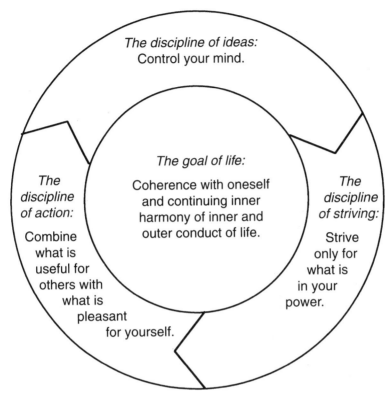

The discipline of ideas:
Control your mind.

The goal of life:

Coherence with oneself and continuing inner harmony of inner and outer conduct of life.

The discipline of action:

Combine what is useful for others with what is pleasant for yourself.

The discipline of striving:

Strive only for what is in your power.

FIGURE 17-3. THE THREE STOIC PRINCIPLES OF PRACTICAL CONDUCT OF LIFE

2. *Strive* only for what is in your power to do and accept that which you cannot control.

3. *Act with justice,* that is, combine what is useful for others with what is pleasant for yourself.

According to Epictetus, it is not the facts themselves that worry us, but the ideas we construct about these facts. As Marcus Aurelius puts it: if you are worried about outer problems, you are depressed not by outer things, but by your judgment about them.[7] This applies to leadership, too. Nothing can disturb a leader if he or she does not want it to do so. Through our value judgment, we influence the value of events; things become what we want them to be. Our representations or ideas have an effect on us, and this only in the case we add a value judgment. The fact, for example, that two of our major competitors are merging is not disturbing; only our judgment, with which we attribute a certain competitive behavior to the new company, can excite us or leave us indifferent. Our value judgments determine our goals and actions. We always have the choice to say to ideas concerning things that are not in our power: What has that to do with me?

The second guiding principle for the conduct of life concerns our aims in life. Stoic philosophy is based on rationality. Marcus Aurelius emphasizes again and again that: The reason shall guide the emotions; the master in one's own house has to be the reason (see Figure 17-4).

If a business leader pays bribes in a developing country, the profit is the *external cause* of his or her action. It cannot, however, be the decisive one, because other companies resist this temptation. The business leader goes to illegal means only if he or she sees positively the idea that the profit is desirable or because it creates jobs or offers other benefits.

The second cause for business action comes from *inner judgment*. The question is whether, in the preceding case, the reason is strong enough to reject the temptation. In real life this depends on many factors. The leader, who on the basis of a core competency, has created a unique position for his or her company and acquired, through work on him or herself, inner strength, safeguards not only the ability

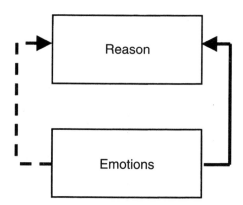

FIGURE 17-4. THE REASON SHALL GUIDE THE EMOTIONS

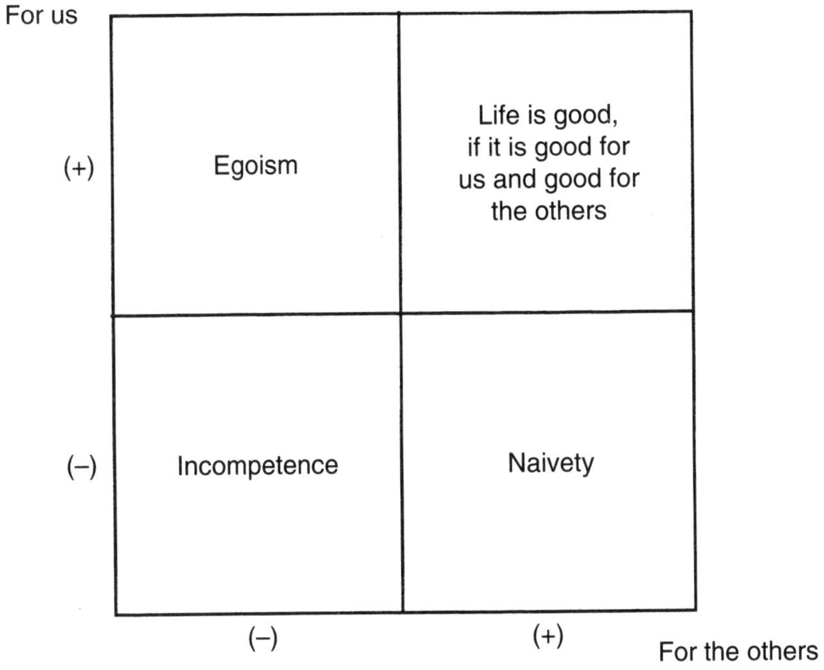

For us

(+)	Egoism	Life is good, if it is good for us and good for the others
(−)	Incompetence	Naivety
	(−)	(+)

For the others

FIGURE 17-5. THE GUIDING PRINCIPLE FOR ACTION

to say, "No," but also the right attitude toward the outside world. We are free, if we carry the true values in ourselves, because this allows us to reject every idea that tries to make us dependent on external factors.

The second guiding principle is best summarized by an American pilgrims' prayer: Lord, give me the strength to change things which are in my power, give me the calmness to accept things which I cannot change, and give me the wisdom to distinguish the one from the other.

The third principle of Stoic conduct of life is shown in Figure 17-5. A leadership life is good if it is good for oneself and good for all key stakeholders of the company.

SUMMARY AND PERSPECTIVES

"You have only one goal: to daily improve yourself."

Seneca

There are significant differences between the American tradition of leadership and the European tradition of partnering leadership. Leadership as partnering is a decision to live a certain way of life. A style of life can be learned by accumulating theoretical propositions and practical experiences. A style of life has to grow daily in work on conscious leadership and work on oneself, which requires time. A philosophy such as Stoicism is a practical one of both reflection and action; it can give leaders the inner strength to master the most difficult situations in life.

The leadership behavior of a CEO or a manager can be recognized not only by the way he or she deals with customers, shareholders, peers, and superiors, but even more in how she or he treats employees and how he or she behaves, for example, toward the porter, the doorman, the waiter in the café, or anyone with a low level of responsibility. True character is best recognized when one observes the behavior of an individual toward the weak and those who are under his or her control. Culture and leadership are demonstrated when leaders communicate with people in subordinate positions twice as modestly and respectfully as with equals, and when they never let less successful people know they are lagging behind. Helmuth Maucher, the former CEO of Nestlé, put it this way: "Co-workers at lower levels of responsibility with a worm's eye view generally have a very clear opinion of their superiors. One notices if his superiors are human and friendly towards modest employees and do not make only great sayings about human relations." Leadership demands the very rare trait of humility.

In conclusion, partnership leadership in the European tradition involves both the heart and reason. It may have its roots in a Stoic philosophy of life, or in one that is Christian: lead others as you would like to be led.

CHAPTER 18

THE GLOBAL LEADER AS PARTNER

MAYA HU-CHAN AND BRIAN O. UNDERHILL

The 1999 study "Global Leadership: The Next Generation" (sponsored by Accenture and Financial Times Knowledge Dialogue) investigated the capabilities required for global leaders of the future. The study's purpose was to identify emerging leadership trends vital in a global work environment. More than 200 high-potential leaders were interviewed, originating from a variety of global for-profit, non-profit, and governmental organizations.

A key finding highlighted the challenges of effectively managing a globally dispersed team. As expected, increasing numbers of our clientele are facing these challenges as their organizations expand to compete in the global marketplace. In 2000, U.S. companies represented 185 of *Fortune* magazine's Global 500 organizations.

Given this reality, how can leaders of globally dispersed teams partner most effectively with their direct reports? In this chapter, we have combined our expertise in the area with interviews of global leaders and their coaches to present solutions for partnering effectively with globally dispersed teams.

Our gratitude goes out to the many individuals providing assistance for this chapter: Jeremy Solomons, Kathleen Curran, Amelie Davis, Bob Silva, Jerry Tucker, Frank Wagner, Mercedes D'Angelo, Mary Hentges, and Marcia Leatham.

THE CHALLENGES OF GLOBALIZATION

Study participants were asked to identify the top three success factors for leaders of the past, present, and future. Although success factors of the past and present tended to focus on the communication and competency of the leader him- or herself (achieve personal excellence, communicate a clear vision, etc.), "understanding the impact of globalization on [their] business" was one of the top three factors identified for future global leaders.

According to the research, the challenge global leaders face is to equip themselves with the skills and resources needed to reach beyond local and national boundaries. Leaders need to know how cultures can work together, gain first-hand experience with other cultures, and even be able to speak foreign languages.

The 1999 study uncovered ten key challenges that global leaders encounter. Even though many of the challenges are common to non-international leaders, they are intensified in a global setting.

1. Change management: work and other paradigms shift constantly without any firm models to base decisions.

2. Role management: leadership and other functions change and combine within organizations at all levels.

3. Career/life management: lifetime employment gives way to life-style employment.

4. Global management: the workforce and clientele become increasingly diverse, with widely differing perspectives, expectations, needs, and contributions.

5. Youth management: workers at all levels, including leaders, become much younger on average and more educated, with a completely different set of values, motivations, and ambitions than their earlier counterparts.

6. Customer management: client relationships become more direct and more exacting.

7. Technology management: the uses and usage of real-time data and communication systems continue to grow exponentially.

8. Knowledge management: privacy, confidentiality, and exclusivity become more and more difficult to maintain in an increasingly open industrial, governmental, and social environment.

9. Time and resource management: technology and competition bring ever shorter deadlines. Everyone needs to do more in less time with fewer resources.

10. Virtual management: physical distances between colleagues and clients spread out around the world so that many people rarely get to meet face-to-face, if at all. Employees and operations will also be much more mobile.

The global leader needs not only to overcome these challenges, but to communicate them to their teams as well. Each member of the team needs to know the environment in which he or she works and understand the role he or she plays in meeting challenges.

THE GLOBAL LEADER AS PARTNER

While partnering effectively as a global leader requires many of the same traits as general leadership, particular competency in certain key traits is essential. The required traits include cultural awareness, leadership approach, distanced empowerment, inspiring the vision, communication, and interpersonal relationships. Aside from effectively demonstrating these key behaviors, the leader must regularly reinforce proper behaviors among team members, thereby creating norms of acceptable "globally smart" behaviors for the team.

Cultural Awareness

The majority of a leader's actions should begin with obtaining the proper cultural awareness of the members of the team and the knowledge about how each of the cultures interacts. First and foremost, a leader needs to know each of his or her people as individuals. While some assumptions can be made based on an individual's cultural background, these should be readily discarded as greater knowledge of the individual as a person is learned.

Failure to do so will likely result in misunderstandings, inefficiencies, or worse. People tend to filter perceptions through their own beliefs and values and make decisions based on those filters. For example, Americans are viewed as relaxed, reckless, emotional, and impulsive by Japanese people, yet they are seen as reserved, cautious, and composed by Brazilians. A global leader needs to consciously analyze and understand these filters to better see things as they are.

Countless books and articles provide guidance to leaders on cultural awareness, many of which are focused on how American managers can better interact with other cultures. While these should be required reading for leaders, it also becomes critical in a team situation for the leader to become familiar with likely dynamics among team members. To that end, we suggest that leaders deliberately study cultural characteristics among each cultural pairing in the team, while better learning about the people as individuals.

Also, assuming that people from nearby regions are similar is a poor substitute for proper research (and can even make matters worse). For example, the culture, people, and business practices between northern and southern Italy or between Japan and Korea are very different. It could be offensive to confuse one with another.

A suggestion is to ensure that meetings rotate locations to allow members to physically visit each other's facilities, thus learning more about them and the cultural context in the process. Key holidays, such as Chinese New Year, Ramadan, etc., should be respected, even celebrated together as a team. A group calendaring function allows members to quickly see each other's schedules, and it can also highlight key holidays.

Key points for the global leader as partner:

➤Study characteristics of all cultures comprising the team.

➤Study likely dynamics arising between each cultural pairing.

➤Spend significant time with each direct report getting to know them as individuals.

➤Question filters and assumptions openly with direct reports and other culturally aware individuals.

Leadership Approach

The eternal dilemma on the most effective leadership approach (authoritative/participatory) becomes more acute in a global setting. In domestic management, properly applying the right style is complicated already. A leader will choose an approach based on knowledge of the subject matter, timeframe required, significance of "buy in," and other factors. However, in a globally dispersed team, leaders face an additional layer of complexity in balancing the proper leadership style necessary for the diverse direct reports of their team.

Simply practicing one style most of the time will likely backfire. For example, an American manager may have learned to regularly practice a collaborative leadership style. This may work for certain direct reports; however, this style is ineffective in many cultures in which the leader is expected to make decisions and "have all the answers," such as Latin America, the Middle East, and Asia. Yet, an authoritarian approach would come across as "dictatorial" in North America and Western Europe.

The global team leader will have to counterbalance the leadership style required in a given situation with the preferred style based on cultural demands. Initially, it is suggested that leaders allow the culturally appropriate style choice to prevail. After time and after trust has been established, the more situationally appropriate style choice should emerge. Of course, the culturally appropriate style will be determined by the makeup of the team and will have to vary by direct report.

Gender issues could also be barriers in global team management. Some cultures are more hierarchical, and traditional businesses are managed and dominated by men. It could be difficult for a male subordinate to report to a female manager. An executive from a multinational pharmaceutical company said, "As a female executive from the U.S., I have to manage several Japanese males in my global team. They sometimes challenge me or even ignore my requests. So I have to change my style and become more authoritative. I also need to build credibility."[1]

Key points for the global leader as partner:

➤A global leader needs to be aware of how his or her style influences team members in various cultures and be prepared to adapt his or her style to one that is effective for each culture.

➤Once the leader has adapted his or her style to suit the culture of the team, the leader should be able to operate appropriately in each situation that arises.

Distanced Empowerment

As the workforce becomes more and more spread out geographically, the global leader needs to be able to do more with less. Leaders cannot be everywhere at the same time; therefore, they must let go of operational details, while still ensuring that the organization is moving in the right direction. Leaders must recruit the best people, motivate them to think and work globally, and empower them to move the organization forward. Leaders must be able to trust people to do their jobs regardless of where they are.

It is also important to understand, however, how empowerment contrasts with the social habits of a particular culture. For example, in China, employee empowerment is a new concept for leadership practice. Several leaders pointed out that it's challenging to delegate and empower Chinese employees to take ownership for their work: "It's my boss's job to make decisions and tell me what to do."[2] Their job is to take orders and get the job done. How do leaders change the mindset and empower people to take responsibility? "Practice what you preach. Hold people accountable for their work. Be patient and consistent with your demands, and then reward people accordingly. It takes time, but it really works!" one leader stated.[3]

Another example from a global leader, "I worked with a Lebanese colleague who was educated in the U.S. and has lived in the U.S. for years, but he never speaks up. He is smart and knowledgeable, but it's very hard to get him to correct or disagree with people. I had to encourage him to speak up by saying 'What you have to say will help us do a better job.' Then he'd share his opinion."[4]

In Japanese culture, during negotiations or communication with third parties, most team members will remain silent, avoid eye contact, and wait for the highest executive to speak for the group. In such an example, global leaders should understand that their direct reports would not usually take a participatory role unless directly instructed to do so.

Key points for the global leader as partner:

➤Empowering team members over a distance will be a necessity.

➤Leaders sometimes have to give permissions and encouragement for people to take initiatives, make decisions, and even speak up.

➤Avoid making assumptions on people based on their behaviors that are different from the Western style.

Inspiring the Vision

Effective leaders are particularly skilled at creating and inspiring people toward a shared vision. In the global environment, leaders must be able to develop a vision that is clearly defined, but broad enough to be suitable across a wide spectrum. It will need to be compelling enough to keep people inspired in between group meetings. "Global leaders must believe in what you do, and love what you do. The passion is contagious. People want to know that you care about the product, about the services, and about the people," emphasized one leader.[5]

Once again, what inspires and motivates people will vary from individual to individual; however, some cultures hold certain elements in high regard. For example, in Western cultures such as the United States and United Kingdom, employees are encouraged to express their opinions, and one's identity is based on individual achievement. It's important for leaders to communicate not only the vision, but also how an individual's work contributes to the overall success of the organization. On the other hand, Chinese and Japanese cultures are more group-oriented. Relationship prevails over task. Loss of "face" for self and group should be avoided at all costs. Identity is based on the social network to which one belongs. Therefore, the company's good reputation and strong team relationships give employees pride and motivation. Using this knowledge, the global leader may be better able to tie the inspiring vision with culturally desirable goals.

The leader must be able to articulate a vision and start an inexorable march toward realizing that vision. As one leader commented, "Keep the energy moving, no matter what."[6] Even still, working toward a vision also demands the ability of a leader to be able to anticipate new strategies and remain nimble enough to go in new directions.

Role modeling will continue to be an integral part of this equation. The leader must "walk the talk" and live by the mission and vision. A key to success for the future leader will be to embody the spirit and intent of the vision so that it becomes instilled in the workforce. Only if the leader can get "buy in" from the workforce can the mission be fully realized.

Key points for the global leader as partner:

➤Ensure the team's vision is clearly defined.

➤Inspiring global team members to the vision requires more creativity than usual; use cultural knowledge of what motivates each individual as a person and motivate to that end.

Communication

Communication is regularly identified as a critical skill for global leaders. Leaders need to communicate frequently and often with all stakeholders. The role of the global leader is to compensate for the complexities of communicating over time zones and language barriers. Given the differences in time zone, distance, cultural barriers, and other factors, leaders have a greater responsibility for communicating effectively over multiple mediums.

The global leader must communicate in ways that are direct, yet diplomatic, without the use of colloquialisms or phrases that convey secondary messages. With the number of language and cultural obstacles that can cause miscommunication between parties, the global leader must maintain a consistent, clear communication style.

For example, in the Latin culture as well as many Asian cultures, there is often an avoidance of saying, "No," primarily as a way of maintaining a positive and cordial relationship. Obviously, when a leader is attempting to reach a conclusion or agreement, this can cause conflicts and misunderstandings. One way around this issue is to summarize conclusions in writing, so that all parties fully understand what has been agreed on.

Like never before, technology allows individuals across the globe to communicate at a moment's notice. It is also true, however, that the more communication relies on technology, the greater the possibility there is for miscommunication. As J.B. Priestly said, "The more we elaborate our means of communication, the less we communicate."[7]

There is an increased need for the global leader to appear "present," even if he or she is not physically present all the time. This requires much travel, heavy use of video and teleconferencing, and rapid response to inquiries through E-mail and other electronic means. Leaders should be perceived as very responsive and ever-present.

Leaders should set the norm of respect for each team member's location. Conference calls should be planned at the most mutually convenient time possible (or rotated). A team leader from a large high-tech company pointed out, "People live in different time zones. Sometimes people would schedule conference calls at the time that's convenient for the U.S. team, but it could be 2 A.M. in another country. Some of our overseas colleagues were too polite to mention it or request a different time."[8]

To be able to listen, understand, and express empathy for other's concerns is critical for global leaders. Conversely, the ability to reach a group with mass appeal through their oratorical abilities is also a needed skill.

Key points for the global leader as partner:

➤A global leader must communicate frequently with each member of her or his team using a variety of mediums.

➤When communicating cross-culturally, leaders must use words that have a clear meaning, practice active listening, and try to explain complex ideas in more than one way.

➤A global leader needs to be aware of nonverbal communication and avoid making assumptions based on his or her own cultural values.

➤When communicating with a multicultural team in English, leaders should slow down, avoid using slang and idioms, and watch for "information overload" among non-native speakers. Give people time to reflect, translate back to their native language, and respond.

Interpersonal Relationships

Global leaders must build an intimate relationship with their team and a deep level of respect, trust, and mutual understanding. A global leader from South America told us, "I always acknowledge success of my global team by E-mail, sharing the good news and congratulating the little people who are often invisible or neglected. I also give people frequent feedback, both positive and negative. It's important to keep building the relationship."[9]

Repeatedly, interviewees commented that the leader should establish a "foundation of trust." This is key in all interpersonal relationships, and ever more so in a relationship of global reach. Building this trust may take more or less time depending on a variety of circumstances, many of them influenced by cultural differences. For example, *Guan-Xi* (the personal and social relationships) is the collective sense that forms the matrix of Chinese behavior by which things are accomplished. Without proper *Guan-Xi,* few things could get done in China. This is the opposite of Western culture, in which task prevails over the relationship, and hiring and promotion decisions are supposed to be based on skills and competence only.

A global leader shared his own experience in building trust with his global team: "A lot of listening and asking questions," he states.[10] Other leaders point out methods to building trust: "Show respect for different opinions, beliefs, and values," "Be supportive, empower people, and allow them to make mistakes," "Walk the talk," and "Demonstrate personal integrity; and avoid political behaviors."[11]

These trust-building measures, however, need to be adapted to the culture of the team. A sympathetic, measured approach is not necessarily the best one. For example, the communication style in the Israeli culture is often very confrontational and emotional. Leaders who do not respond in kind in such an environment risk losing credibility in the eyes of their direct reports. The key to successful interpersonal relationships is to develop an effective relationship within the context of the culture in which the leader works.

Key points for the global leader as partner:

➤Work to build a "foundation of trust" with each team member.

➤Recognize that accomplishing this takes varying methods and length of time given cultural circumstances.

CONCLUSION

Effectively partnering with a globally dispersed team is similar to general leadership; however, the aforementioned behaviors are particularly important. Global leaders need to form alliances between teams and organizations built on trust and focused on the same goals. These leaders need to be able to negotiate, listen, and assess situations continuously. Workforces must become much more collaborative and exist in environments that encourage honest communication and feedback.

In conclusion, the global leaders of tomorrow must not only continuously assess their own communication skills and competence in a given field, but also realize that their future success depends on their ability to understand and communicate in ways that extend beyond convention.

The future leader needs to anticipate how his or her workforce will respond in a given situation and develop a vision in which a diverse workforce can excel. The ability to communicate a clear direction for the organization, so that the workforce can become empowered to move the organization forward, is of paramount concern to global leaders.

CHAPTER 19

LEADERSHIP AND THE RAPIDLY CHANGING GLOBAL ENVIRONMENT

FARIBORZ GHADAR

Watching the Indy 500 pit crews, one can see the ultimate expression of and exhilaration in teamwork. As the racecars pull into the pit, the teams go to work with efficiency and speed worthy of note even in business history. The pit crewmembers don't need to stop to ask for directions or permission to do their jobs. They already have a clearly defined vision of their team's goals, and they have been given the power to act immediately on the needs of the driver and car. Experience, practice, and a clear understanding of their goal and of how their tasks fit into the whole scheme makes the pit team unbelievably efficient. Who is the leader of this team? There must be one. What is his or her role?

Now imagine a much greater degree of uncertainty. Imagine for a moment that the pit crew, after many months of practice on a specific racing car, is told that the race has changed, and it is not known what model car will come into the pit next. In fact, not only is the model unknown, but also the engine may not even be a combustion engine at all. What will happen to this finely tuned team? How does one help develop a winning NASCAR crew when one may not know what type of "racecar" will pull into the pit next? How would you as a leader respond to this challenge? This scenario is similar to what leaders face in today's rapidly changing and dynamic business environment.

From the perspective of the business leader, the legacy of the twentieth century is one of dramatically accelerated product lifecycles and rapidly changing markets. Product lifecycles have shrunk from the leisurely pace of 15 to 20 years about 50 years ago to a mere 2 to 3 years today. At the same time, product development costs have increased 10-fold. It is increasingly more difficult to generate the required return on investment to develop new products, processes, and services. Managers implemented reengineering and downsizing in the 1980s with the hope of making their organizations leaner and more efficient, only to be faced with the globalization and the accelerated pace of business that occurred in the 1990s.[1]

"We realized that we needed to take our products global very quickly, gain market share, and hopefully make our product or service the standard of the industry in order to recoup the rising cost of product development in shorter and shorter life cycles."

This is a statement heard from many a CEO in the past decade. Leaders today realize that to achieve the effectiveness they are seeking, their organization and team must have the ability to respond quickly to changing market needs. They need the ability to act quickly and intelligently—right across the organization. How does one develop a winning NASCAR-type team in this rapidly changing environment?

Astute leaders have realized that accomplishing this requires three interconnected actions. First, decision-makers at all levels of the firm need to share accurate and complete information about the business—they need to be *informed.* Second, they need to develop a collective understanding of the critical factors of business success—they need to be *involved.* Third, they must coordinate and align decision-making to empower their team to do wonderfully effective things for the organization—they need to be *in touch.*

It's not too much to say that the forward-looking, winning company has become a true "learning corporation," which not only shares and disseminates information throughout all levels within the firm, but also has an empowered team that effectively implements action based on its distilled responses.

Again, let's return to our new version of a NASCAR race. An unknown car is ready to pull over. Once that car begins to slow down, the pit crew must anticipate the new car and driver's needs, and all hands, including the crew chief, pitch in to get the job done—a job somewhat different from what they have been used to in the past. From the driver's point of view, it doesn't matter who among the crew has been designated as crew chief, as long as the job is done right.

The pit crew doesn't have time to stop and ask for directions or permission to do their jobs. In this dynamic environment, they must already have a clearly defined image of their team's goals, and they must be empowered to act immediately on the needs of the driver and car. Yet, they must be interconnected in order to share all their information and knowledge, and to help others on their team with their expertise when it is required.

Shifting gears in today's business setting, ensuring that everyone within the organization can act quickly and intelligently, is only the starting point for meeting the challenge of developing new products, producing and distributing them efficiently, and then successfully marketing them on a global scale. Leaders in industries ranging from automotive to financial services are aligning their organizations with other firms to acquire market presence and investment resources. Often, leaders realize that outsourcing business processes and activities that are core elements in their value proposition is not only desirable, but also essential to achieve success for their companies.

This new type of business paradigm requires sharing of timely information and implementing responses not just within the firm itself, but also among its key strategic alliances. Today's successful leader must ensure that his or her team members have bought into a common vision and direction; that they are armed with the information, skills, and tools necessary for appropriate analysis; and that they are encouraged and empowered to respond quickly to the customer.

Our racecar has an oil company's logo prominently displayed on the driver's door. The lubricant specialist at that company knows the engine's precise specifications, so that he or she can recommend the best formula to keep that expensive and intricate motor roaring. If changes to the engine are anticipated, the lubricant specialist is brought onboard immediately. He or she is an integral part of the pit crew as well as an employee of a strategic ally—the oil company.

To many leaders, it probably seems that the rules that governed the race changed just as they were beginning to master them. Throughout their careers, they were led to believe that vision and strategy development were the main responsibilities of the organization's leader. They accepted the dictum that size (often achieved through mergers and acquisitions) was the proven way to achieve economies of scale, and the clear path to respond to the increased usage of technology and the result of shorter product life cycles. These managers believed they had the expertise to assess the factors that drive strategy. They had the scars from their failed attempts. They understood the fundamentals and models. They had the discipline to analyze strategies and make data-driven choices. To their surprise, in the new business environment these qualities no longer assured success.

Whereas strategic plans were once considered the enduring road signs by which corporations determined annual operating plans and budgets, the new business climate requires that strategies be considerably more fluid, innovative, and broader in perspective. Furthermore, plans must be developed with shorter time horizons in step with the dramatically shortened product lifecycles. What was once long term and relatively static is now continuously changing. The new digital economy has further accelerated this effect, resulting in a fundamental shift in the way business strategies are developed, communicated, and executed by the organization. Business is no longer an orderly promenade through the park. It is an expensive, action-packed, thrill-a-minute race. As a result, the role of today's leader in this new environment is more challenging, but it is also more rewarding.

The once well established product positioning dictum argued that if a firm had a mix of products at different international lifecycle stages, it almost certainly had a single dominant product set resulting in a clear overall global competitive position. A firm positioning itself for its core products, whether new, innovative products; customer-focused goods and services; or mature, price-competitive commodities, had little flexibility in offering anything different.

To respond to this strategic dilemma, managers often created separate business units to market their varied products and services. To correct for the likelihood that multiple units would call on the same customers, corporations appointed national and global account managers. Their task was to coordinate the activities relating to major national and global customers. A complex set of solid and dotted reporting lines attempted to coordinate the activities of functional, regional, business unit, and account managers.[2] However, these organizational complexities did not reduce the need for the frontline manager to quickly respond to changing market needs. Often the successful manager acted first and asked for forgiveness later in the event that another manager's ego was bruised.

Currently, the leader's ability to adopt new approaches is made more difficult because so many of the previously deeply held concepts, such as the importance of being number one or two in market share, conflict with the new global business environment. Today's managers are victims of their "learning horizons." They simply never experienced anything like the new digital business model while they were advancing through the ranks. It must be a similar scenario for NASCAR crews when rapidly changing technology comes into use at the racetrack. Because of the extreme conditions created under the hood of a racecar, NASCAR mechanics use extra components that wouldn't be found under the hood of Mom's Pontiac.[3]

While it may be clear that a different approach is needed, it is not necessarily clear what that approach should actually be. Of course each firm's circumstances are sufficiently different that generalized prescriptions are unlikely to apply, but the successful leader of the future needs to ask, "How am I going to develop my own NASCAR pit crew?"

Strategic analysis can no longer be based on static business conditions or previously proven business models. Now technology changes rapidly, new competitors emerge through various capabilities, and customer demands constantly escalate. As Peter Drucker has said, the challenge is that "reality has changed but the theory of the business has not."[4] Leaders who were taught to develop strategies based on long-term assumptions about their business must realize that the long term is much less meaningful in the new environment. Now, disruptive technology and new business models dictate the likely outcome. The test to employ is this: Any strategy that isn't incorporating unanticipated change and providing for a contingency is incomplete.

Just as in the business environment, it would also appear that stock-car racing has its own set of necessary high-risk strategies and corresponding contingency plans. Because the function of the ignition system is paramount to good stock car performance, no driver can afford to have it fail. As a result, NASCAR racecars have two ignition systems with two switches on the dashboard. The backup system can be utilized in the event of mid-race ignition failure. The boxes of the systems are set up on two different timing degrees. With one set higher, the engine runs leaner, but this also creates a bigger threat of engine failure. This chance has been taken into consideration in the successful design of the racecar.

Successful strategies have always put the customer at the heart of all decisions. In the 1980s and 1990s, however, marketplace power shifted from manufacturers to distributors. Wal-Mart was an excellent example of a distributor who controlled the customer. Now, technology is bringing about a further shift of marketplace power to the ultimate buyer.

Opportunities to exploit these new developments abound. In today's environment, we need to employ better customer buying data, microsegmentation, cross-marketing, as well as improved customer relationship management for improved service and cross-selling. The manager must use these tools to respond to fleeting customer desires. At Wal-Mart, store managers today are empowered to respond to numerous individual customer demands—from matching competitors' coupons to responding to individualized complaints—but with detailed input and data from the supercomputers that analyze customer trends and histories. The key, however, is to ensure that the new technology improves the *solution* and not just the products that are offered.

New approaches are particularly evident in the financial services industry in which reduced regulation has brought about many changes. Fidelity Investment Management, known for its creative use of technology with the world's largest family of mutual funds, is seizing this opportunity. Its stated strategy is to provide a full range of services that enables consumers to plan and purchase individualized or mass-customized types of financial services. To achieve this, Fidelity has branched into selling insurance products, including life, auto, and homeowners.

This is not simply a technology matter though, and a far more sophisticated view has emerged. The new business environment puts even greater emphasis on the quality of human capabilities, if for no other reason than to keep up with the rapid pace of change and technology design. Frontline employees are both the pit crew and the crew chiefs in the new approach to strategy. They need to be familiar with and committed to the big picture and intimately knowledgeable of their specific field of expertise.

This new view creates many challenges. It has never been easy to communicate senior management's goals down to the rank-and-file, and in rapidly changing environments, unless there was a burning necessity, enterprises did not change their ways.

The new business environment has gone from "build and sell" to "sense and respond." To keep up with this change, you have to make more decisions, and faster, but now every decision is interconnected with the next one.[5] What would happen if a member of the NASCAR pit crew calibrated the air pressure in the racecar's tires according to the ambient temperature of the track at the beginning of the race and failed to account for the decreased need for air pressure? How would this then affect the car's fuel consumption and how soon would the car have to stop again in the pit to refuel? How would this affect the life of the tires?

Intel's chairman and former CEO, Andy Grove, blames blind belief in existing strategies for Intel's slow exit from the memory chip business in favor of microprocessors. He credits frontline employees for the better approach:

"Our most significant strategic decision was made not in response to some clear-sighted corporate vision but by the marketing and investment decisions of frontline managers who really knew what was going on."[6]

He calls this formulating strategy "with your fingertips." Although companies have tried everything from stock options to casual dress codes to ensure the loyalty and commitment of employees, the real test is whether the rank-and-file feel that they are a part of the company's vision. In other words, are the leaders of the firm also their partners?

Leaders must make their own test of involvement. Ask employees to answer the following five critical questions:

1. What are we trying to accomplish? What's our goal, our "strategic intent," and what will our success look like?

2. What am I supposed to do to contribute to this goal?

3. What help and support will I receive?

4. What are the relevant metrics and how will I be evaluated?

5. In what manner will I be acknowledged and rewarded?

Our research has identified certain principles that guide leaders to address the challenges they face in this dynamic environment: principles refined by leaders who have found ways to align their team to execute successfully within and across functions throughout their organization and across their strategic alliances; leaders who, as a result, have forged ahead of the competition, and have won many a race for their organization.

Frontline teams, those down in the "pit," need to have a clear understanding of the leader's vision and strategic intent. It must also be *their* vision; they must believe in that vision. That vision must be based on identified strengths (core competencies) that are present or will be developed. Teams must have a clear understanding of the values of the leader and of the organization: "What do we stand for?" This in a sense is the brand of the leader. To achieve this requires a leader who inspires his or her team members with an exciting vision, a vision to which they can aspire—a leader who provides them with the tools to accomplish their tasks, supports and rewards them, and is the keeper of their organization's value system.

Today's leader identifies the path and leads the charge, but is also beside us when we need help and assistance and behind us when we need support. In such a rapidly changing environment, even when we follow the vision, base our actions on our core competencies, and act according to our values, we will still occasionally fail. In these instances, the role of the leader is to support and encourage the team to learn from this experience and move forward. In short, we want a leader who is a true partner.

If he or she is *informed, involved,* and *in touch,* then the new leader is truly a partner along the path to success. "Gentlemen, start your engines . . ."

CHAPTER 20

DILEMMAS OF MULTICULTURAL LEADERS

The Need for Transcultural Competence

FONS TROMPENAARS AND PETER WOOLLIAMS

Our recent research reveals that the essential distinguishing characteristic of leaders in a multicultural environment is their propensity to reconcile seemingly opposing values. In contrast, managers (rather than leaders) seem to have solvable problems. Leaders frequently suffered from insomnia because they had not been able to resolve a dilemma they faced. It is difficult "not to have made it," but even more difficult not knowing "what to make." The successful integration of conflicting values, however, frequently leads to the continous creation of one or more new dilemmas.

What are these dilemmas that international leaders face? Of course, leaders should inspire, as well as listen. They need to follow the orders of headquarters to fulfill the global strategy and to succeed at the local level by adapting to regional circumstances. They have to decide when to act alone, but also when and where to delegate. Leaders need to attend to day-to-day tasks and at the same time be passionate about the mission of the organization as a whole. They need to simultaneously use their own analytical power while enabling the contribution of others. Leaders need to develop an excellent strategy while at the same time understanding why a strategy missed its goal.

We thus begin to understand why there are numerous definitions of good leadership. According to Warren Bennis, it is all about vision, mission, and transparency. The French management literature indicates

[207]

that great leaders are functions of their educational background. Compare this with the Asian literature, which suggests that you should be male, senior, and from the University of Tokyo.

With the globalization of organizations, we find that leaders have to face multicultural teams. What style of leadership is effective in those diverse circumstances? We believe that it requires a set of value-free competencies that we identify as *transcultural competence*. We interviewed 21 leaders to provide the underlying schema for our new book, *21 Leaders for the 21st Century*.[1] From this evidence, we performed an in-depth and critical inductive analysis. Thereby, we identified that the significant and common factor among successful leaders today is their competence to reconcile seemingly opposing values of dilemmas that they face on a continuing basis, which are described in the following sections.

THE DILEMMA BETWEEN STANDARD AND ADAPTATION

It is striking how often we found this in many forms. Should we globalize or localize our approach? Is it better for our organization to mass produce or to focus on specialized products? Good leaders, in their transnational organizations, are effective in finding resolutions whereby locally learned best practices are globalized.

Thus, activities might be decentralized, but the information about the activities is centralized. *Mass-customization* has become the credo of the reconciliation between standardized and universal products and customized and particular adaptations.

McDonald's

Jack Greenberg, McDonald's CEO, was able to transform local learning into global products. His company (especially with regard to its U.S. performance) has swiftly turned around during the last three years after a doubtful start in the early 1990s.

What values has Greenberg reconciled? Is it even possible in a company that is known (like Coca-Cola) to stand for an uncompromising approach such as "Be as American as you can be"? McDonald's universalism is reflected in several areas of the business—the promotion of global brands, common systems, and human resources principles around the world.

Universalism fuels the search for the one best way of doing things and releases the synergy of a global corporation. This is an important attribute because without this synergy, it is easy to lose the benefits of operating globally.

At the same time, if not balanced with a healthy dose of particularism, universalism can lead to extremes with "one best way" being pursued at the cost of flexibility in response to the particular circumstances and needs of the local situation. This might explain McDonald's difficulties in the late 1990s. There is also a "particular" relationship at the heart of the company, however, because McDonald's, at its most senior levels, is run by the "family." This interesting bicultural setup has allowed McDonald's to create freedom within a framework of strong values. It enables McDonald's to reconcile the dilemma of how to exploit the common franchise frameworks of the brands (universalize) and how much to leave to local market adaptation (particularize). In Indonesia, The Netherlands, and South Korea, McDonald's offers Big Macs and Happy Meals; in Austria its franchises also contain "McCafes," which offer coffee blends for local tastes. In addition to French fries, it also offers rice in Indonesia. In Amsterdam, McDonald's offers the McKroket, a local Dutch snack. In Seoul, the burger chain sells roast pork on a bun with a garlicky soy sauce. Yet, McDonald's is going beyond the theme that "all business is local." Greenberg and other executives say that they are responding to concerns of too much localization. McDonald's is in tune with its decentralized foreign operations, where it is actively experimenting. From there it takes the best local practices and tries to use them in other areas of the world. It globalizes best local practices. The result is a transnational organization in which exceptions and rules modify the existing principles.

INDIVIDUAL CREATIVITY AND TEAM SPIRIT

International leaders frequently face the integration of team spirit in which cooperation dominates over individual creativity and empowerment. The effective leader knows how to mold an effective team

comprised of creative individuals. In turn, the team is made accountable to support the creativity of individuals as they strive to contribute
their best. This has been described as *coopetition*.

Lego

At Lego, there is no problem in finding enough individuals to generate ideas. The challenge lies with the "business system" or community,
which has to translate those ideas into the reality of viable products
and services. It was not unusual for the community or system to im-
pede the realization of good ideas, especially when ideas came from
senior people, whereas juniors were expected to be concerned solely
with implementation.

Christian Majgard, marketing member of the management team
of Lego, has made a vital intervention. While ideas originate with individuals, it is insufficient to simply pass these down for subordinates
to implement. The latter are inhibited in their criticism and it required
the hiring of consultants to legitimize skepticism. Instead, the origi-
nator must work with critics, implementers, and builders of working
prototypes to help debug his or her idea where necessary.

Majgard has seen that it is ineffective to give higher status to the
idea than to its implementers, otherwise defective ideas will persist to
disappoint their backers. Realization is at least as important as ideal-
ization and the two must be reconciled. You accept testing ideas to
destruction.

We can reconcile this dilemma concerning individual versus community using Majgard's insight, that the membership of teams must
be diverse, consisting of people whose values and endowments are
opposite, yet these teams must achieve a unity of purpose and shared
solutions. Once again we have two polarized extremes in which "prima
donnas" are created and conversely in which solid, viable agreements are the result. According to Majgard, this offers the potential
of creating a solution that has benefited from diverse viewpoints and
novel inputs and quality, which has already cleared the hurdles of
skepticism.

The problem with highly diverse competing individuals is that they
may behave like so many prima donnas, singing their own praises. The

problem with unity and team spirit above all is that diverse and novel inputs is squeezed out. Majgard's reconciliation is to make the super-ordinate goal so exciting and the process of creating new shared reali-ties so passionate and enjoyable that diverse members overcome their differences to realize a unity-of-diversities, which makes the solution far more valuable.

PASSION AND CONTROL

Is a good leader a passionate person or rather a person who controls his or her emotions? We recognize two extreme types. Passionate lead-ers without reason are known as neurotics. Overly controlled leaders without emotions are known as robots or control freaks. Both types are unsuccessful in a multicultural environment. Richard Branson is successful because he continuously checks his passion with reason. If we consider the less emotive Jack Welch, we observe a leader who gives meaning to his control by showing his passion at specific well chosen moments.

Club Med

Club Med's prodigious growth had overstrained its traditional man-agement structure. It had become intoxicated by its self-celebrations week after week, and it was not keeping track of costs or logistics. The company's downward spiral had begun and subsequent chronic under-investment made it worse. The company was not competent in the more neutral, hard side of the business (travel, finance, logistics, etc.). Resorts were not profit centers and several had lost money without anyone realizing this. Many opened too early in the season or not early enough. Moreover, hospitality had simply been increased with no awareness of diminishing returns. The food and wine expenditure had escalated.

When it is about *esprit,* ambience, and all the affective and diffuse aspects of life, leave it to Club Med. Yet, this was also their under-sponsored strength. Philippe Bourguignon was very aware that he had to reconcile these neutral and affective necessities. He helped Club Med to refine the art of placing immaterial experiences above the bits and pieces of the material world, while ensuring that the bits and pieces paid off. The wholeness of experience with its *esprit* is vital. However, taken too far (as in the early 1990s), the personalized and unique vacation was driven to the point of destruction. It had become a vendor of incomparable experiences, but it couldn't survive in a cost-conscious world. But, the opposite, more neutral approach, in which elements are standardized into a reliable, high-volume, and therefore affordable holiday, would risk abandoning Club Med's founding values.

With ever-advancing living standards, the separate elements of luxury and good living are accessible to more and more people. What is often missing, and more elusive, is the integration of these elements into a diffuse and affective sense of satisfaction, a *savoir vivre*. Bourguignon no longer manages villages, but a shared spirit, a seamless scenario of satisfactions, an ambience or atmosphere, like Planet Hollywood or Hard Rock Cafe, augmented by food and wine.

ANALYSIS OR SYNTHESIS: WHOSE BUSINESS ARE WE IN?

Is the leader of the twenty-first century a cool, analytical brain, able to chop the larger whole into piecemeal chunks and strive monolithically for specific shareholder value, or a person who puts everything into a larger context and prioritizes the diffuse stakeholder value? At Shell, van Lennep's concept of Helicopter Quality was introduced to focus on an important quality of the modern leader: the competence to transcend the problem by elevating to higher levels of abstraction, while at the same time, the ability and drive to zoom into certain aspects of the system of problems. Jan Carlzon of SAS called this integration of more specific moments with the ability to go deeper when one approaches a client, moments of truth. Here, also, we find an important new quality of the international leader: the (competence) ability to select where to go deep.

Dell

Pure analysis leads to paralysis and an overdone synthesis leads to aimless holism and protest against action. Michael Dell has had to grasp the dilemma of selling to a broad array or to a special group with whom deep relationships were developed. His newly developed Direct Selling Model has the advantage of being simultaneously very broad and at the same time deep, personal, and customized.

Dell broke with the conventional wisdom that you either aim for many customers or you aim for just a few clients, with complex problems and specialized needs, who need very complex, high-end service. The first strategy is cheap, but rather superficial. The second strategy is intimate and personal, but it is typically niche-oriented and attracts premium prices.

The risk is that if you go for the first strategy, distribution channels might clog very quickly, and there is no differentiation between you and competitors. This strategy runs the risk of swamping the intermediaries. On the other hand, Dell could have focused on creating a very narrow, but deep, strategy with the risk of creating severely limited opportunities in small niche markets.

The reconciliation he created was as powerful as it was simple. By direct sales via face-to-face interaction, telephone, and the Internet, he reconciled breadth with depth and complexity. The genius of direct selling via the Internet is that you reach an ever-increasing spectrum of customers and can use the Net to give personalized, detailed, information-rich services to those customers via premium pages for each.

BEING AND DOING

Getting things done is important for manager performance, but doesn't doing mundane things need to be in balance with our private lives? As a leader, you also need to be able to be yourself. We conclude from our research, however, that our leaders are not different from what they do. They seem to be one with what they do. One of the most important sources of stress is when being and doing are not integrated. An overdeveloped achievement orientation that isn't in harmony with a leader's self and/or lifestyle will lead to ineffective behaviors.

In researching for our book, *Building Cross-Cultural Competence,* we found that successful leaders do things in harmony with whom they feel they are.[2] They reconcile private and work life. This is not easy, but "the servant leader" doesn't use his or her ascribed status only to help people achieve, he or she also uses it to balance family life and business.

SEQUENTIAL OR SYNCHRONIC?

Effective leaders can plan sequentially, but they also have a strongly developed competence to stimulate parallel processes. We all recognize just-in-time management as the method in which processes are synchronized to speed up the sequence. Furthermore, an effective international leader is able to integrate short- and long-term and past, present, and future.

Heineken

The Heineken tradition is significant but at the same time the seeds for decline are present. For more than 100 years, Heineken has appealed to people's taste. Historically, the company's reputation has been maintained at great cost. Recently, however, many special beers have entered the market, jeopardizing the big established names in the trade.

Karel Vuursteen's approach to innovation was therefore cautious. He had to maintain the consistency of Heineken's attraction. He had to change to remain consistent. One way of innovating, in a manner that's not dangerous, is to clear a space for a totally new approach, which is separate from existing success and will not endanger it.

Vuursteen's dilemma is the tension between Heineken's tradition and stability and the elusive nature of its success. He very cleverly embarked on two forms of innovation: *process innovation,* which searches for better and newer means of creating the same result and reserving a safe area for creation; and *product innovation,* which allows new drink products to be invented from scratch, without involving Heineken's premium product in these experiments.

INNER-DIRECTED PUSH OR OUTER-DIRECTED PULL

The final core quality of today's effective leaders is the competence to integrate the feedback from the market and the technology developed in the organization. Again, it is not a competition between technology push or market pull. The modern leader knows that a push of technology will eventually lead to the ultimate niche market—that part of the market without customers. Conversely, a monolithic focus on the market will leave the leader at the mercy of its clients.

Our thinking is that values are not "added" by leaders, since only simple values "add up." Leaders combine values (i.e., a fast and a safe car, good food, yet easy to prepare). Nobody claims that combining values is easy, but it is possible. A computer that is able to make complex calculations can also be customer friendly. It is the more extended systems of values that will be the context in which international leadership will prove its excellence.

Bombardier

Laurent Beaudoin, president of Bombardier (an international transportation company headquartered in Canada), skillfully reconciled his dilemma in this area of inner and outer direction. We might even argue that the reconciliation of this dilemma accounted for much of the success of Bombardier. An acquisition strategy is an advanced form of inner direction with powerful motives, steered from within. Beaudoin has created a company that looked for the rare and valuable. Bombardier was always looking to find this ability coupled with its opposite, the readiness to understand, acknowledge, and respond to the value-creating capacity of an outside system.

Laurent Beaudoin used humility, listening, and patience to learn about the companies Bombardier acquired. He reconciled the inner-directed strategy of bold, new acquisitions with the outer-directed policy of respecting the integrity of acquired companies. He had to let people from the companies he acquired share their dreams, so he could understand what was possible and of how much they were capable. The resolution of these contrasting abilities, hitting the acquisition trail and studying respectfully what you acquire, is the way of the acquiring scholar.

CAN OUR MODEL OF CROSS-CULTURAL COMPETENCE BE DEVELOPED OR IS IT INNATE?

From our extensive reflective critique of our evidence, we conclude that this newly identified competence of reconciling dilemmas is not simply just learned or innate. It needs a systemic approach. The whole organization needs to provide a framework that supports, stimulates, and facilitates people to reconcile.

We have seen individuals with high potential, yet not able to progress further than a lose–lose compromise, because their work environment did not appreciate creative solutions. Conversely, we have found less effective individuals who achieved significant reconciliation by their stimulating and supportive environment.

How do we create such an environment? It begins with leaders who practice what they preach, and it is of utmost importance that rewards be created to motivate individuals and teams to do so. Our message is to link reconciliation to business issues and business results and make it into a continuous process, so that it becomes a way of living rather than a conceptual exercise.

CHAPTER 21

THE LEADER AS PARTNER:
THE REALITY OF POLITICAL POWER

THE RT. HON. KIM CAMPBELL

To speak of "the leader as partner" requires us to understand what leadership is. A leader is able to mobilize people toward a desired end. The means of doing this are many and are determined not only by the particular qualities of the leader, but also by the circumstances in which he or she is attempting to achieve a goal. Absolute power of the "your-wish-is-my-command" type is very rare. Dictators have to be on guard against coups d'etat; CEOs can be fired by their boards of directors; and political leaders need to accommodate many constituencies. Unlike a parliamentary prime minister, the president of the United States cannot lose office if Congress fails to approve his initiatives, but his power to achieve his aims is largely in the hands of the lawmakers in the House of Representatives and the Senate.

The experiences that taught me most about leading through partnership occurred during my career in the federal government of Canada, and in particular, during the three years I spent as minister of justice and attorney general. In the parliamentary system of government, the cabinet secretaries—called ministers—are chosen from among the members of Parliament (MPs) of the majority party by their leader, who is the prime minister. In January 1989, just two months after being elected to Parliament, I was appointed to the cabinet as the minister of state for Indian Affairs and Northern Development. In

[217]

February of 1990, I became the first woman to be named minister of justice.

Cabinet ministers in a parliamentary system of government not only run their departments as members of the executive, but also lead the legislative agendas in their portfolio areas. Canadian criminal law is a federal jurisdiction, and so the minister of justice is responsible for amending the criminal law for the whole country. I soon learned why this role makes a national figure of the minister of justice and also can put her at loggerheads with her parliamentary colleagues.

In December, 1989, just two-and-a-half months before I took over the justice portfolio, a man named Marc Lepine entered the Ecole Polytechnique in Montreal with a Ruger semiautomatic firearm with two 30-shot magazines and killed 14 young female engineering students. As he was carrying out his carnage, he shouted, "You're all feminists." Finally, he took his own life. Canada has regulated firearms since the nineteenth century and our homicide rate is very low, just one tenth of that in the United States, so the entire country was in shock. Only a short time before this event, my predecessor in the justice portfolio had begun reviewing our gun control legislation, which had last been amended in the 1970s. The events at Ecole Polytechnique put the adequacy of our firearms laws on the front burner. Moreover, the misogynist intent of those killings seemed to link the firearms policy to the question of violence against women, which was also a significant justice policy concern at the time.

In the 1970s, a memorandum written for the Justice Minister had claimed that gun control was the most divisive criminal law issue in the country, even more divisive than abortion. Although there are no claims for a constitutional right to bear arms in Canada and we have regulated firearms for most of our history, the divisions are not unlike those found in the United States. In particular, there is an urban–rural split: rural people see hunting and the use of firearms to deal with pests on farms and ranches as an integral part of life. They often regard gun control initiatives as efforts to solve the urban crime problem on the backs of law-abiding country folk. There are those who have no experience with firearms, largely urban-dwellers, who regard any gun owner as a latent homicidal maniac. Then there are those in the middle who think there are legitimate reasons for people to have firearms, who think that some people should not own any guns and some kinds of guns should not be owned by anyone.

In a parliamentary system, the instrument of rule is the *caucus*, the elected members, of the majority party, and the solidarity of this caucus is key. As long as this group of legislators remains united, their party will form the government. That is, their leader will be prime minister, they will be eligible to be members of cabinet, and they will be able to implement their party's platform. I would like to be able to claim that my appointment to cabinet was solely a matter of merit. However, that is not entirely the case. In the 1988 election, two of the cabinet ministers from my province, British Columbia, were not returned to the House of Commons (our House of Representatives). One did not run again and the other was defeated. These two vacancies significantly enhanced my chances of being appointed. Had I been from the neighboring province of Alberta, I would have been out of luck because the three ministers from that province were all reelected and were sufficiently senior that the prime minister would not think of replacing them. For the young, talented Alberta members of Parliament, this meant that they would not have an opportunity to serve in cabinet. So, it behooved me, as it behooves any cabinet minister, to remember that there were many of my colleagues on the backbenches who regarded themselves as just as able as I was and who were eager to take my place if I fell on my face. One of the ways of accomplishing that feat would be to create a division in the caucus that threatened its solidarity.

Gun control is not a partisan issue in Canada. All major parties have their advocates and opponents. It was this reality that I faced when I began my meetings with caucus colleagues to find a legislative formula that would respond to the weaknesses in our gun control laws. I knew where I wanted to go, but I also understood that I would cause a riot if I just barged ahead. The challenge was complicated by the fact that I was the first woman, and an urban woman at that, to lead a legislative initiative on this subject, and so I was deeply suspect in the eyes of those who opposed any firearms initiative. I began my presentation to the caucus by saying, "I don't get to be minister of justice unless you get elected. I am not here to get you defeated in the next election." That recognition that we were all part of the same team was the important basis on which our discussions progressed. At all times, even when the disagreements were sharp, I kept that basic premise. When I had a formula that I believed was sound and that would pass in the House, I continued to work with those of my partisan colleagues who felt they simply could not support the bill. I had enough votes to pass the bill, why should I insist that they vote for it when their constituents were opposed? We negotiated the dissent. Would a colleague vote no, abstain, or be absent from the vote? My bill passed by a healthy majority, and I remained on good terms with my own party members who voted against it.

WHY IT WORKS

How did leading through partnership work in this instance? First of all, I had to make a realistic assessment of my own power in the situation. Just as colleagues in a corporation can sabotage a leader, my own colleagues could have made life difficult for me if they had, for example, gone to the prime minister and threatened to leave the caucus or to withhold support from an important initiative. By acknowledging upfront that they mattered and that I had no desire to get my way "no matter what," I established a basis for negotiation. The detailed consultation on the bill not only enabled me to respond to some of my colleagues' concerns, but it also resulted in a better product. Those of my colleagues who opposed the bill understood the political pressures in favor of the legislation and that they would not win this particular battle. They fought hard for their positions and I for mine, but never as enemies, always as partners.

This process had an interesting aftermath. In 1993, when I became a candidate for the leadership of my party, many of these same caucus colleagues who had opposed this and other of my legislative initiatives supported my candidacy. Why? Because, as they told the press, I was "tough," and as they told me, they had confidence that I would continue to treat them with respect, even when I didn't agree with them. Clearly, leading as a partner did not make me less of a leader in their eyes.

Sometimes "leading as partner" is a way of building relationships for the long term. That was my experience when I presented legislation on sexual assault. The Supreme Court of Canada had struck down the "rapeshield" provisions of the criminal code, which protected the complainant in a sexual assault case from having to testify about prior sexual conduct. Although the judges supported the philosophy of the provision, they felt it was too broadly drafted and could deny a defendant a full and fair defense. Because this provision was essential to give sexual assault victims the confidence that they could press charges without themselves being put on trial, I decided that we should relegislate, bearing in mind the court's concerns, as soon as possible.

Because the rapeshield case had been making its way through the courts for some time, my lawyers in the Department of Justice had already been looking at how the law could be recrafted. When the decision came to strike down the old provision, we were ready with some quite imaginative proposals. To my astonishment, women's groups declared themselves opposed to my legislating so quickly. I was perplexed. Only after a meeting where I could reveal to them the direction I wished to go did I understand. They had assumed that I would just do the minimum, when in their view the law on sexual assault needed a more thorough revision. They assumed that if it didn't happen during this legislative process, it would not be dealt with again for a long time. When they saw what we had in mind, these representatives of various groups concerned with women and the law were astonished. We were much farther ahead than they could have imagined. It would have been tempting to continue on our own path, after all, we were quite proud of what we had produced "in house." However, we proceeded to engage in a very detailed consultation process, which, like that of the gun control legislation, gave us some good ideas to improve the legislation. Equally important, however, we gave a variety of concerned groups the opportunity to participate in crafting the law.

When the law was ultimately passed, these groups that had been so skeptical at the start were vocally supportive. I believe that had they not been invited to participate in the process, they would have been highly critical, notwithstanding the content of the bill. When people devote themselves to advocacy of a cause, their exclusion from an opportunity to develop policy or legislation on that subject seems like a slap in the face. Here, the partnership was not to get the bill passed, but to enable it to take effect with the maximum amount of public support. Although some of the groups, accustomed to pushing against a closed door, were not immediately sure how to respond when the door was opened, the relationships of trust created between these advocacy groups and the Department of Justice were genuine. Our rapeshield bill was numbered Bill C-43 that year. Groups wishing to participate in the development of legal policy still call for a "C-43 consultation," because it was a process that made them feel like partners in developing Canada's criminal law.

To some, the notion of "leader as partner" may seem like a contradiction in terms. Leaders are "in the vanguard," "out in front," "ahead of the game," "on the cutting-edge." In their comic opera *The Gondoliers,* Gilbert and Sullivan make this point when they write of their buffoonish character, the Duke of Plaza-Toro:

> In enterprise of martial kind
> When there was any fighting,
> He led his regiment from behind,
> He found it more exciting!

The point of leadership is not that it is spatial or hierarchical, but that it is imaginative. Leaders often have awesome decision-making responsibilities. A sign on President Harry Truman's desk said, "The buck stops here!" Many of those decisions do have to be taken ultimately by the leader alone, but leadership is not just a matter of taking decisions; it is a matter of making things happen. In the political world, leaders can rarely meet their goals alone; they must know how to bring people into the tent, to woo, to coopt, to share—to be partners. As the sign in President Ronald Reagan's office said, "It's amazing what you can accomplish if you don't care who gets the credit!" (Harry S. Truman).

‒◄○►‒

CHAPTER 22

GLOBAL COMPANIES, GLOBAL SOCIETY: THERE IS A BETTER WAY

NANCY J. ADLER

"You and I belong to the same family. All people on earth belong to the same family. The human family."
—Thor Heyerdahl, Norway[1]

September 2001 was not a good month for the world. The month
opened with the UN-sponsored World Conference Against
Racism in Durban, South Africa.[2] As the world watched with high expectations, the conference drowned in a cacophony of intolerance,
expressed by official delegates from more than 160 countries as well
as by thousands of representatives of nongovernmental organizations.
"The meeting, which was intended to celebrate tolerance and diversity, became an international symbol of divisiveness . . ."[3] According
to the world press, the results "reflect less a new international unity
than a collective exhaustion."[85] As one delegate summarized, "Far too
much of the time at this conference has been consumed by bitter,
divisive exchanges on issues which have done nothing to advance the
cause of combating racism . . . [The final documents] contain language which will do nothing to achieve greater peace . . ."[4]

An earlier version of this chapter was published in the *Journal of Management Inquiry,* September 2002.

One week later, on September 11, terrorists destroyed the World Trade Center and parts of the Pentagon, killing more than 3000 people. In the immediate aftermath, public rhetoric and behavior became increasingly susceptible to simplistic definitions of good and evil and to the call for large-scale military retaliation. The escalation of ignorance-based hatred attempting to pit the Western world against Islamic communities and nations became palpable. Perhaps the danger, absurdity, and pain can best be symbolized by the fate of a woman living far from both Durban and the World Trade Center. As the woman, a Montreal doctor, made her usual hospital rounds the week after the terrorist attacks, she was strangled. Why? For the simple reason that she was Muslim. Her status as a physician and good citizen was obliterated in the eyes of her attacker solely because she practiced a religion he failed to understand. During the same week, miles away in the Middle East, Israeli children admitted to reporters that they no longer "imagine ever having a Palestinian friend," nor do their Palestinian counterparts imagine having an Israeli friend. They do not foresee living in peace. As one 13-year-old murmured, while staring at his hands, "It'll end by war. Either we'll die or they'll die."[5]

After spending a week in Durban, the New York–based director of the Center for the Advancement of Human Rights concluded, "Sadly, hate . . . was all too evident at this global conference in the new South Africa in which so many placed their hopes."[6] Hate and intolerance, optimism reduced to hopelessness, compassion eclipsed by anger, ignorance motivating senseless action: Is this the scenario that will define the twenty-first century? Will this scenario define our children's future? Perhaps, but hopefully it will not.

Although the events of September 2001 may lead us to think otherwise, the twenty-first century is not just a time of terrorism, intolerance, and fear. It also heralds an era of unprecedented global communication, global contact, and global commerce.[7] However, the ability of global companies to work successfully across cultures, while better than the track record of participants at UN racism conferences, remains humbling. Historically, more than 50 percent of all international joint ventures fail.[8] As everyone who has watched the much-touted Daimler/Chrysler debacle knows, in this case, the statistics don't lie. The seeds of failure become particularly evident when one overhears the chorus of Daimler/Chrysler's American managers blaming the company's 50 percent drop in value on the "bull-headed, dominant, and just plain dishonest" German managers, while Daimler/Chrysler's German managers, with equal vehemence, blame the company's problems on the Americans being "unworldly and too-focused-on-the-bottom line."[9] One wonders why societies continue to become more globally interconnected and why companies continue to expand beyond their borders, when the track record of global cross-cultural relationships remains so dismal. Weaving the people of the world together into a global "human family" is not easy. Our historical approaches beg for new perspectives.

NORSKE SKOG: A NEW PERSPECTIVE

Norske Skog, a Norwegian-based global company, may give us a glimpse at just such a new perspective: one with positive implications both for companies and for society.[10] Five years ago, Norske Skog was a domestic paper company with operations almost exclusively in Norway. In the past five years, the company expanded throughout Europe. Last year, following the pattern taken by so many other companies, Norske Skog went global. Among its other acquisitions, they bought a New Zealand–based company with operations throughout Asia and the Americas. In a mere five years, Norske Skog more than doubled its size and went from being a local Norwegian company to the most global firm in its industry. The immediate challenge facing Norske Skog was the same as that facing all newly global companies: How would it create a global organizational culture in which people from throughout the world might work effectively together? How would it benefit from the company's newly acquired global scale, scope, and diversity? How would it reap the benefits of employees' cultural diversity, rather than allowing such diversity to undermine the company's future success?

In many ways, Norske Skog's initial response to creating an organizational culture that would be globally integrated, locally responsive, and skilled at worldwide learning replicated that of other global companies.[11] However, in one fundamental respect, the company's strategy did not follow traditional approaches. Rather than relying solely on Norske Skog's and other companies' experience, or the plethora of global strategies offered by management consultants, Norske Skog went beyond traditional approaches and chose to include the perspectives of children in their thinking. Immediately following its New Zealand acquisition, Norske Skog invited the children of its employees on four continents to help them understand what global cooperation means, and could mean, for society, companies, and individuals. The children did not shy away from the task. In paintings, essays, and sculptural models, they told their parents and the company what it would mean to them to know and to work with people from around the world. They expressed their hopes and fears.[12] For example, Trude Jorid Mosling, an 11-year-old from Norway, told the company:

> We have to be good to the world we live in. Even if we don't have the same culture, and even if some of us are white and some are brown, it doesn't make any difference . . . Actually it's good that there are differences . . . because . . . we can teach each other things . . .

From halfway around the world, another 11-year-old, Julia McKean, of Sydney, Australia, explained that by effectively communicating across cultures, differences among the peoples of the world can become a potential benefit—what managers, but not 11-year-olds, often refer to as *cultural synergy*.[13] Julia wrote:

> I think that people communicating together, freely and happily, is what people need to do to live together in peace. Without communication the world would become one big war. In our world, there are many people who believe in different religions and gods, there are people with different coloured skin, people who speak different languages, and people who look different. If all these people stayed in groups where everyone was the same, our world would not be as good a place to live . . . Without communication the different groups of people would become enemies and fight against each other.

Catherine Goodfellow, a 13-year-old Australian with wisdom well beyond her years—wisdom that appears to have been scarce among the adults deliberating in Durban—added her perspective:

> We will never have a human race that is the same. People will always have different eye, skin and hair colour, [different] race, religion and values. Instead of letting our vast differences draw us apart, we should let them bring us together.

The children, while inherently optimistic, did not shirk from the pain in the world, even when it affected children different from themselves. For example, 12-year-old Nicole Cordova, a Brazilian, reported:

> I am sad when I see thin . . . children on TV, dying of hunger and diseases . . . The mothers have no tears left to cry. It is sad and humiliating to see such scenes.

Nor did the children ignore that different perspectives can lead to conflict. Says Catherine Goodfellow, 13, from Australia:

> It is inevitable that people will have ideas that come into conflict . . . [Yet,] only through the cooperation of people with different cultural roots can greater equality and knowledge be achieved.

Perhaps 8-year-old Canadian Jesse Swanson, in his painting and words, found the essence of global cooperation that has eluded so many companies and countries. (See Figure 22-1.)

The children spoke in words that everyone can understand, and their words and images brought the best of the adults—their parents— into the company's discussions. No longer limited to their professional roles—and thus to their "sophisticated" knowledge of what is not possible—the adults began discussing what their newly formed global company could, and should, accomplish from the broader, more optimistic, and more idealistic perspectives of professionals who are also (or perhaps, foremost) parents and human beings. As the company presented the children's stories, pictures, and sculptural models,

The lamp represents the guiding light in the quest for world peace and cooperation.

The lamp is for everyone to hold.

FIGURE 22-1. THE ESSENCE OF GLOBAL COOPERATION—PAINTING AND WORDS BY 8-YEAR-OLD CANADIAN, JESSE SWANSON. Credit: Norske Skog, Kon-Tiki contest.

they implicitly invited those fuller human beings, with their differences, into the room. Everyone understood that in forming a global organizational culture, they were playing for much greater stakes than merely the success of the company. They were publicly and collectively taking responsibility for the type of world they would pass on to their children. The definition of "winning" far surpassed simply achieving a healthy bottom line. The definition of "winning" was nothing less than the legacy they would be creating for their children and the world's children.

Are the employees and executives at Norske Skog willing to work with each other? Yes. Are they willing to cooperate on a global basis? Yes. Will the company beat the odds against succeeding as an international joint venture? Well, if the initial post-merger results are any indication, the answer will also be yes. Parallel to the impressive growth of Norske Skog in its earlier years, in just one year, 1999 to 2000, operating revenues increased by 48 percent, over two years by 79 percent.[14] Over the same period, operating profits increased by 98 percent over one year and 137 percent over two years.[15] From 1999 to 2001, turnover doubled from approximately $2 billion to an expected $4 billion in 2002. At the same time, earnings more than doubled, with margins being among the highest in the industry.

The positive results are not just financial. Norske Skog has grown from being a modest player to becoming the second largest supplier of newsprint in the world. Production of publication paper is up 40 percent over one year and 87 percent over two years.[16]

The success story to date is not limited to financial and productivity indicators of a healthy bottom line. Norske Skog also leads its industry in environmentally sound practices, including having become the world's largest user of recycled fibers for publication paper and, in the Southern hemisphere, the largest user of plantation (rather than virgin) forests. Similarly, in the area of industrial relations, the company, drawing on its roots in the managerial cultures of Scandinavia, has been able to maintain an organizational culture that strongly encourages employee involvement. Employees currently hold two positions out of nine on the board of directors, and Norske Skog continues to consult and inform union representatives prior to each big expansion and divestment, even during periods of rapid change.

Will Norske Skog do well in the future? No one knows for sure. However, most observers are not willing to bet against them, not when their children's future is at stake.

The same week that Norske Skog held its first-year, global executive meeting in Oslo, the UN Conference on Racism in Durban, South

Africa, was collapsing into racist name-calling, with countries and delegates quitting the meeting in disgust. The contrast to the dynamics at the Norske Skog meeting is immense. Could it be that a for-profit, private-sector company found a way to commit itself to constructive, worldwide communication while many diplomats were failing at the same task?

CONCLUSION

One week after Norske Skog's global executive meeting, terrorists destroyed the World Trade Towers in New York City. No one doubts that too many adults on this planet have failed to live together peacefully while respecting cultural, racial, and national differences. As we listen to the voices of the children—recognizing that many of us have become too jaded and corroded by experience-based cynicism to actually hear the relevance of their perspectives—maybe we should try again not just to listen, but to hear what they are saying. Madeleine Albright, the former United States Secretary of State reminds us " . . . it is our responsibility, not to be prisoners of history, but to create history."[17] Hillel would add, "And if not now, when?"

"The moral universe rests upon the breath of school children."[18]

PART FOUR

---◆---

The Leader as Partner:
Succeeding in a Complex World

CHAPTER 23

THE LEADER AS PARTNER–COACH AND PEOPLE DEVELOPER

JAMES BELASCO

"Partnership" is the leader's highway to success: Leaders partner with many constituencies in their shared journey down the highway of life. We most often think of partnerships with such external groups as customers and suppliers. Equally important, though, are partnerships with internal constituencies, such as employees and teammates. It is my experience that successful leaders are often viewed as co-conspirator partners with their teammates and employees in their growth and development.

Take the example of James Caan, actor extraordinaire.[1] Caan took a sabbatical at the height of his career—fresh from an Academy Award nomination for *The Godfather.* Instead of continuing his acting career, he took up coaching kids' sports. He particularly remembers one nine-year-old named Josh. Josh was big, but he just couldn't hit a baseball, and it really bothered him. Caan spent many one-on-one hours coaching Josh.

As Caan tells it, "The next to the last game of the year Josh comes up to bat. The week before, he had popped it up to the pitcher with the bases loaded. He felt terrible. Anyway, he gets up, and he just creams the ball. And the kid starts running. I'm coaching third base, and he looks up at me when he rounds second. When he saw me waving him on to home, he looks at me—I'll never forget it as long as I live—and there were tears in his eyes. He ran home, jumped up in the

[233]

air, and landed with both feet on the plate. He triumphantly pumped both fists in the air. The whole dugout cleared out to hug him. Nothing replaces that: nothing in the world. I mean to literally change a kid. That was the best time of my life."

Successful leaders, like baseball coach James Caan, who partner with their teammates to help their teammates, like the Joshes of the world, experience fulfillment and joy.

LEADERS BECOME THE VEHICLE/COACH
FOR OTHERS' DEVELOPMENT

In the ancient French language, a *coach* was "a vehicle to transport people." Today's leader is a coach–partner who helps transport people to higher and higher levels of personal and professional fulfillment. Leaders partner with employees and teammates to help them develop career capabilities—the skills and knowledge necessary to succeed in the world of business. In addition, truly successful leader–partner–coaches help others develop life skills, such as learning and working productively with the broadest diversity of peoples and cultures.

Ferid Murad, 1998 Nobel Prize winner in medicine, is an excellent example. Murad was the first member of his family to graduate from high school. On his path to earning an MD, he got lots of coaching and mentoring from individuals, including customers in his family's restaurant. As part of his desire to pay back all the help he'd received from others, he sponsors promising students from less affluent families. One student particularly stands out: a 26-year-old who reported to work in his lab in full biker dress. Nine years later, this student moved with Murad to Stanford University and then went on to head his own medical school department.

Murad said, "Trainees are like offspring, your children. It makes me feel very good when they've done well and when they go on and help others. It's like building a pyramid."[2]

Partnering–coaching–leading isn't reserved to the office. One day, I watched a Reverend teach a sullen and withdrawn teenager a great life lesson. Sunk deep in the typical teenage disease of self-alienation, Billy slouched in the corner, the crotch of his frayed, oversized jeans and big link key chain dragging on the floor. In front of the congregation, the pastor enlisted Billy's reluctant help in an activity that appealed to Billy's strength: an arm-wrestling match between Billy and the reverend.

The two assumed their clasped-hands position at the table, staring at each other. Billy easily won the first round, as the reverend didn't offer any resistance. Billy looked surprised. "Guess you won that one," the reverend said, moving their hands to the initial clasped-hands position. "Billy, I forgot to tell you that your dad promised a quarter a win," the reverend said. In the second round, he offered some initial resistance, but went limp again after a few seconds. Billy won the second round. "Guess that's two quarters for you," he said, moving their hands to the original upright position. This time the reverend offered strong resistance. Billy struggled for an instant, then a smile crossed his face and his hand went limp.

"That's right, Billy," the reverend said smiling. "Now you've caught on. Let's both get lots of quarters. He called out to Billy's father, "Hey, John. Hope you brought a stash tonight." With that, both Billy and the reverend quickly moved their clasped hands back and forth in perfect unison. The audience broke out in laughter and applauded.

"Billy," the reverend asked, "what's the lesson here?"

"Cooperating wins me more money. Dad, you owe me seven bucks."

Here's a great leader–partner–coach in action, co-conspiring with his teammate, in teaching a vital life lesson: "Cooperation wins me more money," to quote Billy.

My mother was another great leader–partner–coach and co-conspirator in my life. She made the best icebox pie in the world with layers of whipped cream and crushed graham crackers. Yum! We kids all fought to get the largest piece. She used her leadership–partnership skills to teach us an important life lesson. One of us would cut the pie and the others choose the slice—and whoever helped prepare the pie got to choose first. All three of us soon learned that the key to getting more pie to eat was to help prepare a larger pie so that each slice could be bigger. My mother taught me an important life lesson: Sharing the pie with all those who helped create it makes a bigger pie for everyone.

Here are five techniques I've learned to be a successful partner–leader–coach and co-conspirator in the growth and development of people.

1. *Focus on progress, not perfection.*

No one's perfect. Just get over it and get on with it! Many successful partner–coaches use the "Weight Watchers approach." Weight Watchers is not about making people feel bad about being overweight. It's about helping people feel good about losing weight. Like Weight Watchers, partner–coaches "weigh in" the people they work with and praise the heck out of those who have achieved their goal. They then help those who didn't realize their expectations figure out what they can do to be more successful next time.

Unfortunately, this is easier said than done. I've heard the following from the podium several times: "Eagles don't have rearview mirrors." I'm also told, "Mountain climbers always look up, focusing on the next hill to climb." Unfortunately, I'm a slow learner. Even though I hear these very plausible messages, I continue to beat myself up about the poor comparisons I make against some arbitrary standard. Take the book I'm writing. I'm feeling bad because I've only gotten two chapters written thus far, and I told the publisher that I'd have five by this time. But they're great chapters and I have a handle on what the balance of the book will be. Yet, I beat myself up for being "behind schedule." My partner–coach (yes, I have not one but several partner–coaches) helps me see that I've made great progress toward my ultimate goal of having a successful book. Great partner–coaches focus on what the individual is becoming, not what he or she isn't.

2. *Create opportunities for people to practice.*

Partner–coaches do much more than ask questions or make suggestions. Partnering–coaching is an active, engaging role. They're in the people-growing business. It takes practices, lots and lots of practice, to develop new skills, capabilities, and attitudes. Successful partner–coaches find and/or create lots of practice venues for the people they are helping to grow and develop.

Shushami, a former student of mine, was an extraordinarily skilled people-relationship builder. She wanted to develop her marketing knowledge and skills to go back to her home country to help her family business. As her partner–coach, I surfaced two internship opportunities. She spent six months with a company in a newly emerging industry, eventually becoming the marketing manager for them. After several years, she returned to her family business, taking a distribution license with her. Today she heads that business for her family.

Dick was the head of a major company in San Diego. He was also the chairman of the United Way. One day over lunch he told me, "I never learned more than when I led the United Way. We had lots of challenges—it was just after the big scandal in New York and the PR was just awful. I learned what it takes to motivate senior folks to volunteer their time: clear goals, lots of positive feedback on their contributions, and effective administrative systems that deliver the materials they need to do their jobs." As his partner–coach, I urged him to take those same lessons into his company. Several months later he told me, "Thanks for your advice. As a result, we dramatically moved the needle."

The world is awash with practice opportunities. Successful partner–coaches identify them and urge their people to "Go for it!"

3. *Continue to raise the bar.*

First-time skiers don't fly down the slope. It takes a great deal of practice to ski. A good partner–coach knows that you can't promise immediate rides down the big hill after the first lesson (except maybe on one's rear end). A good partner–coach sets achievable initial expectations and then raises them slowly (first staying up on the skis, then moving forward on the skis, then . . . well, you get the picture). Incremental steps after successful experiences are the only way to achieve mastery of any skill. Successful coaching partners acknowledge current achievements, while raising the bar for future performance.

Leader–partner–coaches raise the bar by helping people see the bigger picture. Most folks suffer from tunnel vision. I know I do.

It's easy to get caught up in what you're doing and ignore everything else that's going on. For example, one of my relatives decided to move to another city to find work. He ran irrigation pipe for a living and felt that the opportunities would be better there. He packed up his household goods, loaded the wife and kids into the car, and took off. He emailed me a few weeks later looking for some help. It seems that he was having difficulty finding a pipe-laying job. Sensing a partner–coach opportunity, I suggested that he look into related fields, such as plumbing and general maintenance. These ideas, along with his hustling, surfaced several interim opportunities. He got a maintenance supervisor's job at Home Depot, and it has turned out to be the best job he'd ever had. He'd been stuck in identifying himself as an irrigation pipe layer and didn't see the opportunities in the next field. As his partner–coach, I helped him see beyond his self-imposed fences.

4. *Encourage visits to excellence in action and help apply the lessons.*
   It's hard to imagine what excellent performance really looks like, particularly when you have never seen or experienced it. It's like describing lobster to someone who's never tasted it. Hard, isn't it? Seasoned partner–coaches encourage people to experience lobster and excellence in other areas of their lives.
   A mid-range hotel company arranged for their housekeeping and front desk staffs to stay at upscale properties such as the Four Seasons and Ritz Carleton. They paid all the expenses for a two-night stay, providing each person return with at least three ideas they could implement immediately at their property to make their Holiday Inn guests' experience more like that of a Four Seasons or Ritz Carleton. The staffs returned jazzed and ready to be "Ladies and gentlemen serving ladies and gentlemen" (the Ritz Carleton motto). Within months, their hotels were at the top of their regions' customer service and profitability ratings.
   In that situation, as the partner-coach my job was to help the housekeepers and front-desk people translate their experiences and learning into specific, concrete actions. I helped them expand their horizons, gain new insights, and raise the level of their own

expectations of themselves by looking over their own self-imposed wall of "how things are supposed to be." I primed the pump with a few ideas for specific applications. That unleashed the floodgates of ideas. One of the housekeepers said, "I didn't realize I could help a guest find a movie theater in the area. Now I realize that I can also help them find golf places and parks. I'm going to get the concierge's books and study them so I can be ready when a guest asks for advice."

5. *Be the emotional bridge to the future.*

It's very difficult to make the trip to tomorrow when it requires giving up the comforts of today. People generally know what's expected today. Today may not be everything they really want, but it's easier to complain about today than to take steps toward the future. After all, the future is totally uncertain.

That's why the partner–coach is so important. It's scary stepping off into the great unknown. Partner–coaches can't take the risk for the individual, but they can be his or her emotional bridge to that tomorrow. The partner–coach can be there to talk, share, commiserate, and celebrate. He or she can provide the emotional guardrail.

At more times than I'm probably entitled to, I've found a partner–coach to help me through a particularly difficult situation. Once I recall struggling for a long time to help my firm break into the textile dye market. Nothing seemed to work. One day over lunch with my "mastermind" group, an attorney suggested, "Have you thought about interviewing a few of the folks who rejected your offers? Maybe they could tell you you're doing wrong." His idea hit me like a two-ton truck. Of course, talk to the noncustomers. I was too fixated on my efforts. My mental blinders completely prevented me from getting what I wanted. After two conversations with noncustomers, I had a clear picture of what we needed to do. The answer was simplicity itself: Because this was a custom design market, we had to listen more carefully to the customer's needs and tone down the hard-sell approach. But, none of this would have happened without my partner–coach attorney friend. He called me frequently during this difficult time. He encouraged me to keep looking for better answers and helped me handle the negative responses I was getting. His faithful presence made all the difference to me.

Partner–leader–coaches help develop people to be more than they imagine they can be. They are an ear to listen, a smile to encourage, a word to reinforce, and some sage advice to consider. They help individuals focus on the thrill of becoming rather than the despair of what they are now. Successful leaders–partners–coaches help people reach for the stars and gather some moon dust along the way. It is for me, the most satisfying job in my life—and the most valuable use of my time on the planet.

CHAPTER 24

THE POWER OF FOCUS

BRIAN TRACY

The most important responsibility of the leader is to determine clearly what is to be done, and then to convey that to each person who reports to him or her. It is to assure that each person is focused on those tasks that contribute the most to the success of the enterprise.

This is the first of leadership functions and the one task that is most often performed poorly because the leader and his or her team members must be working in partnership with each other if this is to be accomplished. Let me give you an example. In my management seminars, I often ask the participants if they would like to play a game. I explain to them that the name of the game is "Keep Your Job."

I then explain the rules of the game so they can decide, in advance, if they want to play. The rules are simple. Each manager will write down the names of the people who report to him or her. Next to each name, the manager will write the primary responsibilities and priorities of each person.

I will then have managers wait in the room while I go and interview each of their staff members and ask them to tell me what they consider to be their primary responsibilities and priorities. If the answers of the staff members are the same as the answers of the manager, the manager gets to "Keep His Job." After I have explained the name of the game and the rules, I ask if anyone in the room would like to play.

[241]

I have been offering to play this game with managers for several years. I have never seen a hand raised, nor have I ever met a manager who wanted to bet his or her job based on his or her staff being absolutely clear about what they are supposed to do.

THE IMPORTANCE OF CLARITY

In 3300 studies of leadership conducted by James McPhereson, he discovered only one common denominator among leadership qualities. It was consistent and it was mentioned in every study and every report. It was the quality of "vision."

Leaders have vision. Nonleaders do not. Period. Your most important job as a leader is therefore to establish a vision that is clear to yourself and to everyone who is expected to help in fulfilling it. This is essential to effectiveness. As it says in the Bible, "Where there is no vision, the people perish."

What these words mean is that eventually people will lose their spirit and enthusiasm for high performance if they are not clear about the vision toward which the company is working. Clarifying the vision for the organization is a key responsibility of leadership.

The difference between fingers and fists is that the fingers are spread out while the fist is concentrated. The difference between a great organization and an average organization is the same. A great organization is focused and concentrated on achieving important and worthwhile tasks. An average or mediocre organization may have the same people and resources, but its energy is diffused and its impact is weakened: Individuals are not working in partnership with each other toward a common goal.

The one quality of all great leaders is that they have absolute clarity about who they are, what they believe in, where they are going, and how they intend to get there. They have a clear vision of the kind of future they are working to create. They then have the ability to partner with others in order to convey this vision with great clarity and force to the people who they expect to help them to get there. Vision is the key difference between a highly motivated team of employees and a group of people who simply go through the motions each day in order to qualify for a paycheck.

In its simplest terms, a vision is an ideal picture of what the company or department would look like sometime in the future if it were excellent in every respect. It is a summary of your values, mission, purpose, and goals onto an exciting image that motivates and excites people toward making it a reality. What is your vision?

Once you are clear about your vision, the next step in developing your power of focus is to develop absolute clarity about your goals. Think on paper. Make a list of everything that you want to achieve in your position of responsibility, in every area. Write these goals down in the present tense, as if you had already accomplished them.

Once you have a list of goals for what you want to accomplish in your company, and in each area of your position, organize your goals by priority. Which of these goals are input goals and which of these goals are outputs? Which of these goals has to be completed before other goals can be achieved? Which of these goals are more important than any other? Ask others for their input.

You can use a blank sheet of paper and organize your goals in the form of a mind map, with circles, boxes, and arrows linking each one in sequence, very much like a PERT chart. (PERT stands for "Performance Evaluation Review Technique." It is a visual box and arrow representation of a project.) This visual image of what you are trying to accomplish, and the logical sequence in which it has to be accomplished, is very helpful in organizing your thoughts and enabling you to focus with ever greater intensity on the most important tasks and goals before you.

There are five key areas of focus that are important to leading effectively. In each of these areas, the leader is the only person who is tasked to ensure clarity, consensus, and agreement among the team members. The greater clarity you have in each of these areas, the more motivated, empowered, and focused each person will be in achieving the requirements of their individual positions.

FOCUS ON YOUR VALUES

What are your values? What are the values of your company or your department? What are your unifying principles? These are perhaps the most important questions of all, both from a personal and from an organizational standpoint. Men and women with clear values, from which they do not deviate, are far more focused and effective than people whose values are fuzzy and easily compromised.

Each time I bring up the subject of values in a corporate seminar, the whole atmosphere changes. Everyone wants to discuss and debate the values they have and the values that they believe that the organization either has or should have. A brief discussion turns into a two- or three-hour process that very quickly involves everyone.

People are very sensitive about values and about what particular values mean in practice. And the more they discuss them, the more committed they become to practicing them.

Partner with Others to Clarify Values

One of the best exercises you can engage in is to ask each person to bring a list of the five values that they consider to be the most important to a staff meeting.

Collect the slips of paper and write down the values on a flip chart or white board, so that everyone can see them. As you list the values off each sheet of paper, you will discover several repetitions. In a group of five to ten people, you will end up with 15 to 20 different values on the board.

The next part of the exercise is to have each person choose his or her three favorite values from all of those listed. Have them write them on slips of paper and hand them forward. Once again, write these values on the board or flip chart, and put a mark beside each value that is repeated.

In less than half an hour, you will have a clear consensus of the three to five values that everyone considers to be the most important in the operations of your business or department. These values should then become the organizing principles for everything you do, both internally with each other and externally with your customers, suppliers, and other stakeholders.

Decide How You Would Demonstrate a Value

You can take this exercise one step further. Lead a discussion about what each of these values actually means in terms of behavior. How would we behave if we were living and working consistent with this value?

A very successful company that I worked with went through this exercise when the company was being formed. They developed five values and a definition for each of these values. They then printed these values on laminated cards that everyone in the company carried with him or her. Whenever a decision had to be made, even over the telephone, the parties would pull out their "Values Cards" and discuss the decision based on the values to which they had all committed.

As a result of this strict adherence to values in everything they did, this was one of the most cooperative, dynamic, positive, and enthusiastic groups of people I ever worked with. Not only that, they were extremely profitable in a very competitive industry. They were highly respected by everyone who worked with the organization, both inside and outside. They attributed much of their success to their rigid adherence to clear, mutual values from the very beginning.

Determine Your Mission

Once you have clear values to focus on, you can then define your mission. A mission is like a military objective. It is something that can be achieved. It is measurable and time-bounded. A clear mission statement would be something like this: "We produce and distribute high-quality products for the telecommunications industry, are highly respected by everyone who works with us, and achieve a 10 percent market share with 25 percent net profit on sales within five years."

This kind of a mission statement states clearly what you intend to accomplish with your business and how you will measure your success. It makes it clear how people will work together and toward what end. It then becomes easy for you to know how close you are to achieving the mission, and how far you have still to go.

Decide Why You Are in Business

Your purpose flows from your values and your mission. Your purpose is the reason "why" your company is in business in the first place. Your purpose is always defined in terms of how you intend to enrich or improve the life or work of your customers, and is the reason customers choose to partner with you.

If someone were to ask you, "What is your purpose for being in business?" you could answer something like: "We help people to organize their finances, eliminate their debts, and achieve complete financial independence." This is a clear purpose and reason for being.

From that point forward, everything you do for your customers can be compared against your values, your mission, and your purpose. When you have complete clarity in these three areas, it becomes easy for you to make critical decisions regarding the allocation of people and resources. As long as a potential activity or investment is consistent with your vision, mission, and purpose, it is an area to explore and exploit. If it is not consistent with your reasons for being in business, it is something that you can pass on quite easily.

Imagine Your Ideal Future Vision

Your values, mission, and purpose come together to create a vision for the future of your organization. In creating a vision, you continually "idealize" your desired future state. You project forward three to five years into the future and imagine that your entire organization was living its values, achieving its mission, and fulfilling its purpose. What would your organization look like at that time?

Finally, you practice "Back-from-the-Future" thinking. You project forward into the future and then you look back to where you are today and ask yourself, "What steps would we have to take today in order to create the ideal future that we envision?"

It is exciting to be working with an organization that has a great vision to do wonderful things in the world that will ennoble and enrich other people. As Nietzsche once wrote, "A man can bear any *what* if he has a big enough *why*."

Focus on Your Goals

Your goals and objectives are the concrete, measurable, time-bounded steps that you have to take to get from where you are to where you want to go. The greater clarity you have with regard to your long-term vision, the easier it is for you to set specific goals for its realization. This is a key job of leadership.

There are several ways to set goals. The first and easiest is for you to decide what the goals are and then to pass them out, like dealing cards at a blackjack table. However, it is better to partner with others in goal setting, rather than decreeing the goals yourself. There is a direct relationship between participation in the discussion of goals on the one hand, and deep down commitment to achieving those goals on the other.

When I was a young manager, I thought that the process of discussing the work, what needs to be done, how it is to be measured, who is to do it, and when it is to be achieved was too time consuming. I later learned, after much hard experience, that the time that you take to involve others in goal setting saves an enormous amount of time in achieving those goals further down the road.

The critical factor in managing effectively is called "ownership." At the beginning, when you are given your job or responsibility, you own the job completely. You are in control. You are totally responsible for its accomplishment. The buck stops with you. If the job does not get done, you are the person who is held accountable.

The good news is that the more control that you give away to others and the more you partner with others, the more power you have and the more effective you will be. The way that you pass ownership from yourself to your individual staff members is by involving them continually in the process of clarifying and achieving the goals. The more involved they are at the beginning, the more committed they will be throughout.

The more time that you spend talking about the work with your co-workers, colleagues, and staff members, the greater clarity they will have about not only what is to be done, but also why it is to be done. When people understand the why of a goal, they are far more creative and resourceful in developing new and better ways to achieve it.

The fact is that people can't hit a target that they cannot see. Your job as the leader is to set clear goals for your company or department and then to help each person set clear goals for himself or herself that fit into your overall objectives. Clarity is the key.

Goal setting is not a natural skill. Only about 3 percent of adults have written goals and plans that they work on daily. The great majority of people need someone else to help them to set goals at work. Without that partnership, people will always perform below their potential.

Earl Nightingale once wrote that, "Happiness is the progressive realization of a worthy goal, or ideal."

The happier your people are, the more positive, spontaneous, and creative they will be. When you have worked together with them to set clear, specific goals that they are working on each day, they will naturally feel happy and powerful.

Not only that, but people with clear goals have more energy and commitment. They take on more responsibility. They are seldom absent or sick. They develop an inner commitment to the accomplishment of goals that have been entrusted to them. Because you have made them partners in the process of setting goals, they take the accomplishment of the goals personally. They assume ownership. They become more determined and decisive. As they move progressively toward the achievement of their goals, they become more confident and capable. They become top performers and real contributors to your organization.

Key Result Areas

Each job can be broken down into five to seven key result areas. A *key result area* is defined as a specific result that absolutely, positively must be accomplished in order to achieve the overall output goal of the position. In most cases, key result areas are arranged in sequence. First, one must be accomplished, then the second, then the third, and so on. The ultimate result of performing well in each key result area is the accomplished task of the individual.

Each key result area must also have a standard of performance. This standard or measure is what you use to determine how well the result has been accomplished in each area. Remember, you can't manage what you can't measure. Standards of performance give you, and each person, clear metrics by which performance and levels of accomplishment can be regulated and evaluated.

One company I worked with, a very high-spirited and profitable organization, had a series of standards for its staff. The first standard was simply "excellence." An individual had to do an excellent job consistently to be assured of a future within that organization. Each person was continually coached and encouraged by his or her manager to strive for excellence, as clearly defined in advance by both parties.

The next standard above excellence was called "Wow!" It was at this level that bonuses, rewards, and promotions began to kick in. Again, there was a numerical definition and standard for "Wow!" that was clear, objective, and written.

The highest standard of all was called "Double Wow!" This was achieved when the individual went far beyond the standards of excellence and "Wow!" In every case, these measures referred to sales, revenue growth, cost cutting and savings, and profitability. A person's financial contribution to the overall results of the company became the critical determinant of status, rewards, promotion, and increased responsibility.

Coming back to my definition of the game "Keep Your Job," how many of your people are absolutely clear about their key result areas, their goals, and the standards that they need to meet in order to be paid well and promoted faster? When you establish these benchmarks for each person, they then have the ability to bring all of their energies to focus on doing an excellent job for you and the company.

The greater the clarity that the members of your staff have in each of these areas, the greater responsibility they will take on. Your team will function in partnership, like a well-oiled machine, and accomplish more and better results than ever before.

FOCUS ON SPECIFIC ACTIVITIES

The third area in which focus is essential is on the individual activities of your team members. It is absolutely essential that you sit down with your team on a weekly basis and discuss your plans of action. How are your goals and objectives going to be met? How does each person fit into the overall plan? What contributions are expected of each team member?

The very best way to build a peak-performing team is to assign each player to a role that is ideal for his or her talents, abilities, and experience. A person will always do a better job if it is something that he or she really enjoys doing in the first place.

Since most people are primarily visual, you should continually use a flip chart or white board to draw graphs and diagrams outlining and explaining the job that needs to be done and the various tasks that need to be accomplished to achieve the overall results. Ask for input and suggestions. Invite argument and controversy. Be open to changing your mind and to being influenced by your team members. Be flexible and aware of the possibility that you could be wrong or incomplete in your initial assessment.

There is nothing that builds team loyalty faster than for the team members to feel that they have an influence and a voice in how the job is done.

On the other hand, there is nothing that demoralizes a person faster than to know that his or her boss is rigid and inflexible, and once determined to accomplish a task in a particular way is unwilling to partner, change, or accept suggestions from others.

Build and Maintain High Morale

Once a year, and more often if your business situation is changing rapidly, you should have a "Why I Am on the Payroll" meeting with your key team members. In this meeting, everyone writes out an answer to that question, photocopies his or her answer for everyone at the meeting, and then brings it for mutual discussion.

In this job description, under the heading "Why I Am on the Payroll" each person writes down the words "My Primary Responsibilities Are ..."

Under this heading, all team members write out what they feel they have been hired to do, in what order of importance, and to what standard.

The second section starts off with the words, "My Secondary Responsibilities Are ..."

In this section, employees describe their secondary tasks and responsibilities, the jobs they do when they are completely caught up with their primary responsibilities.

Your job as the team leader is to go around the table and lead a discussion of each person's job, in conjunction with everyone else at the table. This is a form of 360-degree management that involves very little stress. It is a positive and productive process that everyone enjoys for this simple reason: Everybody likes to be crystal clear about the tasks by which they are being judged by their boss and others.

For example, I was working for a large conglomerate. The head of a major division resigned abruptly, and the president had to step in and manage the division for several months. He had been out of touch with activities in that division for a couple of years, and he asked me for my ideas on how he could quickly bring himself up to speed on what was really going on within that division.

I suggested that he have each key person complete a "Why I Am on the Payroll" questionnaire and bring it to him for discussion and review. Within one week of taking over, the president, by using this method, had a complete sense for what was really going on at every level of the organization. He told me afterwards that it was the fastest and most effective tool that he had ever used as a senior executive.

The Best Motivator of All

The greatest single motivator in the world of work is "knowing exactly what's expected." When people know exactly what you expect them to do, to what standard, and in what order of priority, they are free to focus all of their energies on high performance.

On the other hand, the greatest single de-motivator in the world of work is "not knowing what is expected." When people are not sure what is expected of them, they always have a nagging feeling of ineffectiveness and confusion. They are never sure if they are doing the right thing or doing it to the right standard. They lose their energy and enthusiasm for the job. They become negative, unhappy, and critical.

Your job as the leader, as a partner to your staff members, is to make it your primary responsibility and goal to assure clarity at all levels. Each person must know exactly why the company exists in terms of the difference that the company intends to make in the lives of the people it serves. Each person must know what his or her goals are and how those goals can be measured. Each person must know what his or her specific job responsibilities are and what the job responsibilities are of the other people in the company. With clarity at all levels, an average group of people can be quickly turned into a Super Bowl team.

FOCUS ON SETTING AN EXAMPLE

Ross Perot once said, "Inventory can be managed, but people must be led."

Ross Perot was a graduate of Annapolis, and his military background shaped his concept of leadership. President Dwight D. Eisenhower was once asked why it was that excellent combat officers always went over the top first. He asked, "Did you ever try to push a string?"

To be a leader, you must lead. The most important thing you do as a team leader is to set an example, to be a role model for the people who look up to you.

If you want people to come in early, you should come in early yourself. If you want people to work on their highest priority tasks, you should be continually working on your highest priority tasks. If you want people to stay focused on their reason for being there, you should be busy and attentive to your tasks most of the time, as well. Whatever you want or expect of others, you should lead the way and demonstrate in your own behavior what you want others to demonstrate in their behavior.

As the leader, there are certain things that only you can do. If you do not do them, neither will anyone else. These are your chief responsibilities. And one of them is for you to make sure that each team member has the resources they need to do his or her job in an excellent fashion.

Some of the most powerful words you can use in working with each team member are the words, "How can I help?"

When everyone is clear about what they are expected to do, and to what standard, and why they are expected to do it, what they need more than anything else from you is your help in removing the obstacles that might hinder their performance. They need your help in getting them the resources they require, so that they can single-mindedly focus on getting the results for which they are responsible.

It is a fixed premise in officer training that the officer always eats last. First of all, the officer makes sure that his or her people have enough to eat, a place to sleep, and that the unit is secure. Only then does the officer provide for his or her own comfort and needs. In this sense, the officer serves his or her people and, as a result, they become loyal and committed to serving the officer when the battle begins.

The concept of "servant leadership" has become very popular in the last few years. As Confucius wrote, "To become the master, you must become the servant of all."

The Best Bosses

In interviews of employees, asking them to describe the best bosses they ever had, the responses continuously mentioned two qualities or characteristics. First, people said that the best boss they ever had was the one who made it extremely clear to them what they were expected to do, to what standard, and they then left them largely alone to do the job. The second characteristic that came out was that the best bosses were very high in consideration. People felt like the boss really cared for them as human beings, as well as employees of the organization.

By practicing the three "C's" of leadership, you will "Bind them to you with hoops of steel." (The three "C's" are caring, courtesy, and consideration.) You can never be too kind, too patient, or too fair when you interact with your people.

Harmony Leads to High Performance

The most important ingredient in a high-performance work environment is harmony. In a harmonious environment, people feel happy, safe, respected, and secure. They feel that they can do their job and make mistakes without being criticized, condemned, or threatened with punishment. They feel that they can express themselves freely with their boss and co-workers without the danger of being ridiculed. In a high-trust environment, characterized by caring, courtesy, and consideration, people feel free to perform at their very best and to put their whole hearts into their work.

The fact is that you do not "raise morale" in an organization. Morale filters down from the top. Everyone watches the boss and patterns their behavior after the boss's behavior. What you do becomes the standard for everyone else. You can never expect the people who report to you to be very much different from you, in the long run.

The very best bosses create an environment in which people say to themselves, "This is a terrific place to work." When you walk through a well-managed department, there is a great deal of laughter and happy conversation. People get along easily with each other. There are open doors, an absence of politics, and directness in communication. The very best compliment you can ever receive is when an employee tells you, "This is a great place to work!"

The way that you behave personally, and the way that you treat others, sets the standard for everyone else. Leaders are always aware that everyone is watching them and patterning their behavior after them. Leaders are highly sensitive to the fact that anything that they say or do is going to be noticed by others. Leaders continually think through their actions and responses to make sure that, if everyone behaved the way *they* did, the organization would be an even better place to work.

FOCUS ON CONTINUOUS IMPROVEMENT

The final key to becoming an excellent leader is for you to not only set high standards, but also to encourage everyone to strive to exceed those standards on a regular basis. Emil Coué revolutionized psychosomatic medicine at his clinic in Geneva at the turn of the century by encouraging every patient to repeat continuously the words, "Every day, in every way, I am getting better and better."

This can be your mantra as well. Encourage everyone around you to look for ways to become better and better every day. When you achieve excellence in one area, set that as your new minimum standard. Create measures of both performance and excellent performance. Continually measure yourself against the very best that you have done in the past, and the very best that anyone else has done.

Michael LeBoeuf, the business writer, once wrote what he called, "The greatest management principle in the world," which was "What gets rewarded gets done."

Make it a practice of setting high standards and then both praising and rewarding everyone and anyone who performs to that standard. Take people out to lunch. Give them a day off. Give them a financial bonus. Lead a hand of applause for them at staff meetings. Practice "One-Minute Praisings," popularized by Ken Blanchard, by bragging about your people's performance to other people while they are standing there.

One of the most important jobs that you have is to be a cheerleader. You should be continually reminding people about how good they are. You should be continually reinforcing excellent performance. You should be continually looking for ways to make people feel terrific about themselves.

THE POWER OF FOCUS—REVISITED

Your ability to focus yourself on the most important results that you can possibly contribute to your organization is the key to a feeling of personal power, high levels of effectiveness, and tremendous self-confidence. You feel terrific about yourself when you know you are accomplishing important results.

As a leader, the kindest and most generous act you can engage in is to make these same feelings possible for each person who reports to you. And you can double and triple your impact on others by involving them as partners both physically and emotionally at each stage.

When each person has an opportunity to share his or her innermost feelings regarding values, vision, mission, and purpose, each person feels a part of the organization and a deep, inner commitment to living and practicing those values in everything he or she does and says to others.

When you involve people in the setting of clear, measurable goals by establishing key result areas and standards of performance, you enable them to focus their energies on accomplishing the most important results required of their positions.

When you openly discuss and determine the specific tasks and activities that people can contribute to the overall success of the organization, you engage them at a deep emotional level and bring out the very best they have to offer.

Throughout, you lead by example. You carry yourself as the role model or standard for everyone else. You treat people with kindness, courtesy, and consideration. You help them get the resources they need to perform at their very best.

Finally, you continue to raise the bar in your work. You set high standards and you encourage each person to meet and exceed those standards on a regular basis. When they do, you praise, reward, and reinforce their accomplishments, so that they are motivated to set and achieve even higher standards in the future.

The fact is that you cannot motivate people to do anything; however, what you can do is to create the kind of environment in which motivation takes place naturally. You can make your company or department a terrific place to work and tap into the spirit of each person who comes in contact with you. This is the real role of leadership.

CHAPTER 25

FIVE TOUCHSTONES TO AUTHENTIC PARTNERING AS A LEADER

KEVIN CASHMAN

While partnering is familiar territory to us all, authentic partnering requires new touchstones to navigate our way. Whether it is the bond that connects family members, the partnering between business entities, the synergy between team members, or the linkages between a business and a vendor, all effective partnering has one thing in common: the "parts" of partnering come together to create a more integrated whole. Why, then, are some of the "wholes" more integrated and why do they create more, whereas others come apart and diminish value?

Over the past 20 years of coaching senior executives and senior teams, we have been fortunate to observe a few underlying dynamics that foster enhanced synergy, connection, and value creation. We call these dynamics the Five Touchstones of Authentic Partnering.

TOUCHSTONE ONE: KNOW YOURSELF AUTHENTICALLY

There is no "part" to connect to another "part," unless we understand exactly what that "part" is and how it can add value by connecting with other "parts."

The phrase *nosce te ipsum,* know thyself, appears throughout the ages in the writings of Ovid, Cicero, and Socrates; in the sayings of the Seven Sages of Greece; on the entrance to the temple of Apollo;

[257]

in Christian writings; and in Eastern texts. One scholar says it was part of Shakespeare's "regular moral and religious diet."

Nosce te ipsum threads its way through history as the preeminent precept in life. Examples include: Chaucer, "Full wise is he that can himself know." Browning, "Trust is within ourselves." Pope, "And all our knowledge is, ourselves to know."[1] Montaigne, "If a man does not know himself, how should he know his functions and his powers?"[2] de Saint-Exupéry, "Each man must look to himself to teach him the meaning of life." Lao Tzu, "Knowledge of self is the source of our abilities."[3]

Contemporary thinkers from Ralph Waldo Emerson and Abraham Maslow to Warren Bennis and Stephen Covey have all carried on the tradition. Emerson wrote, "The purpose of life seems to be to acquaint man with himself."[4] Bennis writes, "Letting the self emerge is the essential task of leaders."[5] Covey says, "It is futile to put personality ahead of character, to try to improve relationships with others before improving ourselves."[6]

If we want to be more effective partners with others, we first need to become a more effective partner with ourselves. Instead of focusing on finding the right partner (in business or relationships), seek to be the right partner.

TOUCHSTONE TWO: LISTEN AUTHENTICALLY

The prerequisite for effective partnerships is to understand where the potential partner is at: What are their needs? What do they require? What are their concerns? Listening is the skill that connects us to these needs and builds the stage for performance together.

How often are we truly present with someone? How often do we set aside all our concerns—past, present, and future—and completely "be there" for someone else? How often do we really hear what the potential partner is saying and feeling versus filtering it heavily through our own immediate concerns and time pressures? Authentic listening is not easy. We hear the words, but rarely do we really listen. We hear the words, but do we also "hear" the emotions, fears, and underlying concerns? Authentic listening is not a technique. It is centered in compassion and in a concern for the partner, which goes beyond our self-centered needs. Listening authentically is centered in the principle of psychological reciprocity: to influence others, we must first be open to their influence. It places the other person's self-expression as primary at that moment. Authentic listening is about being generous—listening with a giving attitude that seeks to bring forth the contribution in the partner versus listening with our limiting assessments, opinions, and judgments. Authentic listening is about being open to the purpose and learning coming to us through the potential partner.

I find it amusing to observe leaders who think that not speaking is the same as really listening. Fidgeting in their chairs and doing several things at once, many leaders give numerous, simultaneous cues that they are anywhere but present with people. One successful senior executive that I was about to coach on how others perceived his poor listening skills was so agitated while listening to me, he actually threw his pen across the room. His impatience and inner distress were so strong, he couldn't even listen to me for a minute without his "dis-ease" bursting through his body and making him fling his Montblanc across my office! It was an embarrassing moment for him, as he saw precisely what other people saw in his behavior. Over time, he learned to relax more and set aside his internal dialogue and time pressure to be more present with people.

Try practicing authentic listening. Be with people and have the goal to fully understand the thoughts and feelings they are trying to express. Use your comments to draw them out, to open them up, and to clarify what is said versus expressing your view, closing them down, and saying only what you want. This will not only help you to understand what value and contribution the other person has, but it will also create a new openness in the relationship that will allow you to self-express more authentically.

Authentic listening creates the platform for true synergy and authentic partnering. Being open to valuing and attending to different perspectives from diverse sources results in a more complete understanding of issues and more effective decisions. Authentic listening is the soul of partnership.

TOUCHSTONE THREE: EXPRESS AUTHENTICALLY

Genuine partnering requires engagement and engagement requires honest self-expression. Authentic expression is a delicate subject for many leaders. I have yet to meet a leader who would admit readily that he or she lacks integrity. I also have yet to meet a leader who has complete integrity in all parts of his or her life. Integrity goes far beyond telling the truth. Integrity means total congruence between who we are and what we do. It is a formidable goal, and most of us will spend our lifetime on the path to getting there. How often have we held back something that we feel is important because we are fearful of expressing it? How often have we expressed something in a slightly more favorable light? How often have we protected someone from what we consider a tough message? How often have we feigned modesty for something of which we were really proud?

Authentic expression is the true voice of the leader. We speak it from our character, and it creates trust, synergy, connection, and partnership with everyone around us. Authentic expression is not about refining our presentation style: it's deeper than that. Some of the most authentic leaders I know stumble around a bit in their delivery, but the words come right from their hearts and experiences. You can feel it. You feel their conviction and the integral connection of who they are and what they say. Benjamin Franklin wrote, "Think innocently and justly, and, if you speak, speak accordingly."[7]

Expressing authentically is about straight talk that creates value. It's not about hurting people with bluntness or insensitivity. Expressing authentically is sharing your real thoughts and feelings in a manner that opens up possibilities for partnering. It's not about delivering only positive messages and avoiding the negatives; sometimes the most difficult messages can open up the most possibilities if shared in a thoughtful, compassionate manner. Expressing authentically is what one CEO I know calls "caring confrontation," the unique blending of straight talk with a genuine concern for people. Carl Jung expressed it this way, "To confront a person in his shadow is to show him his light."[8]

Start observing how authentically you are expressing yourself. How are you doing with your requests and with your promises? One communications expert boiled down his communication paradigm to this: "A human society operates through the expression of requests and promises." Are you authentically expressing your requests? Are you authentically fulfilling your promises? Use this model as a guide to authentic partnering; it is very powerful.

TOUCHSTONE FOUR: APPRECIATE AUTHENTICALLY

In most partnerships, we do too much and appreciate too little. Has a partner of yours (personal or business) ever appreciated you too much? It would probably be safe to say that human beings have an infinite capacity to be appreciated. Lenny Bruce wrote, "There are never enough 'I love you's.'"[9] A mentor of mine once told me, "Love is an extreme case of appreciation." As partners, however, we don't appreciate enough, much less do we love enough. In fact, we have banned the "L" word from business. In spite of the fact that the "L" word is the substance that unifies teams, builds cultures, fosters commitment, knits together partners, and bonds people to an organization, it is not socially acceptable even to say the "L" word in a business context. We can say we hate someone with no repercussions, but if we say we love someone, we may be banished for life! In lieu of this cultural taboo, let's use the word "appreciation." Appreciation is one type of self-expression that creates value. It energizes partners and makes people want to exceed their goals and perceived limits. Criticism is one type of self-expression that usually does not add value. What it does add is fear and insecurity. Criticism may get short-term results, but it rarely adds long-term value. Judging others critically doesn't define them anyway; it defines ourselves. As the Islamic saying goes, "A thankful person is thankful under all circumstances. A complaining soul complains even if he lives in paradise."

When leading a partnering effort, we may want to consider following the advice of William Penn: "If there is any kindness I can show, or any good thing I can do to any fellow being, let me do it now, and not deter or neglect it, as I shall not pass this way again." What would partnership be like if people willingly expressed this type of appreciation for one another?

Studies done by John Gottmann and described in his book, *Why Marriages Succeed and Why Marriages Fail,* found that partnerships that had a 5-to-1 ratio of appreciation to criticism were thriving, healthy, and productive.[10] However, partnerships that were at a 1-to-1 ratio of appreciation to criticism were doomed to failure. Divorce was the inevitable result of falling to a 1-to-1 ratio or lower.

Practice appreciating authentically. Look for what is going well. Point it out and have some fun celebrating the good things as they come up. Shift your analysis of situations from finding fault to finding the value being added. Acknowledge effort and intention even if the results are occasionally lacking. Trust that your appreciation will energize all partners.

TOUCHSTONE FIVE: SERVE AUTHENTICALLY

As the chairman of a fast-growth company, shared with me, "I think one of the key questions every leader must ask himself or herself is, 'How do I want to be of service to others?'"

Ultimately, a leader or partner is not judged so much on how well he or she leads, but by how well he or she serves. All value and contribution are achieved through service. Do we have any other purpose in life but to serve? As leaders, we may think we're "leading," but in reality we're serving. Leadership is a continuum of service. We serve our organization. We serve our people. We serve our customers. We serve our marketplace. We serve our community. We serve our family. We serve our relationships. At the heart of service is the principle of interdependence: Partnerships are effective when mutual benefits are served.

Capturing the essence of serving authentically, Peter Block writes in *Stewardship,* "There is pride in leadership, it evokes images of direction. There is humility in stewardship, it evokes images of service. Service is central to the idea of stewardship."[11]

As leader–partners, when we move from control to service, we acknowledge that we are not the central origin of achievement. This shift is an emotional and spiritual breakthrough. Life flows through us, and we simply play our role. Our real job is to serve all the constituencies in our life and, in the process, to appreciate genuinely the fact that only through our interdependence with others do we create value. The more we serve and appreciate others, the more we cooperatively generate value-added partnering.

As leaders, if we live for ourselves, we will only have ourselves for support. If we live for our organization, we will have people for support. If we live for the world, the whole universe will support us. Serve with purpose and you will marshal far-reaching resources.

A friend of mine had been seeking an opportunity to teach her son about the value of service and giving. The opportunity presented itself after the young boy's birthday party, as he prepared to devour one of his gifts: a multilayered box of chocolates. Approaching her son, my friend asked, "Are you happy with this gift?" Wild-eyed, he immediately responded, "Oh, yes!" My friend probed, "What would make you even happier?" Her son had no idea what possibly could add to his joy. His mother then said, "If you gave someone else a chocolate, they would be as happy as you are, and you could feel even happier." The young boy thought for a minute and said, "Let's go see grandma at the nursing home." Off they went to the nursing home. When the child saw the joy on his grandmother's face and felt how it multiplied his joy, he was hooked. Before he left the nursing home, the entire box was gone, and the boy had learned the joy of service and the power of partnering.

Focus on practicing partnering that serves the most life-enriching outcomes. In this spirit, Bryant Hinckley summed it up well in *Hours with Our Leaders*[12]:

> Service is the virtue that distinguished the great of all times and which they will be remembered by. It places a mark of nobility upon its disciples. It is the dividing line which separates the two great groups of the world—those who help and those who hinder, those who lift and those who lean, those who contribute and those who only consume. How much better it is to give than to receive. Service in any form is comely and beautiful. To give encouragement, to impart sympathy, to show interest, to banish fear, to build self-confidence and awaken hope in the hearts of others, in short—to love them and to show it—is to render the most precious service.

Authentic partnering as a leader goes beyond establishing a successful business transaction or an alliance. It involves bringing our whole person into the business relationship to catalyze long-term, sustainable value for all constituencies involved.

CHAPTER 26

HOW HIGH-IMPACT LEADERS USE THE POWER OF CONVERSATION TO BUILD PARTNERSHIPS

PHIL HARKINS

The difference between high-impact leaders and those who aren't is frequently found in the way that they communicate. We have learned that it's not only what leaders say and what they do, but also what they don't say and do that makes a difference in followership. If it's true that powerful communication advances leadership, then it's a fact that poor communications can get leaders into a lot of trouble. On the one hand, effective communications is an enabler that allows true partnerships to be formed and from this the greatness of leaders can emerge. On the other hand, "stepping into it" by saying the wrong thing at the wrong time can bring a leader down by eroding trust and thus destroying the partnership. This chapter is about the dos and don'ts of effective communication and how they can make and save partnerships for leaders.

MAYOR RUDOLPH GUILIANI

There is no better example of how a leader built partnerships through communication than the crisis of September 11, 2001, in New York City. Here, in the midst of devastation after an outrageous assault, a very good leader transformed himself into an heroic figure. How did he do it? Mayor Guiliani simply used the power of communication to form partnerships with every group with whom he interacted, including state agencies, the federal government, international relief organizations, private companies, and many others. By expressing hope and optimism, he crossed political barriers, formed strategic alliances and joint ventures, and built real partnerships to counterattack the atrocious terrorism immediately and to take committed action to rebuild the city of New York.

Rudy Guiliani's leadership earned him the distinction of "Person of the Year" from *Time* magazine, international fame, knighthood, and perhaps a ticket to any office that he chooses to run for in the United States. His powerful communication throughout the crisis, expressed with both confidence and humility, created a quiet sense of trust that set off a chain reaction of partnerships and overall renewal for New York City and the country. He did this skillfully and with grace. It was not just what he said, but how he said it that made the difference. In a real way, it was how he communicated in crisis that enabled him to create the necessary partnerships to get the job done. As one prominent network news journalist said, "Guiliani learned how to get what he needed by just clicking with people."[1]

What Mayor Guiliani was able to do contains the lessons and secrets of how high-impact leaders use language skillfully to get what they want by giving others what they need. He did this by using language to form partnerships and by following the very basic rules of powerful conversations. Think of what Mayor Guiliani did in forming the partnerships required to navigate through the waters of change necessitated by a quick response.

We went back and traced the conversations. We wanted to understand how this clicking process worked so other leaders can learn from this. Whether it was on CNN in an interview on *Larry King Live,* when he addressed the nation, or when he asked for help and support from the partnerships with relief organizations, we observed three very specific, clear communication patterns. Here is how they are understood and categorized:

➤He was absolutely honest at all times. He said what he was feeling and thinking and told the truth without holding anything back. There was no hidden dialogue.

➤He was very clear about what was needed and what he wanted from others. He also made it clear about what was possible and what wasn't. He didn't mix words. He "really" said what was so.

➤He was totally committed and made that explicitly clear. He also made it clear what commitment meant. There was no question about what the "Let's Go!" was all about.

The Tower of Power

We call this the Tower of Power (see Figure 26-1) in conversations. Notice that "click" is at the top. It's what leaders get when they communicate at their best. In his conversations, Guiliani entered into partnerships by expressing in a logical order, first, "what's up," then "so," then "what's possible," and then he defined the commitments to go forward. He avoided the swamp. He didn't whine about the problems in New York City or complain about the challenges. He said clearly, "We will get through this."

The Tower of Power presented here is a visual representation of how Rudolph Guiliani got partnerships to click by avoiding the swamp and progressing through conversations leading to trusting relationships.

There is so much to learn about what leaders do in crisis to build partnerships through communication. There is equally as much to

FIGURE 26-1: THE TOWER OF POWER

learn from how high-impact leaders communicate every day to build partnerships when there is no crisis. In this chapter, I point out also that the same three specific, clear patterns of communication that Guiliani used in the crisis (absolute candor, clarity, and commitment) apply to leaders in their communications each day. It is also pointed out that the single most destructive aspect of broken partnerships is a breakdown in communication. In fact, more often than not, our analysis shows that as partnerships begin to come apart, so do communications. When communications crumble, conversations are less candid, less clear, and commitments become murky. From this, the fundamental glue that holds partnerships together comes apart. One can hear in language that the trust is gone. For when dialogue decreases, candor, clarity, and commitment suffer in equal amounts. Ultimately, the observable behaviors resulting from breakdowns in communications include suspicion, innuendo, anger, and, if not stopped, other destructive actions that lead to the tearing apart of explicit and implicit agreements.

The work of leaders in forming partnerships is like a marriage. A marriage is a true partnership: each person is a partner and a leader in many ways. Good marriages have open communications. The converse is that bad marriages have closed communications. At the basis of a marriage is a relationship always built on trust. When marriage partners are in full swing, communications are without worry. Marriage partners in good times will often say about their communications, "I can tell my spouse anything. We don't have walls." When the partnership of marriage begins to break down, actions are misinterpreted, because the trust is diminished.

RELATIONSHIPS ARE BUILT ON TRUST

If the basic building block of partnerships is trust, then we must think about how trust works. Consider the following logic points:

➤All partnerships are based on relationships and relationships are built on trust.

➤Trust is a function of communication.

➤So often when partnerships break (and leaders become ineffective), it's because trust disintegrates, people disengage, and the relationship drifts or breaks apart.

Knowing this, leaders must then become masters of building trust through communications.

What Is Trust?

Trust is hard to define, and there are different levels of trust. However, all trust within partnerships is based on absolute candor. The best partnerships have authentic communications at their core. Candor is complemented by consistent clarity about the facts and promises. Most problems with trust in partnerships stem from what is not said or not done, based on what one member of the partnership believed to be the commitment. In the Say/Do Matrix, trust breakdowns are frequently found in the diagonals. (See Figure 26-2.)

There is much to learn from real case situations about how leaders don't form partnerships and how they get themselves into trouble because of breakdowns in trust. At the end of the day, high-impact leaders use candor, clarity, and commitment as powerful tools in their language to build trust. They value relationships by spending time investing in open conversations and always following the Say/Do Matrix. The following case is a good example of how a leader found himself successful yet not trusted and no longer elected to be the leader because he didn't focus on relationships in building partnerships.

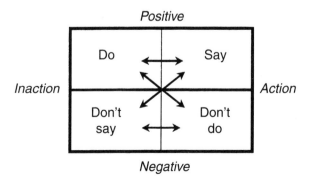

FIGURE 26-2: THE SAY/DO MATRIX

A CASE STUDY

He came to PJH from GE where he was known as a no-nonsense driver. If he could have built stronger relationships at GE, he could have gone to the top, so was his reputation.

Like the poem, when he was good, he was very, very good, and when he was bad, he was awful. That was Wayne at PJH.

He came to run a broken business at PJH. After a year, amazingly, the business had turned around as a result of his management and everyone was pleased. PJH was profitable again; products advanced and sales and marketing topped the industry. His team admired Wayne's success and the company boasted of Wayne's accomplishments.

When Wayne called for coaching help, he was dismayed. The corporation wanted him out by the end of the year. "I feel I deserve to leave when I want. I saved this billion dollar disaster." He felt let down and abandoned. The organization had the turnaround. It had been another pyric victory for Wayne. As he said, "The trust had eroded, relationships were tarnished, and the handwriting was on the wall for me." He was not self-deceptive; he wanted to change and he was asking for help. We investigated.

Background on Wayne's Case

Here's what we learned from interviewing those around Wayne, including his family.

➤Corporate didn't trust him.

➤His team believed in his leadership for the turnaround, but not in him.

➤His family had trouble with his style, too.

He had made it clear that no one was to talk to corporate without his okay. He filtered all information and bullied corporate when they wanted to form relationships with his subordinates. He didn't trust his team to speak to corporate and wanted all information going to corporate to go through him. Corporate felt "he must be hiding something."

Wayne could explode in a moment and his rage caused endless worry about being the next target. In addition, his expectations exceeded reality and no one was sure what it would be like to work for him under normal conditions. They also were afraid to speak to corporate and had told corporate counterparts that they were not allowed to pass on division information without Wayne's permission. This further disturbed corporate and isolated Wayne's team from the corporate team.

At home, his wife of 35 years felt he didn't share anything important with her. His grandchildren felt his impatience. His grown children felt that he was more interested in telling them things than listening to their needs.

Over his career, Wayne had never reached his potential of becoming the "corporate CEO," because he never could get past himself. His focus on results only, and not on relationships, made him "the turnaround guy." He wanted more. Yet, when it came down to running the business, he put the business first and relationships second. Partnerships were conditional, not really based on trust.

Counsel to Wayne

Wayne worked on the following to change his communications style and begin the process of helping him feel "click" and get more "click" going in relationship building.

Corporate

➤Build relationships with one important position in each of the staff functions. Change the stories about you, Wayne, so they see you as a leader–partner.

➤Spend time with people; develop relationships. Invest and demonstrate that you want to be trusted.

Team

➤Before triggers cause you to explode and someone becomes a victim, take those conversations off-line.

➤Always prepare your conversations before going into troublesome situations. Use the Tower of Power to help you prepare.

➤Encourage your team members to form relationships at corporate and not hold back information.

Home

➤Just stop and listen; don't respond with orders.

➤Sit and be there for them.

Wayne knew how to do all of this. He was a master salesman who had leveraged his enormous talents, but never realized his dream. He couldn't hold relationships and create true partnerships based on trust, because he didn't invest consistently. His conversations were not perceived to be candid, clear, or committed. He was winning battles, but at the end of the day there wasn't the "click."

TEN COMMUNICATION TIPS FOR LEADERS TO BUILD TRUSTING RELATIONSHIPS AND PARTNERSHIPS

Here's how to make sure that we can be more like Rudolph Guiliani than Wayne in our leadership . . . and get more "click."

Five Dos

1. Say things at the right time when others are ready to hear the message.

2. Say what's really up—what you are feeling and thinking in a positive way.

3. Build confidence by carefully sharing important information and taking others into your confidence.

4. Make sure you are clear and check back to ensure that there is a mutual understanding.

5. Probe and check into the message, so you really know what's been said.

Five Don'ts

1. Don't tell someone what he or she should be feeling to make your point.

2. Don't hold back important information so that you can win.

3. Don't let others become your mouthpiece in a discussion.

4. Don't say things or write things that you don't really want to see in print when triggers go off.

5. Don't ever, ever divulge a confidence to anyone.

Most importantly, remember that relationships build trust and will get you to "click." So, invest in powerful conversations by using the Tower of Power in your work and life, and "click" will be the reward.

CHAPTER 27

THE LEADER IN THE DIGITAL AGE

ELLIOTT MASIE

The leader in the digital age is smart about technology, is wired to the people who matter within the organization, and understands that business processes are far more important than hardware or software. The leader in the digital age reaches for the technology comfort of the teenager, the powerful and simple view of a senior citizen sending a birthday E-mail to a grandchild, and the care of a buyer spending precious dollars on a trendy item just on the market. The leader in the digital age uses technology to empower relationships and leadership, while using relationships and leadership to appropriately drive technology spending and use within organizations.

THE LEADER'S TECHNOLOGY

I recently sat in an airport club next to a young CEO of one of the still hopeful dot-coms. He had two cell phones, a paper, a Blackberry messenger system, a laptop, and an incredible expression of stress and distraction on his face. Since there were two hours until my flight, it was a perfect opportunity to do some investigation and even some coaching. I asked him a simple question: "How do you use your technology as a leadership tool within your organization?" His answers were revealing in that they contained a flurry of business terms, such as "It speeds my time to market," "It allows me to be continually fac-

[274]

ing our customer." "It moves us to a 24/7 workday." "It gives me the opportunity to work with people anywhere and anyplace." So, I asked him the question again, "How do *you* use your technology as a *leadership tool?*" His answer, "I can stay on top of all the details in my organization, keeping my staff on their toes and myself in the loop continuously." So, I asked the question one more time in a different way, "What style of a leader does your use of technology create?" He put down his cell phone, closed his laptop, and said, "I guess I tend to do more micro-managing then leading with all of this stuff, but that is what my investors want of me."

The next two hours of our dialogue led us into a fascinating conversation about how he spent almost no time reflecting, trusting, or deeply communicating with folks on his staff. His day was spent with an endless set of quick and detail-focused interactions. And, although there was all this "sharing," there was very little true collaboration and almost no talent development going on within his organization.

I am as worried about the CEO of a major life insurance company, who I worked with last month. He proudly said that he still didn't get his own E-mail and that his secretary had a keyboard that would drive the monitor of his desk when he needed to use the Internet or intranet. Both of these extremes worry me, as they are not positively harvesting the gifts of technology. If each of these leaders were to take a few hours to structure a personal approach to the use of technology, he or she would benefit greatly from both a personal and organizational perspective.

It's All About Business and Process!

The challenge is to think about technology from the business and process perspective. Technology is valuable to the organization only to the extent that it changes a human behavior or business process—that results in an added dollar of revenue, a reduced dollar of expense, or an added level of service. My technology closets (at work and at home) are filled with gadgets that were cool and sexy (so I bought them), but I found that they didn't add any value to my business or myself. Likewise, many leaders within organizations approve massive technology investments without really forcing the business and process issues.

If you were asked me to spend $200,000 for a new customer-relationship, management-software package, you should ask to see three things clearly proven:

1. The technology would have to result in *changed behaviors* in our organization. Unless our sales and support staff changed the way they related to customers as a result of this software, it should not get a leader's approval.

2. The technology would result in a payback to the organization, through added revenue or decreased expense, within 18 months. There may be other intermediate indicators, but the key is to push your IT departments to see technology as a short-term return, rather than a long-term investment. Why? It reflects the truer half-life of new systems, and it also deeply constrains "mission creep."

3. The technology purchase decisions should always include a conversation about alternatives to the same end. I may find that spending a smaller amount on training for the current users of an older system may result in greater productivity. We need to do both behavioral and alternative due diligence when driving technology expenditures.

Leaders in the digital age tackle technology investments smartly! They do not see investments as a given, but rather as a strategic intervention to change behaviors and process. As a leader, you don't need to know the technology details, because that is not the level of decision you are making. You do need to provide leadership to the organization to bring technology investments (and usage) in line with the behaviors that would drive the outcomes.

Why We Didn't Get a Plant!

We recently purchased a new house. We informed several companies that provide us with services and products of our new address. Not one of them sent us a "Welcome to Your New House" plant! Think about it. Why wasn't the customer database used to highlight an important life event for a key customer and to leverage it for a moment of marketing and client intimacy? Because the IT manager didn't get evaluated on how well the database drew the organization closer to the customer. The manager's job was done when the system was up and working. However, a leader in the digital age defines "working" as a business result, rather than a new system on the screen.

Behavioral Due Diligence

Make sure your technology works with real people! A large number of high-tech ventures have spent tens of millions of dollars on new systems and never tested them with real people. The number of dot-coms that tested the formulas only in their spreadsheets, without ever testing the concept with real customers, is frightening, if not unethical. Sure, the idea of 29 percent of the population of a state buying 42 percent of their groceries online every week makes for an incredible business plan. But, have we actually asked 50 real people if they are willing to buy bananas online? When you buy the banana and it has spots, you are comfortable with them. However, when you buy them online and there are three more spots than you like, you want the van to pick them up and take them back.

Create a requirement to test any new technology against the behavioral characteristics of real people, either your workforce or your customers. While some behaviors will take time to evolve, you will get a great set of data if you just watch how real people use the systems. Set up a small usability lab in your own conference room and have the IT department bring a few real people in to work with the new technology. Watch them and ask real questions. I know of several CEOs who have started to use their extended families as test panels for new technologies being adopted in their organization. As a leader in the digital age, you have the responsibility to drive the behavioral due diligence of your organization.

Absorbency Rate of Technology and People

We are not elastic when it comes to the human or organizational ability to absorb new technology, processes, or behaviors. The leader in the digital age is acutely aware of the rate at which we drop new technology into our organizations. We tend to underspend on both training and practice time. Techies and IT professionals forget that most people aren't nerds and aren't excited about changes to their screens. Just because we build it, doesn't mean they will come! My colleague Daryl Conner spends his professional life talking about the "nimbleness" of organizations and leaders. He would argue that you have to look at the absorbency rate of a group of people or organizations when making assumptions about their ability to leverage new technology. Keep asking those questions and become an advocate for viewing technology change as organizational change.

DIGITAL BALANCE FOR PROCESSES

The leader should be a walking example of digital balance. He or she is continually looking at leveraging the best of technology with the best of a business process. He or she is continually pushing the organization to find the right blend of technology and human involvement in key business processes. Ask questions such as, "As we drive more and more transactions to the Web, what can we do to touch our customers appropriately?" or "Is there a way we can follow up a new hire interview with an online preorientation to give the applicant a better sense of our energy as a company?" Digital balance is also found in how we do our work! Walk away from the computer screen and keyboard when talking with a colleague, and find places to shut off digital interruption, just as you might find time to answer E-mails without the phone ringing. The leader in the digital age knows how critical and difficult finding balance is and supports the experimentation to get there!

Suggestions for the Digital Leader

We suggest a number of processes that you consider as a leader in the digital age. I'll suggest ways that others and myself have been strategically deploying these technologies:

1. *Instant messenger for core group:* I have 20 people who are on a personal, executive version of Instant Messenger with me. These are a

combination of colleagues, staff, and mentors with whom I want to stay in quite close contact. We have given each other permission to be on each other's "buddy lists," and we use IM from Microsoft. Throughout the day, I have small, targeted dialogues with these folks. Sometimes, it is a friendly hello when I see them log on. Other times, I get a note to read an article in the *Wall Street Journal.* Other times, an instant message asks if it is a good time to talk on the phone or set up a lunch. I can create a deeply intentional circle of resources that help me with my life and work throughout the day.

2. *e-Coaching:* My colleague and coauthor, Marshall Goldsmith, and I have been exploring the world of e-coaching. Basically, think of a business coach who primarily deals with you digitally. I have been experimenting with three different coaches, on diverse topics, who are helping me with key issues that I want to work on as a leader. When I get E-mail from them or set up an online chat, I find myself efficiently focused on the goal that I am seeking. For example, right now I am working on a new venture for our company, and I have a development advisor who is coaching me via Instant Messenger. We have about two contacts every three days, for less than a few minutes each, but the assistance and "tough love" that I am getting is incredible and would not be equal to a series of consulting visits from an expert.

3. *Studio in your office:* There is a small closet, right in my office, which was constructed as a digital broadcast studio. I can walk three feet from my desk, turn on studio lighting, have any background chomakeyed (just like the TV weatherman), and immediately broadcast a video and audio segment. I can use this studio for Internet or ISDN video conferencing; I can send a video segment as a part of an E-mail for a more delicate or complex answer. I even keep a video diary of key events as I am working on a tough project, for review and introspection later. The studio costs less than $15,000 and is a way for a leader to be ready to communicate digitally with employees, customers, or others at a minute's notice.

4. *Digital scouts:* Go out and find yourself some technology scouts that you trust. These are people who will give you multiple perspectives on new and emerging technologies. Reach into your organizations for some employees at every point in the age continuum. Develop a scout in the IT and lines of business who will give you cutting-edge ideas on how to leverage technology and processes. Draft your child or grandchild as well as your parents. Consider hiring a journalist for a few hours, rather than a consultant, to get IT advice. The journalist will not have an invested interest in selling you anything, and you will get some better advice for a cheaper price. And, build a support group of peers from your fields.

5. *Develop skunk works:* Find a place in your organization to try some out-of-the-box concepts of using technology and business processes. Try things prior to large-scale investments. Occasionally, ask the skunk works folks to try using a nontechnology approach and see how it works. Develop the ability to do your own experimentation in the organization to see how technology will really add or subtract from your organizational capabilities.

A FINAL THOUGHT

I will repeat the first paragraph of this chapter. The leader in the digital age is smart about technology, is wired to the people that matter within the organization, and understands that business processes are far more important than hardware or software. The leader in the digital age reaches for the technology comfort of the teenager, the powerful and simple view of a senior citizen sending a birthday E-mail to a grandchild, and the care of a buyer spending precious dollars on a trendy item just on the market. The leader in the digital age uses technology to empower relationships and leadership, while using relationships and leadership to appropriately drive technology spending and use within organizations.

Go out there and lead your company to use technology wisely. I would love to hear your comments and discoveries along the way. Send me a note to emasie@masie.com.

CHAPTER 28

LEGACY CONSCIOUSNESS:
AN ESSENTIAL LEADERSHIP ROLE

BEVERLY KAYE AND BETSY JACOBSON

A classic conundrum asks, "If a tree falls in a forest and nobody is there to hear it, does it make a sound?" Consider the question in an organizational context: If a leader walks out of the office each night, each year, and at the end of a brilliant career, compiling a record of heroic successes, yet leaves no long-term impact on others, did leadership occur?

As the question implies, legacy is a crucial component of leadership. The legacy of a leader is established by leaving something of enduring quality to the organization and its people. Effective leadership occurs when the leader strengthens others' capacity to learn, to reflect, and to make meaning from their learning.

It's not up to the CEO or top management alone to create legacy; everyone has this opportunity based on his or her own experiences and insights. However, to do so requires a new consciousness, a *legacy consciousness*. We want to reframe the notion of legacy as being something that is passed on not only at the end of a career, but that it is passed along throughout a career. Consider these legacy-leaving activities that already take place in organizations:

➤You leave a workflow journal behind when you take a new job.

➤You instill the importance of process improvement in your employees, and when one of them is asked to head a project team, you see them using process improvement tools in the project team's startup.

➤You visit another facility to consult to them, and later find they have adopted your suggested changes.

Occasionally, an individual's contributions "stick" as inventions or innovations that revolutionize operations for years to come. These contributions are legacy-worthy. However, more often a person's contributions are incremental improvements, or an uncommon but effective way of getting things done. From our point of view, these are legacy-worthy as well.

The contention of this chapter is: An organization can capture the valuable experiences and intellectual capital of its high-performing talent for sustained excellence in future years if the organization encourages the long-term, ongoing building, living, and leaving of legacies. An individual's legacy is one's ability to build new ways of thinking and learning in others. This in turn improves the ways daily business is conducted, so that new levels of organizational and individual maturity can be achieved.

LEGACY DEFINED

The legal definition of legacy is not far from our organizational definition. In the laws of wills and trusts, a *legacy* is seen as a bequest, something of value handed down to someone else. In popular use, the term *legacy* usually refers to achievements or actions by which someone will be remembered after they are gone.

We would say legacies are built over time and have a living quality. In other words, your legacy grows and changes as you do. Legacy is a person's contribution, their value-add. Legacies do not automatically result just because something tangible comes into the possession of someone else. Unlike an heirloom, a legacy in our sense must be digested and absorbed by someone else before it can be said to have been "passed on."

Our definition of *legacy* can be stated as follows:

Legacy is the valuable contribution of enhanced thinking and capacity for learning that an individual transfers to others, so that it is available into the organization's future.

Building legacy and living it is crucial to leadership. It is learning in action, and it occurs at all levels of the corporate hierarchy. It is meaning culled from reflection and from interaction with others.

The popular usage of legacy leads most of us to overemphasize the leaving aspects of legacy and to underemphasize the building and living aspects. Each of us has the opportunity to build and live our legacy at any stage of our career.

We see an analogy in the tradition of the elders of certain Native American tribes of the Northwest Pacific Coast who gather for a Potlatch Ceremony. During that celebration, tribal leaders create living legacies by giving away material possessions. The community assesses each elder's value by how much they give away. This is the measure of their wealth. The practice of giving something away is a key part of the ceremony, but the giving takes place while the elder is living.

In the Native American tradition, elders give away physical items. To our organizations we can give knowledge, experience, and information. This is our "mental wealth," and it is best given while we are present to explain, interpret, and instill it in others.

LEGACY: PASSING WISDOM ON

What exactly is it that gets passed along in someone's legacy? We believe it is the sum of knowledge, experience, reflection, and understanding turned into action, along with the ability to create new meaning from one's own actions and the actions of others. Even though many people use their knowledge and can draw on past experience, far fewer can truly reflect upon their actions and translate them into new understandings, new assumptions, or new beliefs. The ability to do this is a kind of wisdom that needs sharing.

For example, in a mentoring program that we conducted, a senior manager spoke at an educational forum that was part of the program. His message was about the importance of having personal boundaries and the ability to say "No" in the face of organizational pressure. He supported his message with his own personal stories and track record. When participants challenged him about the consequences of saying "No," his response was, "Of course there are consequences. Consequences, however, don't signal failure and don't negate the importance of taking the right stand." He was a role model for this message in the organization.

We saw another example in a biotech company in the Silicon Valley. One of the engineers had a reputation for poor interpersonal skills, and, by his own admission, he was a man of few words. He had quite an unorthodox way of running tests, but the results he achieved were consistent and accurate. He had intuition and insight that might never have been captured had he not been given a young college intern who studiously learned his methods. Through her, his unique way of working became common practice in the lab. Despite his lack of effectiveness as a communicator, he was able to leave his legacy when someone else saw he had something to offer to the organization.

Often in our own practice, the question is asked, "How did you know that?" or "Why did you make that intervention then?" The answer comes out of our experience, in which we have integrated theory and practice. As different from the Silicon Valley engineer as we like to think we are, we've reflected on on our experience and made our particular meaning from it. What we give our clients could probably be found in part through a variety of textbooks, but how and why we do what we do is our unique twist. It is our meaning grown out of many books, programs, failures, ideas that came before us, and our own "spin on things." Our legacy is our capacity to articulate this spin and transfer it to our clients, protégés, and colleagues.

LEARNING LOST NEEDLESSLY

When a difficult problem is addressed by an organization, it generates valuable learning. This happens regularly in business, but only rarely, and then generally by accident or anecdote, do leaders and managers cull this learning, talk about it, and perhaps pass it on to others. In most organizations, there is little or no commitment to establishing an awareness of "how-we-did-what-we-did" or "why-it-didn't-work" before the arrival of another important thing to do.

When such learning is lost, managers cannot use it to more effectively address future issues and/or to help develop leaders who will have the benefit of this experience in the future. In other words, learning opportunities that are bypassed translate readily into risks and costs in the form of the following:

➤Failure to leverage intellectual capital for future gains

➤The chance to recreate past problems

➤An inability to build capacity and bench-strength through the ranks of the organization

It doesn't have to be this way. Organizations can capture the experiences and insights of their employees. Even though a great deal of what we call legacy is embodied in the singular spin and style individuals have, their own personal brand on the way they do things, the organization can absorb this as part of its repertoire.

ACTIVATING INTELLECTUAL CAPITAL

When individuals build and leave legacies, the most obvious payoff is for the organization. Building and living legacy activates the store of individual talent that exists within every corporation in a very practical way, and the corporate world is beginning to appreciate the value of this intangible asset.

In his book *Intellectual Capital,* Thomas Stewart notes that American business now depends more on the intellectual assets of employees and less on fixed assets and tangible resources, ushering in an age of intellectual capital in which the most crucial tasks are human tasks.[1] These tasks draw on past experiences and call for interacting about previous successes and failures.

Having people reflect and discuss things together is essential for building current depth and assuring future intellectual assets. As one CIO put it, "I can't prevent turnover, but that doesn't mean we don't feel the impact of people constantly walking out the door. I used to worry that one day I would wake up and the last person with the answers would be gone. Then it dawned on me: I don't need to retain that *person;* I need to capture those *answers.*"

We tend to overlook the important brain trust on which our organizations have become dependant. The organization that does not begin to cull and disseminate its intellectual capital will miss out on an important and valuable opportunity to capture legacy.

INDIVIDUAL BENEFITS

Beyond the organization's needs, there are enormous personal benefits to be gained by those who build and leave legacies. In itself, the act of building the asset of wisdom is challenging and gratifying. The act of disseminating it in a way that builds a legacy for the next generation rewards us with a perception of self-worth (much like the tribal elders discussed earlier in this chapter).

When we have our own reasons for feeling needed (an intrinsic motivation), our sense of purpose changes. We are no longer working simply for the paycheck, but because we have something to offer others. This is a valuable reframing. Our work becomes a part of the legacy we have to give in our lives, literally part of our purpose in life. Perhaps this is why it is that so many millionaires continue working.

In building a legacy, we are focusing on our own passion, helping to define ourselves, "double-clicking" on what is most important to us, and expressing it. Building and living our legacies enables and empowers others around us, as well as ourselves.

A LEGACY FOR EVERYONE

Again, legacy is not the sole province of those the organization recognizes as senior or high-ranking. Leadership is a way of acting, not a position or title. Leadership, and legacy, is for everyone who wants to make an impact beyond the execution of their assigned tasks.

Are you setting direction or pace? Can you reflect on events and, perhaps with others, make sense out of what has happened, and does that help you tackle the next round of events? Are you interested in what you know? Are you grooming others around you in your way of thinking, the meanings you take away, your style? Have you become a storyteller in your organization?

Legacy comes out of an individual's experience and perspective, even if the track record is not a brilliant one. Becoming aware of what you have to give away, and learning to articulate it, will make your legacy valuable. After all, learning from failure has tremendous value too. A young entrepreneur whom we know hired a technology officer for his Internet startup company. The man he hired was a Romanian refugee whose experience was vast in the design and development of e-learning products on the Internet. There was no question that his new employer valued the man for his technology experience. However, his experience also included several failed companies of his own. When this technology officer wanted to draw on his experiences to offer advice on how to market and position the business, his advice was refused.

His experience was discounted because the founders felt he had a poor track record as a businessman. Yet, we would argue that his business acumen growing out of these failures in such a volatile market is a useful part of his value-add. For example, he could head off a misguided strategy in which the founders of his new company proposed to give its product away for free, in an ill-considered imitation of certain well known pioneers, because he could see they had no profit-making follow-on product or service to sell. Unfortunately, his advice is still being overlooked.

Building legacy and sharing it with others requires continuous learning by an individual and continuous transfer of that learning to others. In fact, for a growing percentage of the workforce, who may stay in any one organization for a couple of years at most before moving on or whose career is made up of a series of short-term contracts, legacy is on the short list of "To Do" items. Knowing what your legacy is and bringing it to the organization may be your most important value-added accomplishment.

Legacy is a valuable gift to the organization of leadership sustained, but it is possible only when individuals are aware of the precious and powerful legacies they have to offer. Those in the field of knowledge management have pointed out that knowledge has an unusual property among assets: when you give it away, you don't diminish your own reserve. Legacy, it could be argued, has an even more unusual character in that giving it away actually increases the individual's supply.

CHAPTER 29

CONNECTING WHO WE ARE
WITH WHAT WE DO

RICHARD J. LEIDER

Inside each of us right now is a call waiting to be answered. It has been with us throughout our lives. The call was placed the moment we were born; it has been ringing in the background every day we have lived.

Taking that call, hearing and heeding our calling, is not the easiest path through life, but it is a path filled with fulfillment. It is a path of fulfillment quite different from the traditional conception of jobs and careers with which most of us grew up. If we are going to find meaning in our work, we will do so by approaching our work as a calling. And, if we feel no meaning, it's clear that we have yet to make that approach.

Many people discover a sense of calling in fairly dramatic ways: through sensing an inner voice, in a vision, from a dream, as a result of a near-death experience, or in meditative insight. For others, the call comes more subtly: through an inner knowing, a sense of inner wisdom, or by a process of elimination through the turns and dead-ends of life. In some instances, a teacher's influence is central; sometimes it's a book, a friend, or the example of others. Many people report gaining insight about their calling through spiritual revelation or while traveling to new places. In many instances, our calling comes once we are removed from our everyday routine, when we have the opportunity to listen to what authentically moves us inside.

All callings are, ultimately, spiritual in nature. Each one of us has unique potential—distinct gifts—with which to serve the world. These gifts provide us with a source of identity in the world, but until we connect who we are with what we do, that source remains untapped.

Some people are lucky enough to hear their calling easily and to find work that allows them to express it fully. But what about the rest of us, who listen for our calling but don't hear a thing? Or hear conflicting things? What if I'm in a job that pays well, but brings me little joy? Or a job that pays poorly and provides a sense of fulfillment? What good is a calling if I'm trapped in a dead-end job? What if I'm out of work?

I write an online column in the career center section of *Fast Company* magazine's website (www.fastcompany.com). The following letter is typical of mail I receive on a daily basis.

Dear Richard:
I just got through reading your column and for the first time in my life, I understand what I have been feeling. You actually put it into words, "the music inside of us." What I didn't realize is that most all of us feel that way. I am a baby boomer and at a crossroads in my life. I am looking for a job. Not just a job really, but something I can give my talents to, give my life to, give my 60 percent to. I am searching the Net for that new life. Is it reasonable to assume that I might find what I want? Do some people actually find that music? Can I? Thank you for your inspiration.
Best regards,
Searcher

All of us go through periods of time when our work feels dead and lifeless. All of us have dreamed of winning the lottery and never having to work again. Similarly, most of us have also had some opportunities to feel the joys that follow from doing work that is an expression of our deepest nature. Yet, when it comes to heeding our calling, most of us have the cards stacked against us. Naming our calling, and more importantly, getting paid for living it, seems as unlikely as winning the lottery.

Nevertheless, there are ways to bring your calling to your work. The challenge is to find or create aspects of your work that express your calling, even if the work as a whole leaves something to be desired.

Discovering our calling doesn't mean that we should immediately quit our day jobs. It does, however, require us to work the process of *connecting who we are with what we do.*

Ultimately, the realization of our calling can occur anywhere. No special circumstances are necessary; what matters is a willingness to recognize the call when it occurs, even if our intuition seems to be guiding us in an unexpected direction.

Heeding our life's calling means thriving, not just surviving. It means that we refuse to accept less than full employment of our talents. It means not settling for a relationship with our work that lacks passion.

It means asking, "What are my gifts? What was I born to do?"

The moment we start asking these questions and exerting the energy to answer them, we make a commitment to the expression of our birthright gifts. We begin to clarify our calling when we sincerely ask:

➤What gift do I naturally give to others?

➤What gift do I most enjoy giving to others?

➤What gift, when freely given, causes me to whistle while I work?

A calling is not something you do to impress other people or to get rich quick. It's a labor of love that is intrinsically satisfying. It's something you would happily, do even if it never makes you rich or famous. Of course, there's nothing wrong with making money or being widely acclaimed; however, we should also recognize that there are other ways to pursue a calling, such as helping others, learning, promoting change, or dedicating oneself to an art form.

Any kind of work can provide us with opportunities to express our calling. Our calling isn't our job; it's what we bring to our job. The core idea of a calling is a simple and liberating truth: "It's not what you do that matters; it's how you do it."

To understand your calling more fully, it's helpful to ask yourself the following questions. First, "What do you do?" In other words, what kind of work are you currently performing? How consistent is it with your calling? Should you stay or leave your current job? Next, "How do you do it?" Ask yourself, what part of your job fulfills your sense of calling? How can you give away your gifts even if you're in a job that isn't exactly what you want to be doing? How can you express your calling, even if it's only partially?

Elements of our calling can be expressed in almost any job. When we begin to see what we do as an opportunity for heeding our calling, nothing changes, yet everything changes. We still have our organization to lead, our patients to care for, and our clients to serve. We still have our up days and down days, empowering colleagues and irritating colleagues, and our interesting and boring projects. We still have days when it's hard to get out of bed in the morning; nothing seems to have changed.

On the other hand, everything has changed. By expressing our calling, even in small, partial ways, our work is suddenly more fulfilling. We find meaning in what we do, even when it's not exactly what we were meant to be doing. On occasion, throughout the workday, we feel that we're in the right place, with the right people, doing the right work, on purpose.

When this happens, even for an instant, we experience who we are and what we do as one. We experience the power of heeding our calling. We experience the feeling of aliveness that comes from giving our gifts away to someone who needs them, to create something that wouldn't have existed without us. It's the feeling of whistling while we work!

CHAPTER 30

THE HIGH SELF-ESTEEM LEADER

NATHANIEL BRANDEN

The primary function of a leader in a business enterprise is to persuasively convey a vision of what the organization is to accomplish, and to inspire and empower all those who work for the organization to make an optimal contribution to the fulfillment of that vision and to experience in doing so that they are acting in alignment with their self-interest.

Thus a leader must be a thinker, an inspirer, and a persuader.

The higher the self-esteem of the leader, the more likely it is that she or he can perform this function successfully. A mind that distrusts itself cannot inspire the best in the minds of others. A person who feels undeserving of achievement and success is unlikely to ignite high aspirations in others. Nor can leaders draw forth the best in others if their primary need, arising from their insecurities, is to prove themselves right and others wrong, in which case their relationship to others is not inspirational, but adversarial. Under such conditions, partnership is impossible.

A LEADER'S EGO

It is a fallacy to say that a great leader should be egoless. A leader needs an ego sufficiently healthy that it does not perceive itself as on trial in every encounter—is not operating out of anxiety and defensiveness—so that the leader is free to be task- and results-oriented, not oriented toward self-aggrandizement or self-protection.

A healthy ego asks, "What needs to be done?" An insecure ego asks, "How do I avoid looking bad?"

Which leads us to the subject of self-esteem and its importance to lead and to build partnerships effectively.

Self-Esteem

Self-esteem is the disposition to experience yourself as competent to cope with the basic challenges of life and as being worthy of happiness. It is made of two components: self-efficacy and self-respect. *Self-efficacy* is confidence in the efficacy of your mind, in your ability to think; by extension, it is confidence in your ability to learn, to make choices and decisions, and to respond effectively to change. *Self-respect* is the experience that success, achievement, fulfillment—in a word, *happiness*—are right and natural for you. The survival value of such confidence is obvious. So is the danger when it is missing.

To face life with (reality-based) assurance rather than anxiety and self-doubt is to enjoy an inestimable advantage: your judgments and actions are less likely to be distorted and misguided. A tendency to make irrational decisions, as well as fear of making decisions, are both observable consequences of intellectual self-distrust.

To face human relationships and to build partnerships with a benevolent, nonarrogant sense of your own value is, again, to enjoy an important advantage: self-respect tends to inspire respect from others. A tendency to form destructive relationships—and to experience the suffering they occasion as your destiny—are familiar effects of feeling unlovable and without value.

The level of your self-esteem has profound consequences for every aspect of your existence: how you operate in the workplace, how you partner with people, how high you are likely to rise, how much you are likely to achieve—and, in the personal realm, with whom you are likely to fall in love; how you interact with your spouse, children, and friends; and what level of personal happiness you attain.

Healthy self-esteem correlates with rationality, realism, intuitiveness, creativity, independence, flexibility, and ability to manage change, willingness to admit and correct mistakes, benevolence, and cooperativeness. Poor self-esteem correlates with the opposite traits.

Over four decades of study have led me to identify six practices as the most essential to cultivating or strengthening self-esteem. They may be summarized as follows:

➤ *The practice of living consciously:* Respect for facts; being present to what you are doing while you are doing it (e.g., if your customer, supervisor, employer, employee, supplier, or colleague is talking to you, being present to the encounter); seeking and being equally open to any information, knowledge, or feedback that bears on your interests, values, goals, and projects; seeking to understand the world not only external to self, but also your inner world as well, so that you do not act out of self-blindness. Effective leaders operate at a high level of self-awareness.

➤ *The practice of self-acceptance:* The willingness to own, experience, and take responsibility for your thoughts, feelings, and actions, without evasion, denial, or disowning—and also without self-repudiation; giving yourself permission to think your thoughts, experience your emotions, and look at your actions without necessarily liking, endorsing, or condoning them. If you are self-accepting, you do not experience yourself as always on trial, and what this leads to is nondefensiveness and willingness to hear critical feedback without becoming hostile or adversarial—a trait essential to an effective leader.

➤ *The practice of self-responsibility:* Realizing that we are the authors of our choices and actions; that each one of us is responsible for our own life and well-being and for the attainment of our goals; that if we need the cooperation of other people to achieve our goals, we must offer a value in exchange; and that the question is not, "Who is to blame?" but always, "What needs to be done?" Can anyone be a powerful leader who does not operate at a high level of self-responsibility?

➤ *The practice of self-assertiveness:* Being authentic in your dealings with others. Treating your values and person with decent respect in social contexts; refusing to fake the reality of who you are or what you esteem to avoid someone's disapproval; being willing to stand up for yourself and your ideas in appropriate ways in appropriate circumstances. An effective leader who is afraid of self-assertiveness is a contradiction in terms.

➤*The practice of living purposefully:* Identifying your short-term and long-term goals or purposes and the actions needed to obtain them; organizing behavior in the service of those goals; monitoring actions to be sure you stay on track—and paying attention to outcomes so as to recognize if and when you need to go back to the drawing board. It is impossible to imagine an effective leader who does not operate purposefully, and a leader who does not pay attention to outcome leads his or her organization to catastrophe.

➤ *The practice of personal integrity:* Living with congruence between what you know, what you profess, and what you do. Telling the truth, honoring commitments, exemplifying in action the values you profess to admire; dealing with others fairly and benevolently. A leader who cannot inspire trust cannot lead effectively, and a leader who does not exhibit integrity cannot inspire trust.

A young, newly appointed CEO once hired me to coach him in becoming a better leader. He wanted to know, "Is there a way to work on being a good leader?" I answered that one of the best ways was by working on one's development as a human being—and, in particular, by working on one's self-esteem, by applying the six pillars to the sphere of work and work relationships/partnerships.

For example, to be effective, a leader must be well aligned with reality—open and available to all facts, knowledge, information, data, feedback that bear on the success of the mission of the organization. Openness to facts, pleasant or unpleasant, goes to the heart of what it means to live consciously—and the practice of living consciously is both the source of self-esteem and an expression of self-esteem.

In the past two or three decades, we have seen many examples of once great companies shrink into anemic versions of their former selves, disappear into mergers, or lose significant market share because their leaders refused to confront the fact that strategies that had once been successful were no longer adaptive to the new realities. They were ruled not by a respect for facts, but by their wishes and fears. Rather than respond to clearly apparent changes, they stayed lost in dreams of the good old days. Rather than help their staff to see more clearly, which is a leader's responsibility, they were co-conspirators in organizational blindness.

The first law of self-esteem and the first principle of effective leadership are the same: Thou shalt be aware. Dismissing pertinent realities in the name of short-term comfort is not an acceptable option.

In the professional realm or the personal, any time we choose to confront painful realties that we know need to be addressed—because they bear on our values, goals, and projects—two results follow. Our actions become more appropriate and we grow in self-esteem. We *feel* more effective because we *are* more effective.

Leadership begins with the leader possessing a vision, to which he or she is passionately committed, a specific and concrete agenda for actualizing that vision, and an unrelenting focus on results. After that, many factors contribute to success or failure. No factor, however, is more fundamental than the leader's degree of openness to reality, a respect for reality, and speed of appropriate response to reality.

Nothing is intrinsically irrational about the impulse to pull back from that which is frightening or painful. All of us have such impulses. If we have a well-developed sense of reality and the capacity for self-discipline, however, we recognize that there are circumstances in which it is dangerous to allow fear and pain to have the last word. Sometimes, we need to do things that scare us. Sometimes we need to look at things that are painful. If we don't, the consequences will be bad for us. Understanding this, we know that sometimes all we can do is draw a deep breath and proceed.

What kind of factors might obstruct the process of living consciously? Well, for instance:

➤Fear of our fallibility

➤Fear of taking on new challenges with no guarantee of success

➤Fear of facing truths about ourselves (our thoughts, feelings, or actions) we have been denying or disowning so as to protect our self-esteem or our pretense at it

➤Fear of facing truths about another person (a business partner, an associate, or a spouse) that, if acknowledged, might entail us to rock the boat of the relationship or even to destroy it

➤Fear of not knowing how to deal with realities one is acknowledging (very common both in business and in personal life)

➤Fear of losing face in the eyes of significant others if certain truths about one's self are brought out into the open, so that one conceals past mistakes rather than correcting them

➤Fear of self-responsibility; fear of being held accountable should one's judgment prove to be mistaken

This list is far from exhaustive. I have not mentioned plain laziness or inertia, for instance, or the blindness that can be summoned to obfuscate reluctance to give up power when that is clearly what the situation demands; however, I think that what I have listed is sufficient to make the point.

I do not mean to imply that if only we confront reality we will always know the right action to take. There are no guarantees. But we will increase the odds of discovering the right actions.

Trust

If integrity is one of the cardinal pillars of self-esteem, it is an equally essential pillar of effective leadership. The reason is the intimate relationship that exists between integrity and the ability to inspire trust and thus build partnerships. Studies of leadership—not only in business organizations, but also in the military—clearly show that whereas people can and will perform extraordinary feats for leaders whom they trust, their performance tends to be less impressive when that trust is lacking.

It is no mystery how trust is created. It is a matter of congruence between words and actions. To reduce this issue to its simplest fundamentals:

One tells the truth. One keeps promises. One honors commitments. One's behavior manifests one's professed values. One deals with people fairly and justly.

I once sat with a group of vice presidents at a major brokerage house who were complaining that there was a lack of trust in their organization and were wondering how to correct the situation. I asked them to write down the sentence stem *"If I want to be perceived as trustworthy—"* and then write six to ten endings. Then they all read their completed sentences aloud. There were no surprises and no significant differences of opinion, merely some differences of emphasis. Everyone knew what needed to be done. Here is the essence of what they came up with:

➤Tell the truth and make it safe for others to do so.

➤Keep promises.

➤Walk your talk.

➤Don't just preach "respect for each individual"—exemplify it in your behavior.

➤Manifest integrity and communicate that nothing less is acceptable.

➤Understand that meeting your numbers is not enough; you must also live your professed values (assuming those values include honesty and integrity).

➤Set an example.

➤Exemplify fairness and evenhandedness in all your dealings with people.

When it comes to setting an example, ultimate responsibility necessarily falls on the leader. Unfortunately, few company heads understand or appreciate the extent to which they are role models. They do not realize how closely their smallest moves are noted and absorbed by those around them, not necessarily consciously, and reflected via those they influence throughout the organization. If a leader is perceived to have integrity, a standard is set that others tend to feel drawn to follow. A leader who treats people with respect—associates, subordinates, customers, suppliers, and shareholders—sends a signal of incalculable power, a signal for which no speech or mission statement is a substitute. Conversely, a leader who feels no need to operate with integrity or to be fair and decent in dealings with others also sends a signal that cannot be neutralized by the expression of noble sentiments.

Trust is inspired by consistency and predictability. If we feel we do not know what a leader might do in any particular situation, we cannot feel trust. If someone is sometimes honest and sometimes not, sometimes fair and sometimes not, sometimes values-driven and sometimes not, we may still be able to appreciate that person's other assets—such as intelligence, energy, enthusiasm, creativity—but we will not feel trust. And when we do not trust, we rarely give our best.

At one company—one of the three largest in its industry—the CEO was greatly admired for his energy, innovativeness, and willingness to share power. He was also admired for his generosity. His generosity, however, was deeply impulsive and this created problems in the organization, including the undermining of trust. If he took a personal liking to some employee or was impressed by something the employee had done, he would often bestow an immense bonus that bore no relationship to the official reward system of the organization. Senior managers constantly had to deal with the problem of the CEO's behavior. The CEO was perceived as not walking the talk, not remaining consistent with the system of rewards that he (his organization) proclaimed. Because of his extraordinary generosity, he had difficulty understanding how people could feel his dealings lacked fairness— lacked integrity.

To say it once more: trust requires consistency and predictability.

Leadership needs more than an inspiring vision. It needs the passion and enthusiasm to translate that vision into real-world results. For this, it needs the passion and enthusiasm of other people. Leaders need to partner with others in the vision and its realization. They need to inspire commitment. They cannot do this if they cannot first inspire trust. They do not need to win love, but they do need to win respect—

and better still would be to win admiration. This is more likely to be achieved by leaders who have first earned their own esteem.

A great deal of business activity consists essentially of conversations—between representatives of different institutions, between CEOs and their executives, between managers and the people reporting to them, between salespersons and customers, between purchasing specialists and suppliers, between company negotiators and union representatives. All such conversations entail the understanding that people are accountable for what they say, including what they promise to do, and only to the extent that such understanding is honored is business activity possible.

If we understand this, we see that integrity, trust, and character are not peripheral to business but fundamental, which means that self-esteem is fundamental. Even though this truth is relevant at every level for the long-term success of an enterprise, nowhere does it more urgently need to be kept in constant focus than in the office of the CEO, whose job is to set the standards. CEOs may not usually think of themselves as moral teachers, exemplars, or inspirers—but they are and they should.

During the 1980s, while he was CEO of Chrysler, Lee Iacocca persuaded the union to make major financial concessions on the grounds that the company was caught in hard times. Then, Iacocca turned around and gave himself a gigantic bonus. What signal was he sending to Chrysler employees? Was it a signal to inspire higher levels of moral behavior or lower levels? Did Iacocca raise the level of trust or the level of cynicism? Predictably, the next time the union sat down at the bargaining table, its representatives were ruthlessly unrelenting in their demands and acceded not an inch; all spirit of cooperation was gone.

Apart from the general matter of integrity, one of the ways leaders generate trust is through the clarity of their communications. Do they articulate clearly not only the general vision, but also a concept of how that vision is to be actualized? Do they articulate clearly what they are asking for and requiring from their people—and the ethical and philosophical principles they expect to guide the work—and the nature of the culture they see as the necessary context for their achievements? For example, when Larry Bossidy became CEO of AlliedSignal, he helped design a personal-development program and put 86,000 employees through it. But also, during his first year, he personally spoke to 15,000 people, explaining his vision, helping them to understand markets and market conditions, lecturing, asking questions, arguing, debating, relentlessly pursuing a shared clarity of understanding concerning what AlliedSignal was to achieve. Over a period of six years, he helped increase the market value of his company by 400 percent. He understood that leaders are teachers and that their first obligation is to be clear.

Yet another way leaders inspire trust (and demonstrate integrity) is by the quality of the people with whom they surround themselves. A leader who seeks out the best, most innovative and independent minds to be found, minds who will not be afraid to disagree with the boss and will not be penalized for doing so—and who makes it abundantly clear that their contributions are welcome—sends a strong signal that will reverberate through the entire organization that the focus is not on "Who's right?" but on "What's right?" It is a signal summoning the best in everyone, and thus tends to attract those who have a decent level of self-esteem, which every organization needs, and also to spark the self-esteem that exists in almost all human beings. Here again, we encounter the strong reality-orientation of which I spoke earlier: not inappropriate self-aggrandizement, not turf-protection, not a battle of personalities, but rather a concern with "What's true?" "What needs to be done?" and "What best serves our mission and our values?" Reality, not rank, is given the last word. When a leader embodies this principle, we are witnessing not selflessness, self-abnegation, or "absence of ego," but self-esteem in action.

When this reality-orientation is perceived to be consistent and basic to an organization's culture—because a leader exemplifies it, teaches it, insists on it, rewards it (and punishes its opposite)—people feel safe, they feel honored, and they feel trust. And then they may astonish themselves and others with what they are able to accomplish.

Ability to Tolerate Aloneness

Someone observed that if Moses went up the mountain with a committee, he never would have come back. To be out in front sometimes means to be alone. A leader must understand and accept this responsibility.

Although full consensus is the ideal, it may not always be realizable, not even by a superb teacher or persuader. To invite everyone's feedback does not mean that everyone has equal authority regarding the final decision. As Max DePree, former chairman of Herman Miller, points out, "Participative management is not democratic. Having a say differs from having a vote." After all the respectful talking, listening, debating, and interacting are done, someone has to say, "This is what we are going to do." That is a leader's job.

The ability of leaders to do their job rests on at least two factors. The first, obviously, is trust in their own ability to think, choose, and make appropriate decisions. The second is their ability to manage any desires they may have to be liked or approved that obstruct the perception of what needs to be done or the will to do it.

The desire to be liked is not abnormal. Who would not prefer being liked to being disliked? Although it is true that for some people it is not a desire but an obsession. In any event, the challenge is to avoid being manipulated by that desire in ways that do not serve your long-term interests—for example, making the popular or easy choice rather than the right one.

No leader can be effective who has not learned to manage emotions—whether the emotions pertain to a hunger for popularity, inappropriate exhibitionistic impulses, and competitiveness with subordinates, defensiveness, anger, or fear and insecurity. Emotions need to be recognized, owned, experienced, and accepted (non-self-punitively)—but not acted on when to do so conflicts with more important agendas. A leader's job is to guide the organization to the fulfillment of its mission, and not to indulge in personal catharsis at the expense of this primary commitment. Emotional intelligence is intimately related to self-esteem.

The leader's job is to do what he or she honestly thinks is right for the organization. Sometimes this task will test self-esteem. But if, without repression, denial, or disowning, leaders learn to manage and rise above feelings and emotions that may stand in the way—if they place their firsthand judgment of the realities confronting them above all other considerations—they grow in personal stature and self-esteem, as they grow in professional effectiveness. Such a leader becomes a better person and a better executive at the same time through the same process.

Self-Awareness

The ability to operate in this manner, however, presupposes a reasonable level of self-awareness. You cannot successfully manage feelings of which you are ignorant or which you have denied and disowned. On the contrary, such repressed feelings tend to manage you.

Self-awareness (an aspect of living consciously) is one of the characteristics of effective leaders. Without it, they cannot manage themselves; unable to manage themselves, they cannot properly manage others. They will tend to lack the emotional intelligence that is the foundation of interpersonal competence. Without a commitment to self-examination, a leader operates at a severe disadvantage.

The willingness to look at yourself dispassionately, at your thoughts, feelings, and actions—moved by the desire not to judge or condemn but to be aware, learn, and understand—is both a process that strengthens self-esteem and also one that expresses self-esteem. Of course, the need to do so, and the advantage of doing so, is not confined to leaders.

Focusing only on your strengths and being blind to your weaknesses does not strengthen self-esteem. You need to be aware of both. No one is equally strong in all respects; if you know what your weaknesses are, you can learn to compensate for them—which is precisely what effective leaders do. Ineffective leaders do not see themselves realistically, do not recognize that they have any shortcomings, and therefore do not think their way through to solutions; they merely resort to denial, blaming, and alibiing.

Challenges of Leadership

It takes a significant measure of self-esteem to generate a vision that is rational, uplifting, and involves stepping into the unknown—and persuading others to follow one there. It takes a significant measure of self-esteem to embody and uphold a standard of integrity with such unswerving consistency (regardless of the latest crisis) that it becomes the trademark of an entire organization—thereby creating an internal culture of trust and mutual regard. It takes a significant measure of self-esteem to give away power, to welcome and embrace the talents of others, never to steal their responsibilities, and to be relentless in communicating one's belief in their potential. It takes a significant measure of self-esteem to see oneself—assets and limitations—realistically, and to think strategically about how to transcend shortcomings.

Rarely are such things done easily. They demand courage, energy, perseverance, and commitment.

ABOUT THE AUTHORS

LARRAINE SEGIL is former CEO of an aerospace distribution company, and she has also been president of businesses in mortgage finance and medical services. Segil currently teaches strategic alliances at Caltech (executive education). Considered a thought leader in alliances, she has written two best-selling books on the subject, *Intelligent Business Alliances* and *Fast Alliances*. Also an expert in strategic leadership, she published her book *Dynamic Leader, Adaptive Organization* in 2002.

Segil consults through The Lared Group in Los Angeles to such companies as Compaq, Praxair, Butler Manufacturing, Ericsson, and Verizon, and she speaks on alliances, global leadership, and strategic management worldwide to such organizations as The Royal Mail, Nokia, Sainsbury's, and Standard and Poor. Called "the real deal" by *Fast Company* magazine, Segil acts as an expert resource on alliances and mergers to *Business Week*, the *Los Angeles Times, Dallas Morning News, San Jose Mercury,* as well as to CEO, CFO, and CIO magazines. She is also a commentator on CNBC, CNN, and Yahoo FinanceVision. She's had her own column in *IndustryWeek* magazine, as well as in *IT Malaysia.* Her online interactive program on partnering and alliances is offered by Ninth House Network and PBS, and her video programs by Larraine Segil Productions are distributed worldwide. Contact: lsegil@lsegil.com; www.lsegil.com.

[305]

MARSHALL GOLDSMITH is widely recognized as one of the world's foremost authorities in helping leaders achieve positive, measurable change in behavior—for themselves, their people, and their teams. In 2000, *Forbes* listed Goldsmith as one of five top executive coaches and *Human Resources* rated Goldsmith as one of the world's leading HR consultants. He has also been ranked by the *Wall Street Journal* as one of the "Top 10" executive educators. His work has received national recognition from the Institute for Management Studies, the American Management Association, the American Society for Training and Development, and the Human Resource Planning Society.

Goldsmith is a managing partner of A4SL, the Alliance for Strategic Leadership, a consulting organization that includes more than 100 top professionals in the field of leadership development. He is also the co-founder of the Financial Times Knowledge Dialogue, a video-conference network that connects executives with the world's greatest thinkers. He has a Ph.D. from UCLA. He is on the faculty of the global executive education program for Dartmouth and Oxford (UK) Universities, and he is a partner in Duke Corporate Education's Personal Learning Systems. He is an emeritus member of the Board of the Peter Drucker Foundation.

Goldsmith's 12 recent books include *The Leader of the Future* (a *Business Week* "Top 15" best-seller), *Learning Journeys,* and *Coaching for Leadership.* His book *The Leadership Investment* won the American Library Association's *Choice* award as an "Outstanding Academic Business Book" of 2001. Amazon.com has ranked five of his books as the number-one best sellers in their field. Contact: Marshall@A4SL.com; www.A4SL.com.

JAMES BELASCO is an entrepreneur, best-selling author, and internationally known consultant. Belasco is currently executive director of the Financial Times Knowledge Dialogue, a joint venture that connects the world's leading consultants with global executives in a video conferencing network. He's also starting several other high-tech ventures. Previously, Belasco founded and led a highly successful specialty chemical company and software and services organization. He has written nine books, several of which were on business best-seller lists. They include *Flight of the Buffalo and Teaching the Elephant to Dance.* As a consultant, Belasco coaches executives in developing and implementing breakthrough strategies, creating new cultures and higher levels of performance. He currently coaches leaders of six of the *Fortune 20* companies. Contact: jim@knowledgedialogue.com; www.belasco.com.

———————————◄o►———————————

The Other Contributors

NANCY J. ADLER is a professor of international management at McGill University in Montreal, Canada. She consults and conducts research on global leadership, cross-cultural management, and women as global leaders and managers. She has authored more than 100 articles and produced the film *A Portable Life.* Her book *International Dimensions of Organizational Behavior* (fourth edit., 2002) has over a quarter million copies in print in multiple languages. Adler has also edited the books, *Women in Management Worldwide* and *Competitive Frontiers: Women Managers in a Global Economy.* Her latest book is *From Boston to Beijing: Managing with a Worldview.* In addition to her research and writing, Adler consults with major global companies and government organizations around the world. Contact: adler@management.mcgill.ca.

JOHN R. ALEXANDER is president of the Center for Creative Leadership. He came to the Center in 1990 after an 18-year, award-winning career as a journalist and newspaper editor. During his tenure as a journalist, he served as a correspondent for *Time* magazine in its New York and London bureaus and later as an editorial writer, book editor, and editorial page editor at leading North Carolina daily newspapers. Contact: www.ccl.org.

KEN BLANCHARD is a prominent author, speaker, and business consultant. Author of more than 20 books, Blanchard has had far-reaching impact. His phenomenal best-selling book, *The One Minute Manager,* coauthored with Spencer Johnson, has sold more than nine million copies worldwide and is still on best-seller lists. *The One Minute Manager* is regarded as one of the most successful business books of all time.

Blanchard has received several awards and honors for his contributions in the field of management, leadership, and speaking, including the Distinguished Contribution to Human Resource Development Award from ASTD.

He is chief spiritual officer of The Ken Blanchard Companies, which he and his wife, Dr. Marjorie Blanchard, founded in 1979 in San Diego, California. The Ken Blanchard Companies provides expertise in organizational change management through training programs and processes, seminars, and consulting. Contact: ken.blanchard@kenblanchard.com; www.kenblanchard.com.

NATHANIEL BRANDEN has a Ph.D. in psychology and a background in philosophy. A psychotherapist, corporate consultant, author, lecturer, he is a recognized authority on self-esteem, a field he pioneered four decades ago. He has published 20 books, and his writings have been translated into 18 languages. His books include *The Six Pillars of Self-Esteem, The Art of Living Consciously,* and *Self-Esteem at Work: How Confident People Make Powerful Companies.* Contact: n6666b@cs.com; www.nathanielbranden.net.

W. WARNER BURKE is professor of psychology and education and coordinator for the graduate programs in social–organizational psychology in the Department of Organization and Leadership at Teachers College, Columbia University in New York. He is also senior advisor to the organization and change strategy practice of Pricewaterhouse-Coopers LLP.

Burke has consulted with organizations in business-industry, education, government, religious, and medical systems. A Diplomat in I/O psychology, the American Board of Professional Psychology, he is also a Fellow of the Academy of Management, the American Psychological Society, and the Society of Industrial and Organizational Psychology, and past editor of both *Organizational Dynamics* and the *Academy of Management Executive.* He has authored more than 130 articles and book chapters in organizational psychology, organization change, and leadership, and authored, co-authored, or edited 14 books. His latest book is *Organization Change: Theory and Practice.*

The Right Honourable **KIM CAMPBELL**, P.C., Q.C., served as Canada's nineteenth and first female Prime Minister in 1993. She previously held cabinet portfolios as Minister of State for Indian Affairs and Northern Development, Minister of Justice and Attorney General, and Minister of National Defence and Veterans' Affairs. She was the first woman to hold the Justice and Defence portfolios, and the first woman to be Defence Minister of a NATO country. Campbell participated in major international meetings including the Commonwealth, NATO, the G-7 Summit, and the United Nations General Assembly.

Campbell recently completed a four-year term as Consul General of Canada in Los Angeles serving the states of California, Utah, Nevada, Arizona, Hawaii, and the Territory of Guam. She is a Visiting Professor of Practice at the John F. Kennedy School of Government, Harvard University, where she teaches graduate courses in Gender and Power and Democratic Transition and Consolidation. A long-standing champion of women's rights, Campbell is chair of the Council of Women World Leaders. She is the author of a political memoir, *Time and Chance.* Contact: kim_campbell@ksg.harvard.edu.

KEVIN CASHMAN is CEO of LeaderSource, an international executive coaching and leadership development consultancy based in Minneapolis. He has coached hundreds of senior executives and senior teams to enhance performance, and is the founder of the Executive to Leader Institute@ recognized by *Fast Company* as the "Mayo Clinic" of leadership development for its whole-person, interdisciplinary approach to executive coaching. Cashman is author of *Leadership from the Inside Out,* named one of the best-selling business books of the decade and the number-one best-selling business book of 2000 by CEO-READ. A believer in dynamic life balance, he has completed more than 50 triathlons and has taught meditation over three decades. His forthcoming book, *Awakening the Leader Within* (2003), is an interactive coaching experience that chronicles the transformational journey of a leader to a new way of leading and a new way of life.

STEPHAN A. FRIEDRICH is director of Cell Consulting, a German management-consulting firm. He is also head of Cell Executive

Academy and lecturer of strategic management at the University of Innsbruck, Austria. His research and consulting focuses included leadership, corporate strategy, and restructuring. Contact: stephan. friedrich@cell-consulting.com.

FARIBORZ GHADAR is the William A. Schreyer Chair of Global Management, Policies and Planning and director, Center for Global Business Studies at The Pennsylvania State University Smeal College of Business Administration. He specializes in global corporate strategy and implementation, international finance and banking, and global economic assessment. In particular, Ghadar is a leading authority on the impact of E-business on global firms. He has been a consultant to major corporations, governments, and government agencies and regularly conducts programs for executives of multinational corporations in the United States and abroad.

Ghadar is the author of 11 books and numerous articles, his most recent being the first chapter in *Pushing the Digital Frontier: Insights into the Changing Landscape of E-Business* and *The Dubious Logic of Global Megamergers,* which was the lead article in the July/August (2000) issue of *Harvard Business Review.* Contact: fghadar@psu.edu; www.smeal.psu. edu/cgbs/.

PHIL HARKINS is founder, president, and CEO of Linkage, Inc., an international organizational development learning company that offers educational programs, products, consulting, and coaching services. In his own consulting and executive development work, Harkins focuses on senior leaders and leadership teams. His clients include senior executives and teams at *Fortune 500* companies worldwide. In addition, along with leadership expert Warren Bennis, he is co-chair of the Global Institute for Leadership Development, which has trained and developed more than 4,000 leaders from around the world.

Harkins has written several books, including *Powerful Conversations: How High-Impact Leaders Communicate,* and his newest book, *Click.* He has also authored articles for magazines and journals and speaks frequently on these topics at public and in-house conferences, seminars, and programs. Contact: pharkins@linkage-inc.com; www.linkageinc.com.

SALLY HELGESEN delivers keynotes and consults on issues relating to work, leadership, and women for organizations all over the world. She is the author of five books, including *The Web of Inclusion: A New Architecture for Building Great Organizations*, which was cited in *The Wall Street Journal* as one of the best books on leadership of all time, and *The Female Advantage: Women's Ways of Leadership*, widely hailed as "the classic work" on women's management styles and used as a standard text in colleges and universities. Helgesen's latest book is *Thriving in 24/7: Six Strategies for Taming the New World of Work*. Articles about her work have been featured in *Fortune, Business Week,* and *Fast Company* magazine, and she has appeared on hundreds of radio and television programs. Contact: sally@sallyhelgesen.com; www.SallyHelgesen.com.

HANS H. HINTERHUBER teaches strategy and leadership at the University of Innsbruck in Austria. He is guest professor at the Bocconi-University in Italy. His research focus includes leadership, innovation management, corporate strategy, and internationalization. He is head of the academic advisory board of Cell Consulting and the author of numerous books, including *Leadership—More than Management* and *Corporate Strategy*. Contact: hans.hinterhuber@uibk.ac.at.

MAYA HU-CHAN is an international management consultant, executive coach, leadership development educator, and a founding partner of Alliance for Strategic Leadership (A4SL). She has coached thousands of leaders of Global 100 companies to improve their leadership compentency. Coauthor of *A Study in Excellence: Management in the Nonprofit Human Services* and *Coaching for Leadership: How the World's Greatest Coaches Help Leaders Learn*, she recently completed the research, "Global Leadership: The Next Generation," for Accenture and Keilty, Goldsmith and Company (KGC). The book about this cutting-edge research is scheduled for publication in 2002. Contact: mayahuchan@earthlink.net.

BETSY JACOBSON is president of Betsy Jacobson and Associates a consulting firm based in San Diego, California. A sociologist with an advanced degree in business and management, she is a well respected organization development consultant who has worked extensively with multinational corporations and foreign governments applying a unique blend of learning organization principals and practices to corporate leadership development education and to organization change interventions. She is coauthor of several articles and a frequent speaker at conferences and international meetings.

BEVERLY KAYE is president of Career Systems International, Inc. Such corporations as American Express, Dow Corning, Chevron, Chrysler, Marriott International, and Sears use her management and career development programs. She is a prolific writer, popular lecturer, and management consultant. In the early 1980s, she published her now classic book, *Up Is Not the Only Way*. Her latest research is on management strategies for retaining knowledge workers, and she has recently coauthored *Love 'Em Or Lose 'Em: Getting Good People To Stay*. Kaye has received many honors and awards, including the National Career Development Award of the American Society for Training and Development. She earned a doctorate at UCLA and did graduate work in organization development at the Sloan School of Management at MIT. Contact: www.careersystemsintl.com; www.keepem.com.

ROBERT S. KAPLAN is chairman of the Balanced Scorecard Collaborative and the Marvin Bower Professor of Leadership Development at the Harvard Business School. Kaplan's research, teaching, and consulting focus on linking cost and performance measurement systems to strategy implementation and operational excellence. He has been a co-developer of both activity-based costing and the Balanced Scorecard. He has authored or co-authored ten books and more than 120 papers, for which he has received numerous awards. He also received the 2001 Distinguished Service Award from the Institute of Management Accountants for contributions to the IMA and the academic community.

Kaplan's new, best-selling book, *The Strategy-Focused Organization*, with David Norton, was named best international business book (2000) by Cap Gemini Ernst & Young. *The Balanced Scorecard: Translating Strategy into Action* (1996), with David Norton, won the 2001 Wildman Medal from the American Accounting Association for its impact on practice.

JON KATZENBACH is a founder of Katzenbach Partners LLC, a firm specializing in organization, leadership, team, and workforce performance. Formerly a director of McKinsey & Company, Inc., his activities there included both client and firm leadership roles. His areas of competence include leadership, organization, motivation, and change issues. Katzenbach has served executives of leading companies in forest products, energy, electronics, industrial products, consumer products, medical products, and financial services. He has also served many public institutions, including three New York City hospital and university systems, as well as the New York City Partnership and Miami 2000.

Katzenbach regularly conducts independent research efforts on new approaches to organizational performance. His perspectives on these topics have been presented to numerous executive leadership groups throughout the world. Katzenbach's published works include *The Wisdom of Teams, Real Change Leaders, Teams at the Top, Peak Performance,* and *The Discipline of Teams.* In addition, he is editor of *The Work of Teams* (a *Harvard Business Review* compendium).

JAMES M. KOUZES is co-author (with Barry Posner) of the award-winning and best-selling book, *The Leadership Challenge.* He is also chairman emeritus of the Tom Peters Company and an executive fellow in the Center for Innovation and Entrepreneurship, Leavey School of Business, Santa Clara University.

Kouzes and Posner are also authors of *Credibility, Encouraging the Heart,* and *The Leadership Challenge Planner.* Their 360-degree leadership assessment instrument, The Leadership Practices Inventory (LPI), has helped develop the leadership skills of nearly 1 million people worldwide, and an online version was recently launched (www. ipionline.com). Combining these publications and instruments with several leadership videos (distributed by CRM Learning), and The Leadership Challenge Workshop (offered through the Tom Peters

Company), make Kouzes and Posner's Five Practices of Exemplary Leadership model the most trusted source on becoming a better leader. To learn more about their work, visit www.leadershipchallenge.com.

RICHARD J. LEIDER is a founding principal of The Inventure Group, a coaching and consulting firm. A pioneer in the field of career coaching, he has become an internationally respected author, speaker, and a noted spokesman for "life skills" needed in the twenty-first century. Leider has written or co-written five books, including the international best seller *Repacking Your Bags*, and is a contributing author to *The Leader of the Future*. He is a contributing columnist to *Fast Company* magazine's website (www.fastcompany.com) and has been featured as a speaker at all their RealTime Live events.

An avid hiker and backpacker, Leider leads yearly Inventure Expedition walking safaris in Tanzania, East Africa, where he helped found the Dorobo Fund for leadership and conservation. Contact: info@inventuregroup.com; www.inventuregroup.com.

ELLIOTT MASIE is president of The Masie Center, an international think tank located in Saratoga Springs, NY, focused on technology, learning, and organizational development. Masie serves as an advisor to thousand of organizations on the issues of leveraging technology for performance. He is a member of the White House Advisory Task Force on Expanding Training Opportunities. He writes a free newsletter that is ready by 49,000 executives every week on the Internet. Information is available at www.masie.com.

D. QUINN MILLS teaches leadership, strategy, organizations, and human resources at the Harvard Business School. He advises major corporations and consulting companies. Quinn is the author of many books including *e-Leadership* and *The Empowerment Imperative,* as well as articles for the *New York Times, Wall Street Journal, Chicago Tribune, Los Angeles Times,* and *Business Week.* Quinn's research focus is leadership, transformation management, strategy, human resources, and e-learning. Contact: dmills@hbs.edu.

RUSS S. MOXLEY is a Senior Fellow and Director, Nonprofit Initiatives, at the Center for Creative Leadership, an international, nonprofit educational institution devoted to research and teaching on leadership in the private and public sectors. He is the author of *Leadership and Spirit,* coeditor and one of the authors of the *Center for Leadership Handbook for Leadership Development,* and editor of the Center's *Ideas Into Action* guidebook series. Moxley serves on the governing board of the International Leadership Association, part of the James MacGregor Burns Academy of Leadership at the University of Maryland. Contact: rmoxley@att.net.

BOB NELSON is author of the best-selling books *1001 Ways to Reward Employees, 1001 Ways to Energize Employees,* and *1001 Ways to Take Initiative at Work.* His other books are *Managing for Dummies* and his most recent release, *Please Don't Just Do What I Tell You! Do What Needs to Be Done.* Contact: BobRewards@aol.com; www.nelson-motivation.com.

DAVID P. NORTON is president of Balanced Scorecard Collaborative, Inc., an organization facilitating the global use and effectiveness of the Balanced Scorecard as a value-added management process. A lecturer and writer, Norton's work with the Balanced Scorecard has been the subject of many articles and public conferences. The Balanced Scorecard concept was recently selected by *HBR* as one of the most influential management ideas of the past seventy-five years.

Norton is co-author, with Robert S. Kaplan, of four *Harvard Business Review (HBR)* articles and two books: *The Balanced Scorecard: Translating Strategy into Action* and *The Strategy-Focused Organization: How Balanced Scorecard Companies Thrive in the New Business Environment.* Norton and Kaplan were ranked by the *Financial Times* among the top 15 business world's most important practical and intellectual influences.

DEBRA A. NOUMAIR is an associate professor of psychology and education in the social organizational psychology program in the Department of Organization and Leadership at Teachers College, Columbia University. In collaboration with Executive Education at Columbia Business School, W. Warner Burke Associates/Pricewaterhouse-

Coopers, CDR International, and Leadership Consulting Associates, she conducts leadership development programs and executive coaching using multi-rater feedback methods in a variety of organizations. She also consults to organizations on team effectiveness, intergroup, and inter-organizational relations. A licensed psychologist in the State of New York, Noumair maintains a private practice of organizational consultation and executive coaching.

CHERYL OATES is co-director of the Methods Group at Duke Corporate Education. The Methods Group focuses on understanding and enhancing the ways in which different aggregates of people learn. It develops the capability to design and lead with others, and offers creative and effective learning experiences for individuals, teams, cohorts, communities, and groups of very large scale. Prior to joining Duke Corporate Education, Oates was director of organization capability for the Coca-Cola Company. In that role she worked in the areas of capability, learning, strategy, culture, and change. Contact: cheryl.oates@dukece.com; www.dukece.com.

ELIZABETH PINCHOT is an executive coach, consultant, and author. As co-founder and president of Pinchot & Company, she has coached and trained senior executives in large organizations as diverse as the U.S. Forest Service, Canadian National Railroad, a large computer company, and the New York Stock Exchange. Pinchot has coached entrepreneurs in startups, such as high-tech and social service companies in Moscow, Silicon Valley startups, and consulting companies, and advised the executive directors and senior staff of many nonprofit companies in a consulting capacity.

In earlier years Pinchot was a staff clinician in an outpatient clinic delivering psychological services to individuals, groups, and families. She also maintained a private practice of counseling individuals. Prior to Pinchot & Company, she co-founded and ran several businesses, including a manufacturing business and a teacher training center, and was a founding staff member of the first computer-assisted education project, a joint venture of IBM and Stanford University.

GIFFORD PINCHOT is an author, speaker, coach, and consultant on innovation management and related topics. He has coached teams launching over 500 new products and services, entrepreneurs, intrapreneurs, and leaders of large firms wishing to create a better climate for innovation. His particular specialty is working the interface between difficult business problems and personal growth.

Pinchot's best-selling book, *INTRAPRENEURING: Why You Don't Have to Leave the Corporation to Become an Entrepreneur,* defined the ground rules for an emerging field of enterprise: the courageous pursuit of new ideas within established organizations. The word "intrapreneur," coined by Pinchot to describe the intra-corporate entrepreneur, has been included in the *American Heritage Dictionary* and *Webster's Encyclopedic Unabridged Dictionary.* In his book *The Intelligent Organization,* co-authored with Elizabeth Pinchot, this vision is broadened to include a revolutionary way of organizing all work, from the most innovative to the most mundane. In April 1999, he co-authored *Intrapreneuring in Action A Handbook for Business Innovation.*

BARRY Z. POSNER is co-author (with Jim Kouzes) of the award-winning and best-selling book, *The Leadership Challenge.* He is also Dean of the Leavey School of Business and Professor of Leadership at Santa Clara University (Silicon Valley, California), where he has received numerous teaching and innovation awards, including his school's and his university's highest faculty awards.

They are also authors of *Credibility, Encouraging the Heart,* and *The Leadership Challenge Planner.* Their 360-degree leadership assessment instrument, The Leadership Practices Inventory (LPI) has helped develop the leadership skills of nearly one million people worldwide, and an online version was recently launched (www.lpionline.com). Combining these publications and instruments with several leadership videos (distributed by CRM Learning), and The Leadership Challenge Workshop (offered through the Tom Peters Company), make Kouzes and Posner's Five Practices of Exemplary Leadership model the most trusted source on becoming a better leader. To learn more about their work, visit www.leadershipchallenge.com.

HARVEY ROBBINS, president of Robbins & Robbins in Minnetonka, MN, has been a practicing business psychologist since 1974. His broad experience provides his clients with workshops and consulting service in the areas of team development; change management; collaboration, organization and leadership effectiveness; and interpersonal influence. Robbins also regularly presents at national/international conferences and is listed as a featured speaker with several prominent speaker's bureaus.

Robbins is author/co-author of six books: *Turf Wars, How to Speak and Listen Effectively, Why Teams Don't Work* (co-authored with Michael Finley and winner of the 1995 Financial Times/Booz Allen & Hamilton Global Business Book Award), *Why Change Doesn't Work, Transcompetition,* and the recently released *The New Why Teams Don't Work.* He is currently working on a new leadership book entitled *The Accidental Leader.* Contact: robbi004@tc.umn.edu; www.harveyrobbins.com.

ROBERT ROSEN is an internationally recognized psychologist, bestselling author, researcher, and senior business advisor to world-class companies. Each year he speaks to thousands of executives worldwide and appears regularly in the international media.

Rosen is founder and CEO of Healthy Companies International, a consulting firm that advises individuals, organizations, and communities around the world. His most recent book, *Global Literacies: Lessons on Business Leadership and National Cultures,* was recently chosen as one of *Fortune* magazine's "Best Business Books." His other books include *The Healthy Company: Eight Strategies to Develop People, Productivity, and Profits* and *Leading People: Transforming Business from the Inside Out.* Contact: bob@healthycompanies.com; www.healthycompanies.com.

JUDITH ROSENBLUM is chief operating officer of Duke Corporate Education, responsible for all client-related activities, including the leadership and development of all personnel and alliances integral to designing, developing, and delivering client engagements. For 20 years, she has worked both inside companies and as a consultant in the areas of strategy, capability development, and organizational learning. Her combined background in strategy and learning gives her a unique perspective on how learning experiences can enable strategy. Rosenblum holds a copyright for the "Breakthrough Model," the strategic framework that underpins her work. Contact: www.dukece.com; Judy.Rosenblum@DukeCE.com.

DIRK SEIFERT is a visiting scholar at the Harvard Business School. Together with D. Quinn Mills, he is developing new corporate e-learning formats. Before joining the Harvard Business School, Seifert was Director of the Bertelsmann e-Commerce Group in Hamburg. He has also held senior positions with Procter & Gamble and Bayer. Seifert's research focus is leadership, strategic retail management, efficient consumer response, and e-learning. Contact: dseifert@hbs.edu and seifert-d@gmx.de.

Major General **DONALD W. SHEPPERD** (USAF, Ret.) is a combat fighter pilot with wide experience in industry. He has led and managed men and women in both peace and war. He flew 247 fighter combat missions in Vietnam; was an airline pilot; the National Sales Manager for an aircraft manufacturer; and head of the Air National Guard, one of the Air Force's largest commands with more than 110,000 personnel spread all over the world. Shepperd is a speaker, consultant, and author on the subjects of leadership, corporate culture, coaching of executives, organizational change and development, empowerment and team performance, and leading organizations and people to new levels of performance. He is a military analyst for CNN and is heard over ABC radio.

R. ROOSEVELT THOMAS, JR., has been at the forefront of developing and implementing innovative concepts and strategies for maximizing organizational and individual potential through diversity management for the past 15 years. He currently serves as CEO of R. Thomas Consulting & Training, Inc. and is president of The American Institute for Managing Diversity (AIMD).

Thomas is the author of five published books: *Building a House for Diversity; Redefining Diversity; Differences Do Make a Difference; Beyond Race and Gender: Unleashing the Power of Your Total Work Force by Managing*

Diversity; and his most recent, *Giraffe and Elephant—A Diversity Fable.* He is also the author of several articles, including "From Affirmative Action to Affirming Diversity" (*Harvard Business Review* March–April 1990). Contact: rrthomasjr@aol.com; www.rthomasconsulting.com.

BRIAN TRACY is chairman and CEO of Brian Tracy International, a human resources company specializing in the training and development of individuals and organizations.

He is the best-selling author of 26 books, including *Focal Point* and *Maximum Achievement,* and has written and produced more than 300 audio and video learning programs. Tracy addresses more than 250,000 people each year and has spoken in 23 countries.

He speaks to corporate and public audiences on the subjects of personal and professional development, including the executives and staff of many of America's largest corporations. Prior to founding his company, Brian Tracy International, he was the chief operating officer of a $265 million dollar development company. He has conducted high-level consulting assignments with several billion-dollar-plus corporations in strategic planning and organizational development. Tracy can be reached at 858-481-2977 or at www.briantracy.com.

FONS TROMPENAARS, the original founder of Trompenaars Hampden-Turner Intercultural Management Consulting, based in Amsterdam, first began to research the influence of cultural differences on cross-cultural business during his Ph.D. studies at Wharton School, University of Pennsylvania, using Royal Dutch/Shell as his "laboratory." Now author of several best-selling books and a keynote speaker, Trompenaars is renowned across the world as the leading guru on cross-cultural values. His database of more than 65,000 respondents from all over the world is contained in the THT database, which is one of the richest resources of social constructs. Contact: info@thtconsulting.com; www.thtconsulting.com.

BRIAN O. UNDERHILL, Ph.D., is a senior consultant with Alliance for Strategic Leadership (A4SL). He specializes in leadership development and multirater (360-degree) feedback, executive coaching, and customer service recovery. He has also been involved in the design and delivery of several large-scale executive coaching initiatives, executive team learning experiences, and "next generation" leadership development efforts. He has helped pioneer the use of "mini-surveys"— a unique measurement tool to help impact behavioral change over time. Contact: brian@bunderhill.com; www.bunderhill.com.

PETER WOOLLIAMS is professor of International Business at the Anglia Business School, UK, and visiting professor to THT (Amsterdam). He has worked closely with Dr. Trompenaars over the last 12 years, and has been concerned with the development and analysis of the cross-cultural database, including data mining and neural network analysis. He is a frequent speaker at international conferences on competence and manager development and publishes extensively with Dr. Trompenaars.

NOTES

CHAPTER 1

[1] For a more in-depth discussion of this study and the importance of partnerships, see Goldsmith, M., Robertson, A., Greenberg, C. *Global Leadership: The Next Generation*, 2003.

[2] See "Coaching Free Agents." Goldsmith, M., Sommerville, I., Greenberg-Walt, C. *Coaching for Leadership.* Jossey-Bass, San Francisco, (Marshall Goldsmith, M., Lyons, L., and Freas, A., eds.

[3] Drucker, Peter. *The Essential Drucker.* HarperBusiness, New York, 2001, 78 pp.

[4] Ashkenas, R., Ulrich, D., Jick, T., Kerr, S. *The Boundaryless Organization.* Jossey-Bass, San Francisco, 1995.

[5] Brian Gallagher, personal interview with the author, January 24, 2002.

[6] Goldsmith, M. "On a Consumer Watershed." *Leader to Leader.* No. 5, Summer, 1997. Drucker Foundation, Jossey-Bass, San Francisco.

[7] Ibid.

CHAPTER 2

[1] Kaplan, R. S. and Norton, D. P., "The Balanced Scorecard: Measures that Drive Performance," *Harvard Business Review* (January–February 1992): 71–79.

[2] Kaplan, R. S. and Norton, D. P., "Linking the Balanced Scorecard to Strategy," *California Management Review* (Fall 1996): 53–79; and "Using the Balanced Scorecard as a Strategic Management System," *Harvard Business Review* (January–February 1996): 75–85.

[3] These are described in Chapter 1 of Kaplan, R. S., and Norton, D. P., *The Strategy-Focused Organization: How Balanced Scorecard Companies Thrive in the New Competitive Environment.* Harvard Business School Press, Boston, 2001.

[4] Kaplan, R. S. and Norton, D. P., "Having Trouble With Your Strategy? Then Map It," *Harvard Business Review* (September–October 2000): 167–176.

⁵ The Balanced Scorecard and strategy map have also been extensively applied to public sector and nonprofit organizations. Success for these organizations is not necessarily measured well by growth in budgets and spending. For them, the over-riding objective of increasing shareholder value through profitable growth strategies is replaced by an objective to be more effective organizations: deliver more value to citizens and constituents and improve the benefit-to-cost ratio of services delivered.

⁶ Meliones, J., "Saving Lives, Saving Money," *Harvard Business Review* (November–December, 2000).

⁷ Kaplan, R. S., "Chemical Bank: Implementing the Balanced Scorecard," *Harvard Business School Case* 9-195-210.

⁸ Not all Balanced Scorecards, however, include objectives and measures related to superior supplier relationships. For example, Mobil Marketing and Refining's main purchase was crude oil, a commodity that could be purchased on the spot market, if necessary, from any number of potential suppliers. Many financial institutions obtain their basic input, money, from the government; thus strategic relationships for the acquisition of money is not a critical part of their strategy.

⁹ Not all the focus on environment and safety was altruistic. Environmental and safety incidents are costly to the company and could be motivated, as well, by a cost-improvement objective. Executives also commented to us that safety incidents are usually a leading indicator on process and cost performance, "If employees are not paying attention when their own welfare is at stake, how much attention are they paying to safeguard the company's assets, and operating them efficiently and safely?"

¹⁰ Kaplan, R. S. and Norton, D. P., *The Balanced Scorecard.* Harvard Business School Press, Boston, 1996, p. 35.

¹¹ See Chandler, A. D., Jr., *Scale & Scope: The Dynamics of Industrial Capitalism.* Cambridge, MA, 1990.

CHAPTER 3

¹ Helgesen, S., *The Web of Inclusion: A New Architecture for Building Great Organizations.* Doubleday/Currency, New York, 1995.

² de Geus, A., Talk delivered at Pegasus Conference, Boston, MA, February 1997.

³ *Post Capitalist Society,* HarperBusiness, New York, 1994.

CHAPTER 5

¹ Hyde, L. *The Gift: Imagination and the Erotic Life of Property.* Vintage Books, Vancouver, WA, 1983.

CHAPTER 6

¹ Ken Blanchard originally developed Situational Leadership® with Paul Hersey at Ohio University in 1968. It gained prominence in 1969 in their classic text, *Management of Organizational Behavior,* now in its eighth edition (Prentice Hall, 2001. Coauthored with Dewey E. Johnson). After finding that some critical aspects of the model were not being validated in practice (particularly the use

of coercive power and the absence of leadership as a partnering process), Ken created Situational Leadership® II based on the thinking and research of his colleagues at The Ken Blanchard Companies—Don Carew, Eunice Parisi-Carew, Fred Finch, Patricia Zigarmi, Drea Zigarmi, Margie Blanchard, and Laurie Hawkins—as well as on feedback from thousands of users. *Leadership and the One Minute Manager* (Morrow, 1985), coauthored with Patricia and Drea Zigarmi, marked a new generation of Situational Leadership based on Partnering for Performance for managers everywhere.

2 The terms *Directive Behavior* and *direction* and *Supportive Behavior* and *support* are used interchangeably in this context.

3 The Leader Behavior Analysis II (LBAII) is an instrument designed to measure both self and others' perceptions of leader flexibility, as well as the leader's effectiveness in choosing an appropriate leadership style. D. Zigarmi, Edeburn, C., and Blanchard, K., *Getting to Know the LBAII®: Research, Validity, and Reliability of the Self and Other Forms, 4th edit.* Escondido: The Ken Blanchard Companies, 1997.

CHAPTER 7

1 Bennis, W., "Cultivating Creative Genius." *Industry Week*, August 18, 1997, p. 84.

2 Drucker, P. F., *Management Challenges for the 21st Century.* HarperCollins, New York, 1999, p. 20.

3 Hennan, D. A. and Bennis, W., *Co-leaders: The Power of Great Partnerships.* John Wiley & Sons, New York, 1999.

4 Bennis, W. and Biederman, P. W., *Organizing Genius: The Secrets of Creative Collaboration.* Addison-Wesley, Reading, MA, 1998, p. 3.

CHAPTER 9

1 Throughout this chapter we use the words *cooperate* and *collaborate* synonymously. Their dictionary definitions are very similar. In *Merriam Webster's Collegiate Dictionary, 10th edit.* (Springfield, MA: 2001) the first definition of *cooperate* is: "To act or work with another or others: act together" (p. 254). The first definition of *collaborate* is: "To work jointly with others or together esp. in an intellectual endeavor" (p. 224).

2 As author and university lecturer Alfie Kohn explains: "The simplest way to understand why competition generally does not promote excellence is to realize that *trying to do well and trying to beat others are two different things.*" One is about accomplishing the superior; the other, about making someone else inferior. From Kohn, A., *No Contest: The Case Against Competition.* Houghton Mifflin, Boston, 1992, p. 55.

3 For a history of the Internet, see: Hafner, K. and Lyon, M., *Where Wizards Stay Up Late: The Origins of the Internet* (Touchstone, New York, 1996). For a history of the World Wide Web, see: Berners-Lee, T. with Fischetti, M., *Weaving the Web: The Original Design and Ultimate Destiny of the World Wide Web by Its Inventor* (HarperSanFrancisco, New York, 1999). Bernes-Lee, who is credited with inventing the World Wide Web, says, "The Web is more a social creation than a

technical one. I designed it for social effect—to help people work together—
and not as a technical toy. . . . The essence of working together in a weblike
way is that we function in groups—groupings of two, twenty, and twenty million. We have to learn how to do this on the Web" (pp. 123 and 125).

4 Tiger, L., "Real-Life Survivors Rely on Teamwork." *The Wall Street Journal,* August 2001.

5 Lumet, S., *Making Movies.* Vintage Books, New York, 1996, p. 17.

6 Johnson, D. W. and Johnson, R. T., *Cooperation and Competition: Theory and Research.* Interaction Book Company, Edna, MN, 1989, p. 63.

7 Van de Ven, A., Delbecq, A. L., and Koenig, R. J., "Determinants of Coordination Modes Within Organizations." *American Sociological Review, 41*(2), 322–338
(1976).

8 Homans, G., *The Human Group.* Harcourt Brace Jovanovich, New York, 1950.

CHAPTER 10

1 Our framework draws in part from work completed with the following friends
and colleagues: Terry Hildebrand, Juan Johnson, Bob Ryncarz, Rodolfo Sal-
gado, and others in the Coca-Cola Learning Consortium.

CHAPTER 11

1 Zaccaro, S. J., *The Nature of Executive Leadership: A Conceptual and Empirical
Analysis of Success.* American Psychological Association, Washington, DC, 2001.

2 Jacobs, T. O. and Jaques, E., "Executive Leadership." In R. Gal and A. D. Man-
glesdorff (Eds.), *Handbook of Military Leadership.* John Wiley & Sons, Chich-
ester, England, 1991; Jacques, E., "The Development of Intellectual Capability:
A Discussion of Stratified Systems Theory." *Journal of Applied Behavioral Science,
22,* 361–384 (1986).

3 Bourgeois, L. J. III, "Strategic Goals, Perceived Uncertainty, and Economic
Performance in Volatile Environments." *Academy of Management Journal, 28,*
548–573 (1985); Hambrick, D. C., "Guest Editor's Introduction: Putting Top
Managers Back in the Strategy Picture." *Strategic Management Journal, 10,* 5–15
(1989); Wortman, M. S., "Strategic Management and Changing Leader-follower
Roles." *Journal of Applied Behavioral Science, 18,* 371–383 (1982).

4 Sashkin, M., "The Visionary Leader." In J. A. Conger and R. N. Kanungo (Eds.)
Charismatic Leadership: The Elusive Factor in Organizational Effectiveness. Jossey-
Bass, San Francisco, 1988.

5 Bass, B. M., *Leadership and Performance Beyond Expectations.* Free Press, New
York, 1985.

6 House, R. J., "A 1976 Theory of Charismatic Leadership." In J. G. Hunt and
L. Larson (Eds.), *Leadership: The Cutting Edge.* Southern Illinois Press, Car-
bondale, 1977.

7 Quinn, R. E., *Beyond Rational Management: Mastering Paradoxes and Competing
Demands of High Performance.* Jossey-Bass, San Francisco, 1988.

8 Mintzberg, H., "The Manager's Job: Folklore and Fact." *Harvard Business Review,
53,* 49–61 (1975); Tsui, A. S., "A Multiple Constituency Framework of Man-

agerial Reputational Effectiveness." In J. G. Hunt, D. Hosking, C. Schriesheim, and R. Stewart (Eds.), *Leaders and Managers: International Perspectives on Manager Behavior and Leadership.* (pp. 28–44). New York: Pergamon Press.

9 Burke, W. W. and Litwin, G. H., "A Causal Model of Organizational Performance and Change." *Journal of Management, 19*(3), 532–545, (1992).

CHAPTER 14

1 This version of "The Giraffe and Elephant" fable is compiled from presentations in two books: (1) Thomas, R. R. Jr., *Building a House for Diversity: How a Fable about a Giraffe and an Elephant Offers New Strategies for Today's Workforce.* AMACOM, New York, 1999, pp. 3–5. (2) Thomas, R. R. Jr., *Giraffe and Elephant: A Diversity Fable.* AIMD, Atlanta, 2002.

2 Thomas, R. R. Jr., *Redefining Diversity.* AMACOM, New York, 1996, pp. 57–73.

CHAPTER 15

1 Segil, L. *Dynamic Leader, Adaptive Organization.* John Wiley & Sons, New York, 2002.

2 Author interviews with James Ramo, March 2000 and March 2002.

3 Ibid, March 2000 and March 2002.

4 Author interview with George Fisher, September 1999, "One on One" for Primedia Television.

5 Author interview with Jerome Adams, May 2001.

6 Ibid., May 2001.

CHAPTER 17

1 de Woot, P. "Towards a European Model of Management." In R. Calori and P. de Woot (Eds.), *A European Management Model: Beyond Diversity.* Prentice Hall, Englewood Cliffs, NJ, 1994, pp. 261–277.

2 Hadot, P., *The Inner Citadelle: Meditations of Marcus Aurelius.* Harvard University Press, Boston, 1998.

3 Kirzner, J. M., "The Primacy of Business Leaderial Discovery." In Seldon, A. (Ed.), *The Prime Mover of Progress,* IEA, Westminster, 1980, pp. 3–30.

4 Prokesch, St. E., "Unleashing the Power of Learning: An Interview with British Petroleum's John Browne." *Harvard Business Review,* 75 (5), 132–145 (1997).

5 Hunter, J. C., *The Servant. A Simple Story about the True Essence of Leadership.* Rima, Rocklin, CA, 1998, p. 7.

6 See Note 2.

7 Ibid.

CHAPTER 18

1 Taken from author interviews for the "Global Leadership: The Next Generation" study, Accenture and Keilty, Goldsmith and Company, 1999.

2 Ibid.

3 Ibid.
4 Ibid.
5 Ibid.
6 Ibid.
7 Priestly, J. B., "Televiewing," *Thoughts in the Wilderness.* Kennikat Press, New York, 1957.
8 See Note 1.
9 Ibid.
10 Ibid.
11 Ibid.

CHAPTER 19

1 Ghadar, F. and Leonard, J., "The Digital Economy and 'Black Diamond Management.'" In *Pushing the Digital Frontier.* Edited by Nirmal Pal and Judith M. Ray, Amacom, New York, 2001, pp. 23–24.
2 Ghadar, F., "The Evolving Role of Global Business." *Keynote address at the Thirteenth Annual Institute for the Study of Business Markets,* Center for Global Business Studies, Pennsylvania State University, 1996.
3 Nascar.com, "Getting Started is the Key to Finishing." *Turner Productions, Inc.* (February 28, 2002).
4 Drucker, P., "Theory of the Business." *Harvard Business Review* (September–October 1994), p. 98.
5 Jensen, B., *Simplicity: The New Competitive Advantage in a World of Better, Faster, More.* Perseus Press, San Francisco, 2000, pp. 10, 20.
6 Bartlett, C. and Nanda, A., "The GM's Leadership Challenge: Building a Self-Renewing Institution." *Harvard Business School* July 23, 1996, p. 3.

CHAPTER 20

1 Trompenaars, A. *21 Leaders for the 21st Century.* McGraw-Hill, New York, 2001.
2 Hampden-Turner, C. and Trompenaars, F., *Building Cross-culture Competence.* Yale University Press, New Haven, 2001.

CHAPTER 22

1 Thor Heyerdahl is most known for his many explorations on the *Kon-Tiki,* each with crews of different creeds and cultural backgrounds. His voyages show that people can live and work together in peace.
2 The official title of the conference was the United Nations' World Conference Against Racisim, Racial Discrimination, Xenophobia and Related Intolerance.
3 Swarns, R. L., "Race Talks Finally Reach Accord on Slavery and Palestinian Plight." *New York Times,* September 9, p. A1 (2001).
4 Slackman, M., "Divisive U.N. Race Talks End in Accord." *Los Angeles Times,* September 9, p. A1 (2001).

[5] Ibid, pp. A1/A12.

[6] Hockstader, L., "Eighth Grade in Mideast: A Curriculum of Hatred." *International Herald Tribune,* September 6, p. 6 (2001).

[7] Gaer, F. D., director of the Jacob Blaustein Center for the Advancement of Human Rights, as reported in Rachel L. Swarns' "Race Talks Finally Reach Accord On Slavery and Palestinian Plight." *New York Times,* September 9, 2001, p. 14.

[8] Friedman, T. L., *The Lexus and the Olive Tree: Understanding Globalization.* Anchor Books, New York, 2000.

[9] For research on the instability of international joint ventures, see summary by A. Yan and M. Zeng in "International Joint Venture Instability: A Critique of Previous Research, A Reconceptualization, and Directions for Future Research." *Journal of International Business Studies, 30* (2), 397–414 (1999). Although the definitions (complete termination versus significant change of ownership) and overall results vary, numerous studies have reported substantial international joint venture instability, including 55 percent termination reported by K. R. Harrigan in "Strategic Alliances and Partner Asymmetries," in F. Contractor and P. Lorange (Eds.), *Cooperative Strategies in International Business* (Lexington Books, Lexington, MA, 205–226, 1988), 49 percent termination reported by H. Barkema and F. Vermeulen in "What Differences in the Cultural Backgrounds of Partners Are Detrimental for International Joint Ventures?" *Journal of International Business Studies, 28* (4), 845–864 (1997); and 68 percent instability through termination or acquisition reported by S. H. Park and M. V. Russo in "When Competition Eclipses Cooperation: An Event History Analysis of Joint Venture Failure," *Management Science, 42* (6), 875–90 (1996). Also see G. Hammel's 1991 classic article "Competition for Competence and Inter-Partner Learning Within International Strategic Alliances," *Strategic Management Journal, 12* (1), 83–103.

[10] Among many other reports on Daimler/Chrysler, see B. Jamison's "Far from a merger of equals." ABCnews.com, January 25, 2001.

[11] Norske Skog is listed on the Oslo Stock Exchange, and its affiliated company, Norske Skog Canada Ltd., where Norske Skog controls 36.2 percent, is listed on the Toronto Stock Exchange.

[12] Bartlett, C. and Sumantra, G., *Managing Across Borders: The Transnational Solution.* Harvard Business School Press, Boston, 1989.

[13] All children's quotes are published in the Norke Skog company booklet, "Only Through The Cooperaton of People With Different Cultural Roots Can Greater Equality and Knowledge Be Achieved." Norske Skog, Oslo, Norway, 2001.

[14] See N. J. Adler's *International Dimensions of Organizational Behavior,* 4th edit. (Southwestern, Cincinnati, OH, 2001) and *From Boston to Beijing: Managing with a World View* (Southwestern, Cincinnati, OH, 2002).

[15] Based on company statistics, operating revenues were 14,908 NOR in 1998, 18,054 in 1999, and 26,635 in 2000. For the first six months of 2001, operating revenues were 16,796 NOR (NOR: Norwegian Kronar).

[16] Based on company statistics, operating profits for 2000 were 4211 NOR, 2129 NOR in 1999, and 1780 NOR in 1998. Operating profits for the first six months of 2001 were 2956 NOR (NOR: Norwegian Kronar).

[17] Based on company statistics, production of publication paper in 1000 tonnes was 4080 in 2000, 2918 in 1999, and 2181 in 1998. For the first six months of 2001, production of publication paper was 2593.

[18] From Madeleine Albright's Commencement Address at Harvard University in Cambridge, Massachusetts on June 5, 1997.

[19] Based on Psalm VIII, 3, and Deuteronomy XXXI, 12, as traditionally interpreted by the Rabbis and cited in *The Petatech and Haftorahs*, edited by J. H. Hertz, 2nd edit. Socino Press, London, 1971, p. 888.

CHAPTER 23

[1] Sussman, E. "24 Things To Do Before You Die." *Worth*, September, 1999, pp. 112–124.

[2] Ibid.

CHAPTER 25

[1] Pope, A., *Poetry and Prose of Alexander Pope*. Riverside Editions, Houghton Mifflin College. Market Paperback, June 1969.

[2] De Montaigne, M., *The Complete Essays*. (Penguin Classics), Penguin USA, 1993.

[3] Tzu, L., *Tao Te Ching of Lao Tzu*. St Martin's Press, New York, 1996.

[4] Emerson, R. W., *The Collected Works of Ralph Waldo Emerson*. Belkoop, Cambridge, MA, 1984.

[5] Bennis, W., *On Becoming a Leader*. Addison-Wesley, Reading, MA, 1990.

[6] Covey, S. R., *The Seven Habits of Highly Effective People*. Simon & Schuster, New York, 1990.

[7] Franklin, B., *Benjamin Franklin: Writings* Library of America, 1987.

[8] Jung, C. G., *Basic Writings of C.G. Jung*. Random House, New York, 1993.

[9] Bruce, L., *The Essential Lenny Bruce*. Panther.

[10] Gottman, J. M. and Silver, N. (contributor), *Why Marriages Succeed or Fail and How You Can Make Yours Last*. Fireside, New York, 1995.

[11] Block, P., *Stewardship: Choosing Service Over Self-Interest*. Berrett-Koehler, San Francisco, 1996.

[12] This material is housed in the Mormon Archives, Salt Lake City, UT.

CHAPTER 26

[1] *Larry King Live*. CNN, 2002.

CHAPTER 28

[1] Stewart, T., *Intellectual Capital: The New Wealth of Organizations*. Bantam Books, New York, 1997.

INDEX